THE ALL-SUFFICIENCY OF CHRIST

THE ALL-SUFFICIENCY OF CHRIST

CHARLES HENRY MACKINTOSH

ISBN: 978-93-89582-86-4

Published: 1898

LECTOR HOUSE LLP
E-MAIL: lectorpublishing@gmail.com

THE ALL-SUFFICIENCY OF CHRIST

BY

CHARLES HENRY MACKINTOSH

**MISCELLANEOUS WRITINGS OF
C. H. MACKINTOSH
VOLUME I**

CONTENTS

FORGIVENESS OF SINS: WHAT IS IT?

Oh, the blessedness! transgression forgiven—sin covered! This truly is blessedness; and without this, blessedness must be unknown. To have the full assurance that my sins are all forgiven is the only foundation of true happiness. To be happy without this is to be happy on the brink of a yawning gulf, into which I may at any moment be dashed forever. It is utterly impossible that any one can enjoy solid happiness until he is possessed of the divine assurance that all his guilt has been canceled by the blood of the cross. Uncertainty as to this must be the fruitful source of mental anguish to any soul who has ever been led to feel the burden of sin. To be in doubt as to whether my guilt was all borne by Jesus, or is yet on my conscience, is to be miserable.

Now, before proceeding to unfold the subject of forgiveness, I should like to ask my reader a very plain, pointed, personal question, namely, Dost thou believe that thou canst have the clear and settled assurance that thy sins are forgiven? I ask this question at the outset, because there are many, now-a-days, who profess to preach the gospel of Christ, and yet deny that any one can be sure that his sins are forgiven. They maintain that it is presumption for any one to believe in the forgiveness of his sins; and, on the other hand, they look upon it as a proof of humility to be always in doubt as to this most momentous point. In other words, it is presumption to believe what God says, and humility to doubt it. This seems strange in the face of such passages as the following: "Thus it is written, and thus it behooved Christ to suffer, and to rise from the dead the third day; and that repentance and remission of sins should be preached in His name among all nations, beginning at Jerusalem" (Luke xxiv. 46, 47); "In whom *we have* redemption through His blood, *the forgiveness of sins*, according to the riches of His grace." (Eph. i. 7; Col. i. 14.)

Here we have remission, or forgiveness, of sins (the word is the same in the three passages) preached in the name of Jesus, and possessed by those who believed that preaching. A proclamation was sent to the Ephesians and Colossians, as belonging to the "all nations," telling them of forgiveness of sins, in the name of Jesus. They believed this proclamation, and entered on the possession of the forgiveness of sins. Was this presumption on their part? or would it have been piety and humility to doubt the forgiveness of sins? True, they had been great sinners—"dead in trespasses and sins," "children of wrath," "aliens and foreigners," "enemies by wicked works." Some of them had doubtless bowed the knee to Diana. They had lived in gross idolatry and all manner of wickedness. But then, "forgiveness of sins" had been preached to them in the name of Jesus. Was this preaching true, or was it not? Was it for them, or was it not? Was it all a dream—a shadow—a myth? Did it mean nothing? Was there nothing sure, nothing certain, nothing solid about it?

These are plain questions, demanding a plain answer from those who assert that no one can know for certain that his sins are forgiven. If, indeed, no one can know it now, then how could any one have known it in apostolic times? If it could be known in the first century, then why not in the nineteenth? "David describeth the blessedness of the man unto whom God imputeth righteousness without works, saying, Blessed are they whose iniquities are forgiven, and whose sins are covered. Blessed is the man to whom the Lord will not impute sin." (Rom. iv. 6-8.) Hezekiah could say, "Thou *hast cast all my sins* behind Thy back." (Isaiah xxxviii. 17.) The Lord Jesus said to one, in His day, "Son, be of good cheer; thy sins be forgiven thee." (Matt. ix. 2.)

Thus at all times forgiveness of sins was known with all the certainty which the word of God could give. Any one of the cases aduced above is sufficient to overthrow the teaching of those who assert that *no one* can know that his sins are forgiven. If I find from Scripture that any one ever knew this marvelously precious blessing, that is quite enough for me. Now, when I open my Bible, I find persons who had been guilty of all manner of sins brought to the knowledge of forgiveness; and I therefore argue that it is possible for the very vilest sinner to know now, with divine certainty, that his sins are forgiven. Was it presumption in Abraham, in David, in Hezekiah, in the palsied man, and in numbers besides, to believe in the forgiveness of sins? Would it have been a sign of humility and true piety in them to doubt? It will perhaps be argued that these were all special and extraordinary cases. Well, it matters not, so far as our present question is concerned, whether they were ordinary or extraordinary. One thing is plain—they completely disprove the assertion that *no one* can know that his sins are forgiven. The word of God teaches me that numbers, subject to like passions, like infirmities, like failures, and like sins as the writer and reader, were brought to know and rejoice in the full forgiveness of sins; and hence those who maintain that no one can be sure on this momentous question have no scriptural foundation for their opinion.

But is it true that the cases recorded in the Holy Scriptures are so special and extraordinary as not to afford any precedent for us? By no means. If any case could be so regarded, it is surely that of Abraham, and yet of him we read that "it was not written for his sake alone, that righteousness was imputed to him: *but for us also,* to whom it shall be imputed, if we believe on Him that raised up Jesus our Lord from the dead; who was delivered for our offences, and was raised again for our justification." (Rom. iv. 23-25.) Abraham "believed in the Lord; and He counted it to him for righteousness." (Gen. xv. 6.) And the Holy Ghost declares that righteousness shall be imputed to us also if we believe,—"Be it known unto you therefore, men and brethren, that through this man is preached unto you the forgiveness of sins; and by Him all that believe are justified from all things from which ye could not be justified by the law of Moses" (Acts xiii. 38, 39.); "To Him give *all the prophets* witness, that through His name *whosoever believeth* in Him shall receive remission of sins." (Acts x. 43.)

Now, the question is, What did the apostles Peter and Paul mean when they so unreservedly preached the forgiveness of sins to those who listened to them?

Did they really mean to convey to their hearers the idea that no one could be sure that he possessed this forgiveness of sins? When in the synagogue of Antioch, Paul said to his audience, "We declare unto you *glad tidings*," did he entertain the notion that no one could be sure that his sins were forgiven? How could the gospel ever be called "glad tidings" if its only effect were to leave the soul in doubt and anxiety? If indeed it be true that no one can enjoy the assurance of pardon, then the whole style of apostolic preaching should be reversed. We might then expect to find Paul saying to his hearers, Be it known unto you therefore, men and brethren, that no one can ever know, in this life, whether his sins are forgiven or not. Is there aught like this in the entire range of apostolic preaching and teaching? Do not the apostles everywhere set forth, in the fullest and clearest manner, remission of sins as the necessary result of believing in a crucified and risen Saviour? Is there the most remote hint of that which is so much insisted upon by some modern teachers, namely, that it is a dangerous presumption to believe in the full forgiveness of all our sins, and that it argues a pious and humble frame of soul to live in perpetual doubt? Is there no possibility of ever enjoying, in this world, the comfortable certainty of our eternal security in Christ? Can we not rely upon God's word, or commit our souls to the sacrifice of Christ? Can it be possible that the only effect of God's glad tidings is to leave the soul in hopeless perplexity? Christ has put away sin; but I cannot know it! God has spoken; but I cannot be sure! The Holy Ghost has come down; but I cannot rely upon His testimony! It is piety and humility to doubt God's word, to dishonor the atonement of Christ, and to refuse the faith of the heart to the record of the Holy Ghost! Alas! alas! if this is the gospel, then adieu to peace and joy in believing. If this is Christianity, then in vain has "the dayspring from on high visited us, to give the knowledge of salvation through the remission of our sins." (Luke i.) If no one can have this "knowledge of salvation," then to what end has it been given?

And let my reader bear in mind that the question before us is not whether a person may not deceive himself and others. This would be at once conceded. Thousands, alas! have deceived themselves, and thousands more have deceived others; but is that any reason why I cannot possess the absolute certainty that what God has said is true, and that the work of Christ has availed to put away all my sins?

Men have deceived themselves, and therefore I am afraid to trust Christ! Men have deceived others, and therefore I am afraid that God's word will deceive me! This is really what it all amounts to, when put into plain language. And is it not well to have things thus put? Is it not needful, at times, to strip certain propositions of the dress in which legality and fleshly pietism would clothe them, so that we may see what they are? Does it not behove us, when men stand forth as the professed and authorized exponents of a sound and enlightened Christianity, to test what they say by the unerring standard of Holy Scripture? Assuredly it does. And if they tell us we can never be sure of salvation; and that it is presumption to think of such a thing; and, further, that the very utmost we can attain to in this life is a faint hope that, through the mercy of God, we may get to heaven when we die; we must utterly reject such teaching, as being in direct opposition to the Word of God.

False theology tells me I can never be sure, God's Word tells me I can. Which am I to believe? The former fills me with gloomy doubts and fears; the latter imparts divine certainty. That casts me upon my own efforts; this, upon a finished work. To which shall I attend? Is there a shadow of foundation, throughout the entire volume of God, for the notion that no one can be sure of his eternal salvation? I most fearlessly assert there is not. So far from this, the Word of God, in every section of it, sets before us, in the clearest way, the privilege of the believer to enjoy the most unclouded certainty as to his pardon and acceptance in Christ.

And, let me ask, is it not due to God's faithful Word and Christ's finished work, that the soul confiding therein should enjoy the fullest assurance? True, it is by faith that any one can so confide, and this faith is wrought in the heart by the Holy Ghost. But all this in nowise affects our present question. What I desire is, that my reader should rise from the study of this paper with a full and firm conviction that it is possible for him to possess the present assurance that he is as safe as Christ can make him. If any sinner ever enjoyed this assurance, then why may not my reader now enjoy it? Is Christ's work finished? Is God's Word true? Yes, verily. Then, if I simply trust therein, I am pardoned, justified and accepted. All my sins were laid on Jesus when He was nailed to the cursed tree. Jehovah made them all meet on Him. He bore them and put them away, and now He is up in heaven without them. This is enough for me. If the One who stood charged with *all* my guilt is now at the right hand of the Majesty in the heavens, then, clearly, there is nothing against me. All that divine justice had against me was laid on the Sin-bearer, and He endured the wrath of a sin-hating God that I might be freely and forever pardoned and accepted in a risen and glorified Saviour.

These are glad tidings. Does my reader believe them? Say, beloved, dost thou heartily believe in a dead and risen Christ? Hast thou come to Him as a lost sinner, and put thy heart's full confidence in Him? Does thou believe that "He died for our sins according to the Scripture, and that He was buried and rose again the third day according to the Scriptures"? If so, thou art saved, justified, accepted, complete in Christ. True, thou art, in thyself, a poor feeble creature, having an evil nature to contend with every moment; but Christ is thy life, and He is thy wisdom, and thy righteousness, thy sanctification, thy redemption, thy all. He ever lives for thee up in heaven. He died to make thee clean. He lives to keep thee clean. Thou art made as clean as His death can make thee, and thou art kept as clean as His life can keep thee. He made Himself responsible for thee. God sees thee to be what Christ has made thee to be. He sees thee in Christ and as Christ. Wherefore, then, I pray thee, tread no more those gloomy corridors of legalism, pietism, and false theology, which have resounded for ages with the sighs and groans of poor sin-burdened and misguided souls; but, seeing the fullness of thy portion, and the completeness of thy standing in a risen and victorious Christ, rejoice in Him all thy days upon earth, and live in the hope of being with Him forever in His own mansions of heavenly glory.

Having thus sought to establish the fact that it is possible for one to know, upon divine authority, that his sins are forgiven, we shall now, in dependence upon the teaching of the Spirit of God, proceed to consider the subject of forgiveness of sins, as unfolded in the Word, and, in doing so, we shall present it under the three following heads; namely,

First, the *ground* on which God forgives sins.

Secondly, the *extent* to which He forgives sins.

Thirdly, the *style* in which He forgives sins. There is value in this threefold presentation, as it gives clearness, fullness and precision to our apprehension of the subject as a whole. The more clearly we understand the ground of divine forgiveness, the more shall we appreciate the extent, and admire the style thereof.

May God the Spirit now be our guide while we ponder, for a little,

THE GROUND OF DIVINE FORGIVENESS.

It is of the very last importance that the anxious reader should understand this cardinal point. It is quite impossible that a divinely convicted conscience can enjoy true repose until the ground of forgiveness is clearly seen. There may be certain vague thoughts respecting the mercy and goodness of God, His readiness to receive sinners and pardon their sins, His unwillingness to enter the place of judgment, and His promptness to enter the place of mercy,—all this there may be; but until the convicted soul is led to see how God can be just and yet the Justifier—how He can be a just God and yet a Saviour-God—how He has been glorified with respect to sin—how all the divine attributes have been harmonized, it must be a stranger to the peace of God which truly passeth all understanding. A conscience on which the light of divine truth has poured itself in convicting power, feels and owns that sin can never enter into the presence of God—that sin, wherever it is found, can only be met by the just judgment of a sin-hating God. Hence, until the divine method of dealing with sin is understood and believed, there must be intense anxiety. Sin is a reality, God's holiness is a reality, conscience is a reality, judgment to come is a reality. All these things must be looked at and duly considered. Justice must be satisfied; conscience, purged; Satan, silenced. How is all this to be done? Only by the cross of Jesus.

Here, then, we have the true ground of divine forgiveness. The precious atonement of Christ forms the base of that platform on which a just God and a justified sinner meet in sweet communion. In that atonement I see sin condemned, justice satisfied, the law magnified, the sinner saved, the adversary confounded. Creation never exhibited aught like this. There, the creature enjoyed the manifestation of power, wisdom and goodness; but the fairest fields of the old creation presented nothing like "grace reigning through righteousness"—nothing like a glorious combination of "righteousness and peace, mercy and truth." It was reserved for Calvary to display all this. There, that grand and all-important question, How can God be just and the Justifier? received a glorious reply. The death of Christ furnishes the answer. A just God dealt with sin at the cross, in order that a justifying God might deal with the sinner on the new and everlasting ground of resurrection. God could not tolerate or pass over a single jot or tittle of sin; but He could put it away. He has condemned sin. He has poured out His righteous wrath upon sin, in order that He might pour the everlasting beams of His favor upon the believing sinner.

> "On Jesus' cross this record's graved,
> Let sin be judged and sinners saved."

Precious record! may every anxious sinner read it with the eye of faith. It is a record which must impart settled peace to the heart. God has been satisfied as to sin. This is enough for me. Here my guilty, troubled conscience finds sweet repose. I have seen my sins rising like a dark mountain before me, threatening me with eternal wrath; but the blood of Jesus has blotted them all out from God's view. They are gone, and gone forever—sunk as lead into the mighty waters of divine forgetfulness, and I am free—as free as the One who was nailed to the cross for my sins, but who is now on the throne without them.

Such, then, is the ground of divine forgiveness. What a solid ground! Who or what can touch it? Justice *has* owned it. The troubled conscience *may* rest in it. Satan *must* acknowledge it. God has revealed Himself as a Justifier, and faith walks in the light and power of that revelation. Nothing can be simpler, nothing clearer, nothing more satisfactory. If God reveals Himself as a Justifier, then I am justified through faith in the revelation. When the moral glories of the cross shine upon the sinner, he sees and knows, believes and owns, that the One who has judged his sins in death, has justified him in resurrection.

Anxious reader, see, I beseech thee, that thou apprehendest the true ground of the forgiveness of sins. There is no use in our proceeding to consider the *extent* and *style* until thy poor troubled conscience has been led to rest upon the imperishable *ground* of forgiveness. Let me reason with thee. What is to hinder thee, from this very moment, resting on the foundation of accomplished atonement? Say, does thy conscience need something more to satisfy it than that which satisfied the inflexible justice of God? Is not the ground on which God reveals Himself as a righteous Justifier sufficiently strong for thee to stand upon as a justified sinner? What sayest thou, friend? Art thou satisfied? Is Christ sufficient for thee? Art thou still searching for something in thyself, thy ways, thy works, thy thoughts, thy feelings? If so, give up the search as utterly vain. Thou wilt never find any thing. And even though thou couldst find something, it would only be an encumbrance, a loss, a hindrance. Christ is sufficient for God, let Him be sufficient for thee likewise. Then—but not until then—wilt thou be truly happy.

May God the Holy Ghost cause thee to rest, this moment, upon an all-sufficient sacrifice, as the only ground of divine forgiveness, so that thou mayest be able to enter, with real intelligence and interest, upon the examination of the second point in our subject, namely,—

THE EXTENT OF DIVINE FORGIVENESS.

Very many are perplexed as to this. They do not see the fullness of the atonement; they do not grasp the emancipating fact of its application to all their sins; they do not enter into the full force of those lines, which perhaps they often sing,—

> "All thine iniquities who doth
> Most graciously forgive."

They seem to be under the impression that Christ only bore some of their sins, namely, their sins up to the time of their conversion. They are troubled as to the question of their daily sins, as if these were to be disposed of upon a different ground from their past sins. Thus they are at times much cast down and sorely beset. Nor could it be otherwise with them until they see that in the death of Christ, provision was made for the full forgiveness of ALL their sins. True it is that the child of God who commits sin has to go to his Father and confess that sin. But what does the apostle say in reference to one so confessing his sins? "God is faithful and just to forgive us our sins and to cleanse us from all unrighteousness." Now, why does he say, "Faithful and just"? Why does he not say, "Gracious and merciful"? Because he speaks on the ground that the entire question of sin was gone into and settled by the death of Christ, who is now up in heaven as the righteous Advocate. On no other ground could God be faithful and just in connection with the forgiveness of sins. The sins of the believer have *all* been atoned for on the cross. If one had been left out, he should be eternally lost, inasmuch as it is impossible that a single sin, however trifling, can ever enter the precincts of the sanctuary of God. And, further, let me add, if all the believer's sins were not atoned for in the death of Christ, then, neither by confession, nor by prayer, nor by fasting, nor by any other means, could they ever be forgiven. The death of Christ is the *only* ground on which God could, in faithfulness and justice, forgive sin; and we know He must either do it in faithfulness and justice, or not at all. This is to His praise and our exceeding comfort.

But I can imagine my reader exclaiming, "What! do you mean to say that my *future* sins were all atoned for?" To this I reply that all our sins were future when Christ bore them on the accursed tree. The sins of all believers, for the last eighteen centuries, were future when Christ died for them. Hence, if the idea of future sins presents a difficulty in reference to what we may commit, if left here, it presents just as great a difficulty in reference to what we have committed.[1] But, in truth, all this perplexity about future sins arises very much from the habit of looking at the cross from our own point of view instead of God's—looking at it from earth instead of from heaven. Scripture never speaks of future sins. Past, present, and future are only human and earthly. All is an eternal now with God. All our sins were before the eye of infinite Justice at the cross, and all were laid on the head of Jesus, the Sin-bearer, who, by His death, laid the eternal foundation of forgiveness of sins, in order that the believer, at any moment of his life, at any point in his history, at any stage of his career, from the time at which the hallowed tidings of the gospel fall upon the ear of faith, until the moment in which he steps into the glory, may be able to say, with clearness and decision, without reserve, misgiving, or hesitation, "Thou hast cast all my sins behind Thy back." To say this, is but faith's response to God's own declaration, when He says, "Their sins and their iniquities will I remember no more;" "Jehovah hath made to meet on Him the iniquities of us all."

Let us, by way of illustration, take the case of the thief on the cross. When

[1] Let it be remembered that all the value of the atoning sufferings of Christ on the cross are ever before God, and the soul of the believer will there find the unchanging foundation of the blessed words of Rom. viii. 34: *"Who is he that condemneth? It is Christ that died, yea rather, that is risen again, who is even at the right hand of God, who also maketh intercession for us."*

he, as a convicted sinner, cast the eye of faith upon that blessed One who hung beside him, was he not, then and there, rendered fit to enter the paradise of God? Was he not furnished with a divine title to pass from the cross of a malefactor into the presence of God? Unquestionably. Did he need anything more to be done for him, in him or with him, in order to fit him for heaven? By no means. Well, then, suppose that, instead of passing into heaven, he had been permitted to come down from the cross,—suppose the nails had been extracted and he allowed to go at liberty; he would have had sin in his nature, and, having sin in his nature, he would have been liable to commit sin, in thought, word, and deed. Now, could he ever lose his title, his fitness, his meetness? Surely not. His title was divine and everlasting. All his sins were borne by Jesus. That which had fitted him to enter heaven at the first, had fitted him once and forever, so that if he had remained on earth for fifty years, he would, at any moment, have been equally fit to enter heaven.

True it is, if the pardoned sinner commits sin, his communion is interrupted, and there must be the hearty confession of that sin ere his communion can be restored. "If we say that we have fellowship with Him, and walk in darkness, we lie, and do not the truth." But this is obviously a different point altogether. My communion may be interrupted, but my title can never be forfeited. All was accomplished on the cross. Every trace of sin and guilt was atoned for by that peerless, priceless sacrifice. By that sacrifice, the believer is transferred from a position of guilt and condemnation into a position of justification and perfect favor. He is translated from a condition in which he had not a single trace of righteousness, into a condition in which he has not a single trace of guilt, nor ever can have. He stands in grace, he is under grace, he breathes the very atmosphere of grace, and he never can be otherwise, according to God's view. If he commits sin (and who does not?) there must be confession. And what then? Forgiveness and cleansing, on the ground of the faithfulness and justice of God which have had their divine answer in the cross. *All is founded on the cross.* The faithfulness and justice of God, the advocacy of Christ, our confession, our full forgiveness, our perfect cleansing, the restoration of our communion, all rests upon the solid basis of the precious blood of Christ.

My reader will bear in mind that we are, at present, occupied with the one point, namely, the extent of divine forgiveness. There are other points of great importance which might be looked at in connection, such as the believer's oneness with Christ, his adoption into the family of God, the indwelling of the Holy Ghost, all of which necessarily imply the full forgiveness of sins; but we must confine ourselves to our immediate theme, and having endeavored to set forth the ground and the extent, we shall close with a few words on

THE STYLE OF DIVINE FORGIVENESS.

We are all conscious of how much depends upon the style of an action. Indeed, there is frequently far more power in the style than in the substance. How often have we heard such words as these, "Yes, I own he did me a favor; but then he did it in such a way as to take away all the good of it." Now, the Lord has His style of doing things, blessed be His name. He not only does great things, but He does them in such a way as to convince us that His heart is in the doing of them. Not only is the substance of His acts good, but the style most charming.

Let us have a sample or two. Look, for instance, at Christ's touching word to Simon the Pharisee, in Luke vii. "When they had nothing to pay, he *frankly* forgave them both." Now, so far as the mere matter of the debt was concerned, the result would have been the same whatever style had been adopted. But what heart does not perceive the moral power of the word "frankly"? Who would part with it? Who could bear to see the substance stripped of its style? The creditor might forgive with a murmur about the amount. That murmur would, in the judgment of a sensitive heart, rob the act of all its charms. On the other hand, the frankness of the style enhances, beyond expression, the value of the substance.

Again, look, for a moment, at that familiar but ever fruitful section of inspiration, Luke xv. Each of the parables illustrates the power and beauty of style. When the man finds his sheep, what does he do? Does he complain of all the trouble, and commence to drive the sheep home before him? Ah, no! this would never do. What then? "He layeth it on His shoulders." How? Complaining of the weight or the trouble? Nay; but *"rejoicing."* Here we have the lovely style. He showed that He was glad to get His sheep back again. The sheep would have been safe on the shoulder however it had been placed there; but who would part with the word "rejoicing"? Who would bear to see the substance of the action stripped of its charming style?

So, also, in the case of the woman and her lost piece of silver. "She lights a candle, sweeps the house, and seeks." How? With dullness, weariness and indifference? By no means; but "diligently," like one whose whole heart was in her work. It was quite manifest that she really wanted to find the lost piece of silver. Her style proved this.

Lastly, mark the style of the father in receiving the poor returning prodigal. "When he was yet a great way off, his father saw him, and had compassion, and *ran* and fell on his neck and kissed him." He does not send out a servant to tell the erring one to turn aside into one of the out-offices, or betake himself to the kitchen, or even to confine himself to his own room. No; he himself *runs*. He, as it were, lays aside his paternal dignity, in order to give expression to his fatherly affection. He is not satisfied with merely receiving the wanderer back: he must prove that his whole heart is in the reception; and this he does, not merely by the substance of the act, but by his style of doing it.

Various other passages might be adduced to illustrate the style of divine forgiveness, but the above will suffice to prove that God graciously recognizes the power which style has to act upon the human heart. I shall, therefore, in closing this paper, make an earnest appeal to my reader, as to what he now thinks of the ground, the extent, and the style of divine forgiveness.

Beloved reader, thou seest that the ground is as stable as the very throne of God itself, that the extent is infinite, and the style all that the heart could possibly desire. Say, therefore, art thou satisfied as to the great question of the forgiveness of sins? Can you any longer doubt God's willingness to forgive, when He has set before you, in such a way, the ground on which, the extent to which, and the style in which, He forgives sin? Can you hesitate when He actually

> "Opens His own heart to thee,
> And shows His thoughts how kind they be"?

He stands with open arms to receive thee. He points thee to the cross, where His own hand laid the foundation of forgiveness, and assures thee that all is done, and beseeches thee to rest now, henceforth and for evermore, in that which He has wrought for you. May the blessed Spirit lead thee to see these things in all their clearness and fullness, so that thou mayest not only believe in the forgiveness of sins, but believe also that all thy sins are frankly and forever forgiven.

C. H. M.

REGENERATION: WHAT IS IT?

There are few subjects which have given rise to more difficulty and perplexity than that of regeneration, or the new birth. Very many who are themselves the subjects of this new birth are at a loss to know what it is, and filled with doubt as to whether they have ever really experienced it. Many there are who, were they to clothe their desires in words, would say, "Oh, that I knew for certain that I had passed from death unto life. If only I were sure that I was born again, I should be happy indeed." Thus they are harassed with doubts and fears from day to day and from year to year. Sometimes they are full of hope that the great change has passed upon them; but, anon, something springs up within them which leads them to think their former hopes were a delusion. Judging from feeling and experience rather than from the plain teaching of the word of God, they are, of necessity, plunged into uncertainty and confusion as to the whole matter.

Now, I would desire to enter, in company with my reader, upon an examination, in the light of Scripture, of this most interesting subject. It is to be feared that very much of the misapprehension which prevails in reference thereto, arises from the habit of preaching regeneration and its fruits instead of Christ. The effect is put before the cause, and this must always produce derangement of thought.

Let us, then, proceed to consider this question. What is regeneration? How is it produced? What are its results?

I. And, first, What is regeneration? Very many look upon it as a change of the old nature, produced, no doubt, by the influence of the Spirit of God. This change is gradual in its operation, and proceeds, from stage to stage, until the old nature is completely brought under. This view of the subject involves two errors; namely, first, an error as to the real condition of our old nature; and, secondly, as to the distinct personality of the Holy Ghost. It denies the hopeless ruin of nature, and represents the Holy Ghost more as an influence than as a Person.

As to our true state by nature, the word of God presents it as one of total and irrecoverable ruin. Let us adduce the proofs. "And God saw that the wickedness of man was great in the earth, and that *every* imagination of the thoughts of his heart was *only* evil *continually*." (Gen. vi. 5.) The words *"every," "only,"* and *"continually,"* set aside every idea of a redeeming feature in man's condition before God. Again, "The Lord looked down from heaven upon the children of men, to see if there were any that did understand, and seek God. They are *all* gone aside, they are *all* together become filthy: there is *none* that doeth good; no, not one." (Ps. xiv. 2, 3.) Here, again, the expressions *"all," "none," "no, not one,"* preclude the idea of a single redeeming quality in man's condition, as judged in the presence of God. Having thus drawn a proof from Moses and one from the Psalms, let us take one or two from the prophets. "Why should ye be stricken any more? Ye will revolt more and more: the *whole* head is sick, and the *whole* heart faint. From the sole of the foot even unto the head there is no soundness in it." (Is. i. 5, 6.) "The voice said, 'Cry.' And he said, 'What shall I cry?' *All* flesh is grass, and all the goodliness thereof is as the flower of the field." (Isa. xl. 6.) "The heart is deceitful above all things, and desperately wicked: who can know it?" (Jer. xvii. 9.)

The above will suffice from the Old Testament. Let us now turn to the New. "Jesus did not commit Himself unto them, because He knew all, and needed not that any should testify of man: for He knew what was in man." (John ii. 24, 25.) "That which is born of the flesh is flesh." (John iii. 6.) Read, also, Romans iii. 9-19. "Because the carnal mind is enmity against God: for it is not subject to the law of God; neither, indeed, can be." (Rom. viii. 7.) "Having no hope, and without God in the world." (Eph. ii. 12.) These quotations might be multiplied, but there is no need. Sufficient proof has been adduced to show forth the true condition of nature. It is "lost," "guilty," "alienated," "without strength," "evil only," "evil continual-ly."

How, then, we may lawfully inquire, can that which is spoken of in such a way ever be changed or improved? "Can the Ethiopian change his skin, or the leopard his spots?" "That which is crooked cannot be made straight." The fact is, the more closely we examine the word of God, the more we shall see that it is not the divine method to improve a fallen, ruined thing, but to bring in something entirely new. It is precisely thus in reference to man's natural condition, — God is not seeking to improve it. The gospel does not propose, as its object, to better man's nature, but to give him a new one. It seeks not to put a new piece upon an old garment, but to impart a new garment altogether. The law looked for something in man, but never got it. Ordinances were given, but man used them to shut out God. The gospel, on the contrary, shows us Christ magnifying the law and making it honorable; it shows Him dying on the cross, and nailing ordinances thereto; it shows Him rising from the tomb, and taking His seat as a Conqueror, at the right hand of the Majesty in the heavens; and, finally, it declares that all who believe in His name are partakers of His own life, and are one with Him who is risen. (See, carefully, the following passages: John xx. 31; Acts xiii. 39; Rom. vi. 4-11; Eph. ii. 1-6; iii. 13-18; Col. ii. 10-15.)

It is of the very last importance to be clear and sound as to this. If I am led to believe that regeneration is a certain change in my old nature, and that this change is gradual in its operation, then, as a necessary consequence, I shall be filled with continual anxiety and apprehension, doubt and fear, depression and gloom, when I discover, as I surely shall, that nature is nature, and will be nought else but nature to the end. No influence or operation of the Holy Ghost can ever make the flesh spiritual. "That which is born of the flesh is flesh," and can never be aught else but "flesh"; and "all flesh is as grass," — as withered grass. The flesh is presented in Scripture not as a thing to be improved, but as a thing which God counts as "dead," and which we are called to "mortify," — subdue and deny, in all its thoughts and ways. In the cross of the Lord Jesus Christ we see the end of everything pertaining to our old nature. "They that are Christ's have crucified the flesh with the affections and lusts." (Gal. v. 24.) He does not say, They that are Christ's are improving, or trying to improve, the flesh. No; but they "have crucified it." It is utterly unimprovable. How can they do this? By the energy of the Holy Ghost, acting not *on* the *old* nature, but *in* the new, and enabling them to keep the old nature where the cross has put it, namely, in the place of death. God expects nothing from the flesh; neither should we. He looks upon it as dead; so should we. He has *put* it out of sight, and we should *keep* it so. The flesh should not be allowed to show itself. God does not own it. It has no existence before Him. True, it is in us, but God gives us the precious privilege of viewing and treating it as dead. His word to us is, "Likewise reckon ye also yourselves to be dead indeed unto sin, but alive unto God through Jesus Christ our Lord." (Rom. vi. 11.)

This is an immense relief to the heart that has struggled for years in the hopeless business of trying to improve nature. It is an immense relief, moreover, to the conscience which has been seeking a foundation for its peace in the gradual improvement of a totally unimprovable thing. Finally, it is an immense relief to any soul that may, for years, have been earnestly breathing after holiness, but has looked upon holiness as consisting in the improvement of that which hates holiness and loves sin. To each and all of such it is infinitely precious and important to understand the real nature of regeneration. No one who has not experienced it can conceive the intensity of anguish and the bitterness of the disappointment which a soul feels, who, vainly expecting some improvement in nature, finds, after years of struggling, that nature is nature still—ever the same. And just in proportion to the anguish and disappointment will be the joy of discovering that God is not looking for any improvement in nature,—that He sees *it* as dead, and *us* as alive in Christ,—one with Him, and accepted in Him, forever. To be led into a clear and full apprehension of this is divine emancipation to the conscience and true elevation for the whole moral being.

Let us, then, see clearly what regeneration is. It is a new birth,—the imparting of a new life,—the implantation of a new nature,—the formation of a new man. The old nature remains in all its distinctness, and the new nature is introduced in all its distinctness. This new nature has its own habits, its own desires, its own tendencies, its own affections. All these are spiritual, heavenly, divine. Its aspirations are all upward. It is ever breathing after the heavenly source from which it has emanated. As in nature water always finds its own level, so in grace the new—the divine—nature always tends toward its own proper source. Thus regeneration is to the soul what the birth of Isaac was to the household of Abraham (Gen. xxi.). Ishmael remained the same Ishmael, but Isaac was introduced; so the old nature remains the same, but the new is introduced. "That which is born of the Spirit is spirit": it partakes of the nature of its source. A child partakes of the nature of its parents, and the believer is made "a partaker of the divine nature." (2 Peter i. 4.) "*Of His own will* begat He us." (James i. 18.)

In a word, then, regeneration is God's own work, from first to last. God is the Operator; man is the happy, privileged subject. His co-operation is not sought in a work which must ever bear the impress of one almighty hand. God was alone in creation, alone in redemption, and He must be alone in the mysterious and glorious work of regeneration.

II. Having endeavored to show, from various passages of Scripture, that regeneration, or the new birth, is not a change of man's fallen nature, but the imparting of a new—a divine—nature, we shall now, in dependence upon the blessed Spirit's teaching, proceed to consider how the new birth is produced,—how the new nature is communicated. This is a point of immense importance, inasmuch as it places the word of God before us as the grand instrument which the Holy Ghost uses in quickening dead souls. "By the word of the Lord were the heavens made," and by the word of the Lord are dead souls called into new life. The word of the Lord is creative and regenerating. It called worlds into existence; it calls sinners from death to life. The same voice which, of old, said, "Let there be light," must, in every instance, say, "Let there be life."

If my reader will turn to the third chapter of John's gospel, he will find, in our Lord's interview with Nicodemus, much precious instruction in reference to the mode in which regeneration is produced. Nicodemus held a very high place in what would be termed the religious world. He was "a man of the Pharisees," "a ruler of the Jews," "a master of Israel." He could hardly have occupied a more elevated or influential position. But yet, it is very evident that this highly privileged man was ill at ease. Despite all his religious advantages, his heart felt a restless craving after something which neither his Pharisaism, nor yet the entire system of Judaism could supply. It is quite possible he might not have been able to define what he wanted; but he wanted something, else he never would have come to Jesus by night. It was evident that the Father was drawing him, by a resistless though most gentle hand, to the Son; and the way He took of drawing him was by producing a sense of need which nothing around him could satisfy. This is a very common case. Some are drawn to Jesus by a deep sense of guilt, some by a deep sense of need. Nicodemus, obviously, belongs to the latter class. His position was such as to preclude the idea of anything like gross immorality; and hence it would not, in his case, be so much guilt on his conscience as a void in his heart. But it comes to the same in the end: the guilty conscience and the craving heart must both be brought to Jesus, for He alone can perfectly meet both the one and the other. He can remove, by His precious sacrifice, every stain from the conscience; and He can fill up, by His peerless Person, every blank in the heart. The conscience which has been purged by the blood of Jesus is perfectly clean, and the heart which is filled with the Person of Jesus is perfectly satisfied.

However, Nicodemus had, like many beside, to unlearn a great deal ere he could really grasp the knowledge of Jesus. He had to lay aside a cumbrous mass of religious machinery ere he could apprehend the divine simplicity of God's plan of salvation. He had to descend from the lofty heights of Rabbinical learning and traditionary religion, and learn the alphabet of the gospel in the school of Christ. This was very humiliating to "a man of the Pharisees,"—"a ruler of the Jews,"—"a master of Israel." There is nothing of which man is so tenacious as his religion and his learning; and, in the case of Nicodemus, it must have sounded passing strange upon his ear when "a teacher come from God" declared to him, "Verily, verily, I say unto thee, Except a man be born again, he cannot see the kingdom of God." Being *by birth* a Jew, and, as such, entitled to all the privileges of a son of Abraham, it must have involved him in strange perplexity to be told that he must be born again,—that he must be the subject of a *new birth*, in order to see the kingdom of God. This was a total setting aside of all his privileges and distinctions. It called him down at once from the very highest to the very "lowest step of the ladder." A Pharisee, a ruler, a master, was not one whit nearer to, or fitter for, this heavenly kingdom, than the most disreputable of the children of men. This was deeply humbling. If he could carry all his advantages and distinctions with him, so as to have them placed to his credit in this new kingdom, it would be something. This would secure for him a position in the kingdom of God far above that of a harlot or a publican. But then, to be told that he must be born again left him nothing to glory in. This, I repeat, was deeply humbling to a learned, religious, and influential man.

But it was puzzling as well as humbling. "Nicodemus saith unto Him, 'How can a man be born when he is old? Can he enter the second time into his mother's womb, and be born?'" Surely not. There would be no more gained by a second natural birth than by a first. If a natural man could enter ten thousand times into his mother's womb and be born, he would be nought but a natural man after all, for "that which is born of the flesh is flesh." Do what you will with flesh,—with nature,—and you cannot alter or improve it. Nothing could change flesh into spirit. You may exalt it to the rank of a Pharisee, a ruler of the Jews, a master of Israel,—and you could hardly make it higher,—but it will be flesh notwithstanding. If this were more generally and clearly apprehended, it would prove the saving of fruitless labor to hundreds. Flesh is of no value whatever. In itself it is but withered grass; and as to its most pious endeavors, its religious advantages and attainments, its works of righteousness, they have been pronounced by the pen of inspiration to be as "filthy rags." (Isaiah lxiv. 6.)

But let us see the mode in which our blessed Lord replies to the "how?" of Nicodemus. It is peculiarly interesting. Jesus answered, "Verily, verily, I say unto thee, Except a man be born of water and of the Spirit, he cannot enter into the kingdom of God. That which is born of the flesh is flesh, and that which is born of the Spirit is spirit. Marvel not that I said unto thee, 'Ye must be born again.' The wind bloweth where it listeth, and thou hearest the sound thereof, but canst not tell whence it cometh, and whither it goeth: so is every one that is born of the Spirit." (John iii. 5-8.) Here we are distinctly taught that regeneration, or the new birth, is produced by "water and the Spirit." A man must be born of water and of the Spirit ere he can see the kingdom of God, or enter into its profound and heavenly mysteries. The keenest mortal vision cannot "see" the kingdom of God, nor the most gigantic human intellect "enter" into the deep secrets thereof. "The natural man receiveth not the things of the Spirit of God; for they are foolishness unto him: neither can he know them, because they are spiritually discerned." (1 Cor. ii. 14.) "Except a man be born of water and of the Spirit, he cannot enter the kingdom of God."

It may be, however, that many are at a loss to know what is meant by being "born of water." Certainly the expression has been made the ground of very much discussion and controversy. It is only by comparing scripture with scripture that we can ascertain the real sense of any particular passage. It is a special mercy for the unlettered Christian—the humble student of the inspired volume—that he need not travel outside the covers of that volume in order to interpret any passage contained therein.

What, then, is the meaning of being "born of water"? We must reply to this question by quoting two or three passages from the Word. In the opening of John's Gospel we read, "He came unto His own, and His own received Him not. But as many as received Him, to them gave He power to become the sons of God, even to *them that believe on His name: which were born*, not of blood, nor of the will of the flesh, nor of the will of man, but *of God*." (John i. 11-13.) From this passage we learn that every one who believes on the name of the Lord Jesus Christ is born again,—born of God. This is the plain sense of the passage. All who, by the power of God the Holy Ghost, believe on God the Son, are born of God the Father. The source of the testimony is divine; the object of the testimony is divine; the power of receiving the testimony is divine; the entire work of regeneration is divine. Hence, instead of being occupied with myself, and inquiring, like Nicodemus, "How can I be born again?" I have simply to cast myself, by faith, on Jesus; and thus I am born again. All who put their trust in Christ have gotten a new life—are regenerated.

Again, "Verily, verily, I say unto you, *He that heareth My word, and believeth on Him that sent Me*, HATH everlasting life, and shall not come into judgment; but is passed from death unto life." (John v. 24.) "Verily, verily, I say unto you, He that believeth on Me hath everlasting life." (John vi. 47.) "But these are written that ye might believe that Jesus is the Christ, the Son of God; and that, *believing, ye might have life through His name*." (John xx. 31.) All these passages go to prove that the only way in which we can get this new and everlasting life is by simply receiving the record concerning Christ. All who believe that record, *have* this new, this eternal life. Mark, it is not those who merely *say* they believe, but those who actually *do believe*, according to the sense of the word in the foregoing passages. There is life-giving power in the Christ whom the Word reveals, and in the Word which reveals Him. "Verily, verily, I say unto you, The hour is coming, and now is, when the dead shall hear the voice of the Son of God; and they that hear shall live." And then, lest ignorance should marvel or skepticism sneer at the idea of dead souls hearing, it is added, "Marvel not at this: for the hour is coming, in the which all that are in the graves shall hear His voice, and shall come forth: they that have done good, unto the resurrection of life; and they that have done evil, unto the resurrection of judgment." (John v. 25, 28, 29.) The Lord Christ can make dead souls, as well as dead bodies, hear His quickening voice. It is by His mighty voice that life can be communicated to either body or soul. If the infidel or the skeptic reasons and objects, it is simply because he makes his own vain mind the standard of what ought to be, and thus entirely shuts out God. This is the climax of folly.

But the reader may feel disposed to inquire, What has all this to do with the word "water," in John iii. 5? It has to do with it, inasmuch as it shows that the new birth is produced, the new life communicated, by the voice of Christ,—which is really the word of God, as we read in the first chapter of James, "Of His own will begat He us *with the word of truth.*" (ver. 18.) So also in 1 Peter, "*Being born again, not of corruptible seed, but of incorruptible, by the word of God,* which liveth and abideth forever." (Pet. i. 23.) In both these passages the Word is expressly set forth as the instrument by which the new birth is produced. James declares that we are begotten "by the Word of truth"; and Peter declares that we are "born again by the word of God." If, then, our Lord speaks of being "born of water," it is obvious that He represents the Word under the significant figure of "water,"—a figure which "a master of Israel" might have understood, had he only studied aright Ezekiel xxxvi. 25-27.

There is a beautiful passage in the epistle to the Ephesians, in which the Word is presented under the figure of water. "Husbands, love your wives, even as Christ also loved the Church, and gave Himself for it; that He might sanctify and cleanse it with *the washing of water by the Word.*" (Chap. v. 25-26.) So also in the epistle to Titus: "Not by works of righteousness which we have done, but according to His mercy He saved us, by the washing of regeneration, and renewing of the Holy Ghost; which He shed on us abundantly, through Jesus Christ our Saviour; that, being justified by His grace, we should be made heirs according to the hope of eternal life." (Chap. iii. 5-7.)

From all these quotations we learn that the word of God is the grand instrument of which the Holy Ghost makes use in calling dead souls into life. This truth is confirmed, in a peculiarly interesting manner, by our Lord's conversation with Nicodemus; for, instead of replying to the repeated inquiry, "How can these things be?" He sets this "master of Israel" down to learn the simple lesson taught by "the brazen serpent." The bitten Israelite of old was to be healed by simply *looking* at the serpent of brass on the pole: the dead sinner now is to get life by simply looking at Jesus on the cross and Jesus on the throne. The Israelite was not told to look at his wound, though it was the sense of his wound that made him look: the dead sinner is not told to look at his sins, though it is the sense of his sins that will make him look. One look at the serpent healed the Israelite: one look of faith at Jesus, who hung on the cross of Calvary, quickens the dead sinner. The former had not to look a second time to be healed: the latter has not to look a second time to get life. It was not the way he looked, but the object he looked at, that healed the Israelite: it is not the way he looks, but the object he looks at, that saves the sinner: "*Look* unto ME, and be ye saved, all the ends of the earth."

Such was the precious lesson which Nicodemus was called to learn, such the reply to his "how?" If a man begins to reason about the new birth, he must be confounded; but if he believes in Jesus, he is born again. Man's reason can never understand the new birth; but the word of God produces it. Many are astray as to this. They are occupied with the process of regeneration, instead of the Word which regenerates. Thus they are perplexed and confounded. They are looking at self instead of at Christ; and as there is an inseparable connection between the object at which we look and the effect of looking at it, we can easily see what must be the effect of looking in upon one's self. What could an Israelite have gained by looking at his wound? Nothing. What did he gain by looking at the serpent? Health. What does a sinner gain by looking at himself? Nothing. What does he gain by looking at Jesus? "Everlasting life."

III. We come now to consider, in the third and last place, the results of re-generation,—a point of the deepest interest. Who can estimate aright the glorious results of being a child of God? Who can unfold those affections which belong to that high and hallowed relationship in which the soul is placed by being born again? Who can fully explain that precious fellowship which the child of God is privileged to enjoy with his heavenly Father? "Behold, what manner of love the Father hath bestowed upon us, that we should be called the sons of God: therefore the world knoweth us not, because it knew Him not. Beloved, now are we the sons of God, and it doth not yet appear what we shall be: but we know that, when He shall appear, we shall be like Him, for we shall see Him as He is. And every man that hath this hope in Him purifieth himself, even as He is pure." (1 John iii. 1-3.) "For as many as are led by the Spirit of God, they are the sons of God. For ye have not received the spirit of bondage again to fear; but we have received the Spirit of adoption, whereby we cry, Abba, Father. The Spirit itself beareth witness with our spirit, that we are the children of God: and if children, then heirs; heirs of God and *joint-heirs* with Christ; if so be that we suffer with Him, that we may be also glorified *together*." (Rom. viii. 14-17.)

It is most important to understand the distinction between *life* and *peace*. The former is the result of being linked with Christ's *Person*; the latter is the result of His *work*. "He that hath the Son hath *life*," (1 John v. 12); but, "being *justified* by faith, we have *peace*," (Rom. v. 1),—"having made peace through the blood of His cross." (Col. i. 20.) The very moment a man receives into his heart the simple truth of the gospel, he becomes a child of God. The truth which he receives is the "incorruptible seed" of "the divine nature." (1 Pet. i. 23; 2 Pet. i. 4.) Many are not aware of all that is involved in thus simply receiving the truth of the gospel. As in nature, the child of a nobleman may not know the varied results of the relation-ship, so it is, likewise, in grace. I may be ignorant both as to the relationship and its results; but I am in it notwithstanding; and being in it, I have the affections which belong to it, and I ought to cultivate them, and allow them to entwine themselves artlessly around their proper object, even Him who has begotten me by the Word of truth. (James i. 18.) It is my privilege to enjoy the full flow of parental affection emanating from the bosom of God, and to reciprocate that affection, through the power of the indwelling Spirit. "Now *are* we the sons of God." He has made us such. He has attached this rare and marvelous privilege to the simple belief of the truth. (John i. 12.) We do not reach this position "by works of righteousness which we have done," or could do, but simply "according to His mercy He saved us, by the washing of regeneration, and renewing of the Holy Ghost; which He shed on us abundantly through Jesus Christ our Saviour; that being justified by His grace, we should be *made heirs* according to the hope of eternal life." (Titus iii. 5-7.) We are "*called sons*" and "*made* heirs," and all this simply by the belief of the truth of the gospel, which is God's "incorruptible seed."

Take the case of the very vilest sinner, who up to this moment has been living a life of gross wickedness. Let that person receive into his heart the pure gospel of God,—let him heartily believe "that Christ died for our sins according to the Scriptures; and that He was buried, and that He rose again the third day according to the Scriptures"—and he there, then and thus becomes a child of God, a thoroughly saved, perfectly justified, and divinely accepted person. In receiving into his heart the simple record concerning Christ, he has received new life. Christ is the truth and the life; and when we receive the truth we receive Christ, and when we receive Christ we receive life,—"he that believeth on the Son *hath* everlasting life." (John iii. 36.) When does he get this life? The very moment he believes,—"*believing* ye might have life through His name." (John xx. 31.) The truth concerning Christ is the seed of eternal life, and when that truth is believed, life is communicated.

Observe, this is what the Word of God declares—it is a matter of divine testimony, not merely of human feeling. We do not get life by *feeling* something in ourselves, but by *believing* something about Christ; and that something we have on the authority of God's eternal Word—"the Holy Scriptures." It is well to understand this. Many are looking *in* for evidences of the new life, instead of looking *out* at the object which imparts that life. It is quite true that "he that believeth on the Son of God hath the witness in himself" (1 John v. 10.); but, be it remembered, it is "the witness" of a life which is received by "*believing* on the Son of God," not by looking in upon one's self; and the more undividedly I am occupied with Christ, the more distinct and satisfactory will be "the witness" in myself. If I make the witness my object, I shall be plunged in doubt and uncertainty; but if I make Christ my object, I have the witness in all its divine integrity and power. There is special need of clearness as to this, because of the strong tendency of our hearts to make something *within* the ground of our peace and contentment, instead of building, absolutely and exclusively, upon Christ. The more simply we cling to Christ, apart from all beside, the more peaceful and happy we shall be; but directly we take the eye off Him, we become unhinged and unhappy.

In a word, then, my reader should seek to understand, with scriptural accuracy, the distinction between *life* and *peace*. The former is the result of the connection with Christ's *Person*; the latter is the result of believing in His finished *work*. We very frequently meet with quickened souls who are in sad trouble and disquietude as to their acceptance with God. They really do believe on the name of the Son of God, and, believing, they have life; but, from not seeing the fullness of the work of Christ as to their sins, they are troubled in conscience—they have no mental repose. Take an illustration. If you place a hundredweight upon the bosom of a dead man he does not feel it. Place another, and another, and another, he is wholly unconscious. Why? Because there is no *life*. Let us suppose, for a moment, the entrance in of life, and what will be the result? A most distressing sensation occasioned by the terrible weight upon the bosom. What then will be needful in order to the full enjoyment of the life which had been imparted? Clearly, the removal of the burden. It is somewhat thus with the sinner who receives life by believing on the Person of the Son of God. So long as he was in a state of spiritual death he had no spiritual sensations—he was unconscious of any weight pressing upon him. But the entrance of spiritual life has imparted spiritual sensibilities, and he now feels a burden pressing upon his heart and conscience, which he knows not exactly how to get rid of. He sees not as yet all that is involved in believing on the name of the only begotten Son of God. He does not see that Christ is at once his righteousness and his life. He needs a simple view of the finished atonement of Christ, whereby *all* his sins were plunged in the waters of eternal oblivion, and he himself introduced into the full favor of God. It is this, and this alone, that can remove the heavy burden off the heart, and impart that profound mental repose which nothing can ever disturb.

If I think of God as a judge, and myself as a sinner, I need the blood of the cross to bring me into His presence, in the way of righteousness. I must fully understand that every claim which God, the righteous Judge, had upon me, a guilty sinner, has been divinely answered and eternally settled by "the precious blood of Christ." This gives my soul peace. I see that, through that blood, God can be "just and the justifier of him which believeth in Jesus." (Rom. iii. 29.) I learn that in the cross God has been glorified about my sins—yea, that the whole question of sin was fully gone into and perfectly settled between God and Christ amid the deep and awful solitudes of Calvary. Thus my load is taken off, my weight removed, my guilt canceled: I can breathe freely; I have perfect peace; there is literally nothing against me; I am as free as the blood of Christ can make me. The Judge has declared Himself satisfied as to sin by raising the sinner's Surety from the dead, and placing Him at the right hand of the Majesty in the heavens.

But, then, there comes another thing of immense value. I not only see myself as a guilty sinner provided with a way of access to God as a righteous Judge, but I see God, in pursuance of His eternal counsels of electing love, begetting me through the Word of truth, making me His child, adopting me into His family, and setting me before Him in such a way as that I can enjoy communion with Him as my Father in the midst of all the tender endearments of the divine family circle. This is obviously another phase of the believer's position and character. It is no longer a question of his coming to God in the full and settled consciousness that every just claim has been met—this in itself is ineffably precious to every sin-burdened heart—but there is far more than this: God is my Father and I am His child. He has a Father's heart, and I can count on the tender affections of that heart in the midst of all my feebleness and need. He loves me, not because of what I am enabled to do, but because I am His child.

Look at yonder tottering babe, the object of ceaseless care and solicitude, wholly unable to promote his father's interests in any one way, yet so loved by the father that he would not exchange him for ten thousand worlds; and if it be thus with an earthly father, what must it be with our heavenly Father? He loves us, not for aught that we are able to do, but because we are His children. He has begotten us of His own will, by the Word of truth. (James i. 18.) We could no more earn a place in the heart of the Father than we could satisfy the claims of the righteous Judge. All is of free grace. The Father has begotten us, and the Judge has found a ransom. (Job xxxiii. 24.) We are debtors to grace for both the one and the other.

But, be it remembered, while we are wholly unable to earn, by our works, a place in the Father's heart, or to satisfy the claims of the righteous Judge, we are, nevertheless, responsible to "believe the record which God has given of His Son." (1 John v. 9-11.) I say this lest, by any means, my reader should be one of those who intrench themselves behind the dogmas of a one-sided theology, while refusing to believe the plain testimony of God. Many there are—intelligent people, too—who, when the gospel of the grace of God is pressed upon their acceptance, are ready to reply, I cannot believe unless God gives me power to do so; nor shall I ever be endowed with that power unless I am one of the elect. If I belong to the favored number, I *must* be saved; if not, I *can't*.

This is a thoroughly one-sided theology; and not only so, but its one side is turned the wrong way—yea, it is so turned as to wear the form of an absurd but most dangerous fatalism, which completely destroys man's responsibility, and casts dishonor upon God's moral administration. It sends man forth upon a wild career of reckless folly, and makes God the author of the sinner's unbelief. This is, in good truth, to add insult to injury. It is, first, to make God a liar, and then charge Him with being the cause of it. It is to reject his proffered love, and blame Him for the rejection. This is, in reality, the most daring wickedness, though based, as I have said, upon a one-sided theology.

Now, does any one imagine that an argument so flimsy will hold good for a moment in the presence of the king of terrors, or before the judgment-seat of Christ? Is there a soul throughout the gloomy regions of the lost that would ever think of charging God with being the author of its eternal perdition? Ah, no! it is only on earth that people argue thus. Such arguments are never breathed in hell. When men get to hell, they blame themselves. In heaven they praise the Lamb. All who are lost will have to thank *self*; all who are saved will have to thank *God*. It is when the impenitent soul has passed through the narrow archway of time into the boundless ocean of eternity, that it will enter into the full depth and power of those solemn words,

"I would, ... but ye would not."

In truth, human responsibility is as distinctly taught in the Word of God as is divine sovereignty. Man finds it impossible to frame a system of divinity which will give each truth its proper place; but he is not called upon to frame systems, but to believe a plain record, and be saved thereby.

Having said thus much by way of caution to any who may be in danger of falling under the power of the above line of argument, I shall proceed to unfold a little further the results of regeneration, as seen in the matter of the discipline of the Father's house.

As the children of God, we are admitted to all the privileges of His house; and in point of fact the discipline of the house is as much a privilege as anything else. It is on the ground of the relationship in which God has set us that He acts in discipline towards us. A father disciplines his children because they are his. If I see a strange child doing wrong, I am not called upon to chasten him. I am not in the relationship of a father to him, and as a consequence I neither know the affections nor the responsibilities of that relationship. I must be in a relationship in order to know the affections which belong to it. Now, as our Father, God, in His great grace and faithfulness, looks after us in all our ways, He will not suffer aught upon us or about us which would be unworthy of Him and subversive of our real peace and blessedness. "Furthermore, we have had fathers of our flesh which corrected us, and we gave them reverence: shall we not much rather be in subjection unto the Father of spirits, and live? For they verily for a few days chastened us after their own pleasure; but He for our profit, that we might be partakers of His holiness." (Heb. xii. 9, 10.) Thus the discipline is a positive privilege, inasmuch as it is a proof of our Father's care, and has for its object our participation in the divine holiness.

But then, we must ever bear in mind that the discipline of our Father's hand is to be interpreted in the light of our Father's countenance, and the deep mysteries of His moral government to be contemplated through the medium of his tender love. If we lose sight of this, we shall be sure to get into a spirit of bondage as respects ourselves, and a spirit of judgment as respects others, both of which are in direct opposition to the spirit of Christ. All our Father's dealings with us are in perfect love. When He furnishes us with bread, it is in love; and when He takes down the rod, it is in love also. *God is love.* It may frequently happen that we are at a loss to know the why and the wherefore of some special dispensation of our Father's hand. It seems dark and inexplicable. The mist which enwraps our spirits is so thick and heavy as to prevent our catching the bright and cheering beams from our Father's countenance. This is a trying moment—a solemn crisis in the soul's history. We are in great danger of losing the sense of divine love through inability to understand the profound secrets of divine government. Satan, too, is sure to be busy at such a time. He will ply his fiery darts, and throw in his dark and diabolical suggestions. Thus, between the filthy reasonings which spring up within and the horrible suggestions which come from without, the soul is in danger of losing its balance, and of getting away from the precious attitude of artless repose in divine love, let the divine government be what it may.

Thus much with reference to our own souls while under any special visitation of the hand of God. The effect as to others is equally bad. How often may we have detected ourselves in the habit of cherishing a spirit of judgment in reference to a child of God whom we found in circumstances of trial, either of "mind, body, or estate." This should be carefully guarded against. We ought not to imagine that every visitation of the hand of God must necessarily be on account of some special sin in the person. This would be an entirely false principle. The dealings of God are preventive as well as corrective.

Take a case in point. My child may be in the room with me, enjoying all the sweet intimacies which belong to our relationship. A person enters who I know will utter things which I do not wish my child to hear. I therefore, without assigning any reason, tell my child to go to his room. Now, if he has not the fullest confidence in my love, he may entertain all manner of false notions about my act; he may reason about the why and wherefore to such a degree as almost to question my affection. However, directly the visitor takes his leave, I call the child into my presence and explain the whole matter to him, and in the renewed experience of a father's love he gets rid of the unhappy suspicions of a few dark moments.

Thus it is often with our poor hearts in the matter of the divine dealings both with ourselves and others. We reason when we ought to repose: we doubt when we ought to depend. Confidence in our Father's love is the true corrective in all things.

We should ever hold fast the assurance of that changeless, infinite, and everlasting love which has taken us up in our low and lost estate, made us "sons of God," and will never fail us, never let us go, until we enter upon the unbroken and eternal communion of our Father's house above. May that love dwell more abundantly in our hearts, that so we may enter more fully into the meaning and power of regeneration—what it is, how it is produced, and what are its results. God grant, it for Christ's sake! Amen.

C. H. M.

IN THE FATHER'S HOUSE (POEM)

"The wanderer no more will roam,
The lost one to the fold hath come,
The prodigal is welcomed home,
O Lamb of God, through Thee!

"Though clothed in rags, by sin defiled,
The Father did embrace His child;
And I am pardoned, reconciled,
O Lamb of God, through Thee!

"It is the Father's joy to bless;
His love has found for me a dress,
A robe of spotless righteousness,
O Lamb of God, in Thee!

"And now my famished soul is fed,
A feast of love for me is spread,
I feed upon the children's bread,
O Lamb of God, in Thee!

"Yea, in the fulness of His grace,
God put me in the children's place,
Where I may gaze upon His face,
O Lamb of God, in Thee!

"Not half His Love can I express,
Yet, Lord, with joy my lips confess,
This blessed portion I possess,
O Lamb of God, in Thee!

"Thy precious name it is I bear,
In Thee I am to God brought near,
And all the Father's love I share,
O Lamb of God, in Thee!"

SANCTIFICATION: WHAT IS IT?

To minister peace and comfort to those who, though truly converted, have not laid hold of a full Christ, and who, as a consequence, are not enjoying the liberty of the gospel, is the object we have in view in considering the important and deeply-interesting subject of sanctification. We believe that very many of those, whose spiritual welfare we desire to promote, suffer materially from defective, or erroneous, ideas on this vital question. Indeed, in some cases, the doctrine of sanctification is so entirely misapprehended as to interfere with the faith of the believer's perfect justification and acceptance before God.

For example, we have frequently heard persons speak of sanctification as a progressive work, in virtue of which our old nature is to be made gradually better; and, moreover, that until this process has reached its climax, until fallen and corrupt humanity has become completely sanctified, we are not fit for heaven.

Now, so far as this view of the question is concerned, we have only to say that both Scripture and the truthful experience of all believers are entirely against it. The Word of God never once teaches us that the Holy Spirit has for His object the improvement, either gradual or otherwise, of our old nature—that nature which we inherit, by natural birth, from fallen Adam. The inspired apostle expressly declares that, "The natural man receiveth not the things of the Spirit of God; for they are foolishness unto him: neither can he know them, because they are spiritually discerned." (1 Cor. ii. 14.) This one passage is clear and conclusive on the point. If "the natural man" can neither "receive" nor "know" "the things of the Spirit of God," then how can that "natural man" be sanctified by the Holy Ghost? Is it not plain that, to speak of "the sanctification of our nature" is opposed to the direct teaching of 1 Cor. ii. 14? Other passages might be adduced to prove that the design of the Spirit's operations is not to improve or sanctify the flesh, but there is no need to multiply quotations. An utterly ruined thing can never be sanctified. Do what you will with it, it is ruined; and, most assuredly, the Holy Ghost did not come down to sanctify a ruin, but to lead the ruined one to Jesus. So far from any attempt to sanctify the flesh, we read that "The flesh lusteth against the Spirit, and the Spirit against the flesh; and these are contrary the one to the other." (Gal. v. 17.) Could the Holy Ghost be represented as carrying on a warfare with that which He is gradually improving and sanctifying? Would not the conflict cease so soon as the process of improvement had reached its climax? But does the believer's conflict ever cease so long as he is in the body?

This leads us to the second objection, to the erroneous theory of the progressive sanctification of our nature, namely, The objection drawn from the truthful experience of all believers. Is the reader a true believer? If so, has he found any improvement in his old nature? Is it a single whit better now than it was when he first started on his christian course? He may, and should through grace, be able to subdue it more thoroughly; but it is nothing better? If it be not mortified, it is just as ready to spring up and show itself in all its vileness as ever. "The flesh" in a believer is in no wise better than "the flesh" in an unbeliever.—And if the Christian does not bear in mind that *self* must be judged, he will soon learn, by bitter experience, that his old nature is as bad as ever; and, moreover, that it will be the very same to the end.

It is difficult to conceive how any one who is led to expect a gradual improvement of his nature, can enjoy an hour's peace, inasmuch as he cannot but see, if he only looks at himself in the light of God's holy Word, his old self—the flesh—is the very same as when he walked in the moral darkness of his unconverted state. His own condition and character are, indeed, greatly changed by the possession of a new, yea, a "divine nature," (2 Pet. i. 4.) and by the indwelling of the Holy Ghost, to give effect to its desires; but the moment the old nature is at work, he finds it as opposed to God as ever. We doubt not but that very much of the gloom and despondency, of which so many complain, may be justly traced to their misapprehension of this important point of sanctification. They are looking for what they can never find. They are seeking for a ground of peace in a sanctified nature instead of in a perfect sacrifice—in a progressive work of holiness instead of in a finished work of atonement. They deem it presumptuous to believe that their sins are forgiven until their evil nature is completely sanctified; and, seeing that this end is not reached, they have no settled assurance of pardon, and are therefore miserable. In a word, they are seeking for a "foundation" totally different from that which Jehovah says he has laid, and, therefore, they have no certainty whatever. The only thing that ever seems to give them a ray of comfort is some *apparently* successful effort in the struggle for personal sanctity. If they have had a good day—if they are favored with a season of comfortable communion—if they happen to enjoy a peaceful, devotional frame, they are ready to cry out, "Thou hast made my mountain to stand strong; I shall never be moved." (Ps. xxx.)

But, ah! these things furnish a sorry foundation for the soul's peace. They are not Christ; and until we see that our standing before God is *in Christ*, there cannot be settled peace. The soul that has really got hold of Christ is desirous indeed of holiness; but if intelligent of what Christ is to him, he has done with all thoughts about sanctified nature. He has found his all in Christ, and the paramount desire of his heart is to grow into His likeness. This is true, *practical* sanctification.

It frequently happens that persons, in speaking of sanctification, mean a right thing, although they do not express themselves according to the teaching of holy Scripture. There are many also, who see one side of the truth as to sanctification, but not the other; and, although we should be sorry to make any one an offender for a word, yet it is always most desirable, in speaking of any point of truth, and especially of so vital a point as that of sanctification, to speak according to the divine integrity of the word. We shall, therefore, proceed to quote for our readers a few of the leading passages from the New Testament in which this doctrine is unfolded. These passages will teach us two things, namely, what sanctification is, and how it is effected.

The first passage to which we would call attention is 1 Cor. i. 30,—"But of Him are ye in Christ Jesus, who of God is made unto us wisdom, and righteousness, and *sanctification*, and redemption." Here we learn that Christ "is made unto us" all these things. God has given us, in Christ, a precious casket, and when we open that casket with the key of faith, the first gem that glitters in our view, in this wisdom of God is "righteousness;" then, "sanctification;" and lastly, "redemption." We have them all *in Christ*. As we get one so we get all. And how do we get one and all? By faith. But why does the apostle name redemption last? Because it takes in the final deliverance of the body of the believer from under the power of mortality, when the voice of the archangel and the trump of God shall either raise it from the tomb, or change it, in the twinkling of an eye. Will this act be progressive? Clearly not; it will be done "in the twinkling of an eye." The body is in one state now, and "in a moment" it will be in another. In the brief point of time expressed by the rapid movement of the eyelash, will the body pass from corruption to incorruption; from dishonor to glory; from weakness to power. What a change! It will be immediate, complete, eternal.

But what are we to learn from the fact that "sanctification" is placed in the group with "redemption?" We learn that what redemption *will be* to the body, that sanctification *is* now to the soul. In a word, sanctification, in the sense in which it is here used, is immediate, and complete, a divine work. The one is no more progressive than the other. The one is as immediate as the other. The one is as complete and as independent of man as the other. No doubt, when the body shall have undergone the glorious change, there will be heights of glory to be trodden, depths of glory to be penetrated, wide fields of glory to be explored. All these things shall occupy us throughout eternity. But, then, the work which is to fit us for such scenes will be done in a moment. So also is it, in reference to sanctification. The *practical* results of it will be continually developing themselves; but the thing itself, as spoken of in this passage, is done in a moment.

What an immense relief it would be to thousands of earnest, anxious, struggling souls to get a proper hold of Christ as their sanctification! How many are vainly endeavoring to work out a sanctification for themselves! They have come to Christ for righteousness after many fruitless efforts to get a righteousness of their own; but they are seeking after sanctification in a different way altogether. They have gotten "righteousness without works," but they imagine that they must get sanctification with works. They have gotten righteousness by faith, but they imagine they must get sanctification by effort. They do not see that we get sanctification in precisely the same way as we get righteousness, inasmuch as Christ "is made unto us" the one as well as the other. Do we get Christ by effort? No; by faith. It is "to him that worketh *not*." (Rom. iv. 5.) This applies to all that we get in Christ. We have no warrant whatever to single out from 1 Cor. i. 30, the matter of "sanctification," and place it upon a different footing from all the other blessings which it enfolds. We have neither wisdom, righteousness, sanctification, nor redemption in ourselves; nor can we procure them by aught that we can do; but God has made

Christ to be unto us all these things. In giving us Christ, He gave us all that is in Christ. The fullness of Christ is ours, and Christ is the fullness of God.

Again, in Acts xxvi. 18, the converted Gentiles are spoken of as "receiving forgiveness of sins and an inheritance among them which *are* sanctified by faith." Here, faith is the instrument by which we are said to be sanctified, because it connects us with Christ. The very moment the sinner believes on the Lord Jesus Christ he becomes linked to Him. He is made one with Him, complete in Him, accepted in Him. This is true sanctification and justification. It is not a process. It is not a gradual work. It is not progressive. The word is very explicit. It says, "them which *are* sanctified by *faith* which is in me." It does not say, "which *shall be* sanctified," or, "which are being sanctified." If such were the doctrine it would have been so stated.

No doubt, the believer grows in the knowledge of this sanctification, in his sense of its power and value, its practical influence and results, the experience and enjoyment of it. As "the truth" pours its divine light upon his soul, he enters into a more profound apprehension of what is involved in being "set apart" for Christ, in the midst of this evil world. All this is blessedly true; but the more its truth is seen, the more clearly we shall understand that sanctification is not merely a progressive work, wrought in us by the Holy Spirit, but that it is one result of our being linked to Christ, by faith, whereby we become partakers of all that He is. This is an immediate, a complete, and an eternal work. "Whatsoever God doeth, it shall be forever: nothing can be put to it, nor anything taken from it." (Eccles. iii. 14.) Whether He justifies or sanctifies, "it shall be forever." The stamp of eternity is fixed upon every work of God's hand: "nothing can be put to it," and, blessed be His name, "nothing can be taken from it."

There are passages which present the subject in another aspect, — the *practical result* in the believer of his sanctification in Christ, and which may require fuller consideration hereafter. In 1 Thess. v. the apostle prays for the saints whom he addresses, "And the very God of peace sanctify you wholly; and I pray God your whole spirit, and soul, and body, be preserved blameless unto the coming of our Lord Jesus Christ." Here, the word is applied to a sanctification admitting of degrees. The Thessalonians had, along with all believers, a perfect sanctification in Christ; but as to the practical enjoyment and display of this, it was only accomplished in part, and the apostle prays that they may be wholly sanctified.

In this passage, it is worthy of notice, that nothing is said of "the flesh." Our fallen, corrupt nature is always treated as a hopelessly ruined thing. It has been weighed in the balance and found wanting. It has been measured by a divine rule and found short. It has been tried by a perfect plummet and proved crooked. God has set if aside. Its "end has come before him." He has condemned it and put it to death. (Rom. viii. 3.) Our old man is crucified, dead, and buried. (Rom. vi. 8.) Are we, then, to imagine for a moment, that God the Holy Ghost came down from heaven for the purpose of exhuming a condemned, crucified, and buried thing, so that He might sanctify it? The idea has only to be named, to be abandoned forever by every one who bows to the authority of Scripture. The more closely we study the Law, the Prophets, the Psalms, and the entire New Testament, the more closely

we shall see that the flesh is wholly unmendable. It is, absolutely, good for nothing. The Spirit does not *sanctify* it, but he enables the believer to *mortify* it. We are
told to "*put off* the old man." This precept would never have been delivered to us if
the object of the Holy Ghost were the sanctification of that "old man."

We trust that no one will accuse us of entertaining a desire to lower the standard
of personal holiness, or to weaken the soul's earnest aspirations after a growth in
that purity for which every true believer must ardently long. God forbid! If there is
one thing above another which we desire to promote in ourselves and others, it is
a full personal purity—a godly practical sanctity—a whole-hearted separation to
God—from all evil,—in every shape and form. For this we long, for this we pray,
in this we desire to grow daily.

But then we are fully convinced that a superstructure of true, practical holiness can never be erected on a legal basis; and hence it is that we press 1 Cor. i. 30,
upon the attention of our readers. It is to be feared that many who have, in some
measure, abandoned the legal ground, in the matter of "righteousness," are yet
lingering thereon for "sanctification." We believe this to be the mistake of thousands, and we are most anxious to see it corrected. The passage before us would, if
simply received into the heart by faith, entirely correct this serious mistake.

All intelligent Christians are agreed as to the fundamental truth of "Righteousness without works." All freely and fully admit that we cannot, by any efforts of our own, work out a righteousness for ourselves before God. But it is not
just so clearly seen that righteousness and sanctification are put upon precisely the
same ground in the Word of God. We can no more work out a sanctification than
we can work out a righteousness. We may try it, but we shall, sooner or later, find
out that it is utterly vain. We may vow and resolve; we may labor and struggle; we
may cherish the fond hope of doing better to-morrow than we have done to-day;
but, in the end, we must be constrained to see, and feel, and own, that as regards
the matter of sanctification, we are as completely "without strength" as we have
already proved ourselves to be in the matter of righteousness.

And, oh! what sweet relief to the suffering one who has been seeking for sat-
isfaction or rest in his own holiness to find, after years of unsuccessful struggle,
that the very thing he longs for is treasured up in Christ for him,—his own this
moment, even a complete sanctification to be enjoyed *by faith*! Such an one may
have been battling with his habits, his lusts, his tempers, his passions; he has been
making the most laborious efforts to subdue his flesh and grow in inward holiness,
but alas! he has failed.[2] He finds, to his deep sorrow, that *he* is not holy, and he
reads that "Without holiness no man shall see the Lord." (Heb. xii.) Not, observe,
without a certain measure, or attainment in holiness, but without the thing itself;
which every Christian has, from the moment he believes, whether he knows it or
not. Perfect sanctification is as fully included in the word "salvation" as is "righteousness, or redemption." He did not get Christ by effort, but by faith; and when
he laid hold on Christ he received all that is in Christ. Hence, it is by abiding in

---

[2] The divine picture of this experience and conflict is given us in the seventh chapter
of Romans. For a full consideration of this subject, see the pamphlet entitled, "Deliverance,
What is it?" Price, five cents.—[Ed.]

Christ he finds power for the subjugation of his lusts, passions, tempers, habits, circumstances, and influences. He must look to Jesus for all.

All this is simple to faith. The believer's standing is in Christ, and if in Christ for one thing, he is in Christ for all. I am not in Christ for righteousness, and out of Christ for sanctification. If I am a debtor to Christ for righteousness, I am equally a debtor to Him for sanctification. I am not a debtor to legality for either the one or the other. I get both by grace, through faith, and all in Christ. Yes, all—all in Christ. The moment the sinner comes to Christ, and believes on Him, he is taken completely off the old ground of nature; he loses his old legal standing and all its belongings, and is looked at as in Christ. He is no longer "in the flesh" but "in the Spirit." (Rom. viii. 9.) God only sees him in Christ, and as Christ. He becomes one with Christ forever. "As he is, so are we in this world." (1 Jno. iv.) Such is the absolute standing, the settled and eternal position, of the very feeblest babe in the family of God. There is but one standing for every child of God, every member of Christ. Their knowledge, experience, power, gift, and intelligence, may vary; but their standing is one. Whatever of righteousness or sanctification they possess, they owe it all to their being in Christ; consequently, if they have not gotten a perfect sanctification, neither have they gotten a perfect righteousness. But 1 Cor. i. 30, distinctly teaches that Christ *"is made"* both the one and the other to all believers. It does not say that we have righteousness and *"a measure* of sanctification." We have just as much scripture authority for putting the word "measure" before righteousness as before sanctification. The Spirit of God does not put it before either. Both are perfect, and we have both in Christ. God never does anything by halves. There is no such thing as a half justification. Neither is there such a thing as a half sanctification. The idea of a member of the family of God, or of the body of Christ, wholly justified, but only half sanctified, is at once opposed to Scripture, and revolting to all sensibilities of the divine nature.

It is not improbable that very much of the misapprehension which prevails, in reference to sanctification, is traceable to the habit of confounding two things which differ very materially, namely our *standing* and our *walk*, or position and condition, The believer's standing is perfect, because it is the gift of God in Christ. His walk, alas, may be very imperfect, fluctuating, and marked with personal infirmity. Whilst his position is absolute and unalterable, his practical condition may exhibit manifold imperfections, inasmuch as he is still in the body, and surrounded by various hostile influences which affect his moral condition from day to day. If, then, his standing be measured by his walk, his position by his condition, what he is in God's view by what he is in man's, the result must be false. If I reason from what I am in myself, instead of from what I am in Christ, I must, of necessity, arrive at a wrong conclusion.

We should look carefully to this. We are very much disposed to reason upward from ourselves to God, instead of downward from God to us. We should bear in mind that

> "Far as heaven's resplendent orbs
> Beyond earth's spot extend,
> As far My thoughts, as far My ways,

Your ways and thoughts transcend."

God looks on His people, and acts toward them, too, according to their standing in Christ. He has given them this standing. He has made them what they are. They are His workmanship. Hence, therefore, to speak of them as half justified would be a dishonor cast upon God; and to speak of them as half sanctified would be just the same.

This train of thought conducts us to another weighty proof drawn from the authoritative and conclusive page of inspiration, namely, 1 Cor. vi. 11. In the verses preceding, the apostle draws a fearful picture of fallen humanity, and he plainly tells the Corinthian saints that they had been just like that. "Such were some of you." This is plain dealing. There are no flattering words—no daubing with untempered mortar—no keeping back the full truth as to nature's total and irretrievable ruin. "Such were some of you: but ye *are* washed, but ye *are* sanctified, but ye *are* justified, in the name of the Lord Jesus, and by the Spirit of our God."

What a striking contrast between the two sides of the apostle's *"but!"* On the one side, we have all the moral degradation of man's condition; and, on the other side, we have all the absolute perfectness of the believer's standing before God. This, truly, is a marvellous contrast; and be it remembered that the soul passes in a moment, from one side to the other of this "but." "Such *were* some of you: but ye *are*," now, something quite different. The moment they received Paul's gospel, they were "washed, sanctified, and justified." They were fit for heaven; and, had they not been so, it would have been a slur upon the divine workmanship.

> "'Clean every whit,' thou saidst it, Lord;
> Shall one suspicion lurk?
> Thine, surely, is a faithful word,
> And Thine a finished work."

This is divinely true. The most inexperienced believer is "clean every whit," not as a matter of attainment, but as the necessary result of being in Christ. He will, no doubt, grow in the knowledge and experience of what sanctification really is. He will enter into its practical power; its moral effects upon his habits, thoughts, feelings, affections, and associations: in a word, he will understand and exhibit the mighty influence of divine sanctification upon his entire course, conduct, and character. But, then, he was as completely sanctified, in God's view, the moment he became linked to Christ by faith, as he will be when he comes to bask in the sunlight of the divine presence, and reflect back the concentrated beams of glory emanating from the throne of God and of the Lamb. He is in Christ now; and he will be in Christ then. His sphere and his circumstances will differ. His feet shall stand upon the golden pavement of the upper sanctuary, instead of standing upon the arid sand of the desert. He will be in a body of glory, instead of a body of humiliation; but as to his standing, his acceptance, his completeness, his justification, and sanctification, all was settled the moment he believed on the name of the only begotten Son of God—as settled as ever it will be, because as settled as God could make it. All this seems to flow as a necessary and unanswerable inference from 1 Cor. vi. 11.

It is of the utmost importance to apprehend, with clearness, the distinction between a truth and the practical application and result of a truth. This distinction is ever maintained in the word of God. "Ye *are* sanctified." Here is the absolute truth as to the believer, as viewed in Christ. The practical application of it, and its results in the believer, we find in such passages as these. "Christ loved the church, and gave Himself for it; that He might sanctify and cleanse it with the washing of water by the Word." (Eph. v. 25, 26.) And "the very God of peace sanctify you wholly." (1 Thess. v. 23.)

But how is this application made, and this result reached? By the Holy Ghost, through the written Word. Hence we read, "Sanctify them through thy truth." (Jno. xvii.) And again, "God hath from the beginning chosen you to salvation, through sanctification of the Spirit and belief of the truth." (2 Thess. ii. 13.) So also, in Peter, "Elect according to the foreknowledge of God the Father, through sanctification of the Spirit." (1 Pet. i. 2.) The Holy Ghost carries on the believer's practical sanctification on the ground of Christ's accomplished work; and the mode in which He does so is by applying to the heart and conscience the truth as it is in Jesus. He unfolds the truth as to our perfect standing before God in Christ, and, by energizing the new man in us, He enables us to put away everything incompatible with that perfect standing. A man who is "washed, sanctified, and justified," ought not to indulge in any unhallowed temper, lust, or passion. He is separated to God and should "cleanse himself from all filthiness of the flesh and spirit." It is his holy and happy privilege to breathe after the very loftiest heights of personal sanctity. His heart and his habits should be brought and held under the power of that grand truth that he is perfectly "washed, sanctified, and justified."

This is true practical sanctification. It is not any attempt at the improvement of our old nature. It is not a vain effort to reconstruct an irretrievable ruin. No; it is simply the Holy Ghost, by the powerful application of "the truth," enabling the new man to live, and move, and have his being in that sphere to which he belongs. Here there will, undoubtedly, be progress. There will be growth in the moral power of this precious truth—growth in spiritual ability to subdue and keep under all that pertains to nature—a growing power of separation from the evil around us—a growing meetness for that heaven to which we belong, and toward which we are journeying—a growing capacity for the enjoyment of its holy exercises. All this there will be, through the gracious ministry of the Holy Ghost, who uses the Word of God to unfold to our souls the truth as to our standing in Christ, and as to the walk which *comports with* such standing. But let it be clearly understood that the work of the Holy Ghost in practical sanctification, day by day, is founded upon the fact that believers "*are* sanctified through the offering of the body of Jesus Christ once." (Heb. x. 10.) The object of the Holy Ghost is to lead us into the knowledge, the experience, and the practical exhibition of that which was true of us in Christ the very moment we believed. As regards this, there is progress; but our standing in Christ is eternally complete.

"Sanctify them through Thy truth; Thy Word is truth." (Jno. xvii. 17.) And again, "The very God of peace sanctify you wholly." (1 Thess. v. 23.) In these passages, we have the grand practical side of this question. Here we see sanctification presented, not merely as something absolutely and eternally true of us in Christ, but also as wrought out in us, daily and hourly, by the Holy Ghost through the Word. Looked at from this point of view, sanctification is, obviously, a progressive thing. I should be more advanced in personal holiness next year than I was in this. I should, through grace, be advancing, day by day, in practical holiness. But what, let me ask, is this? What, but the working out in me of that which was true of me in Christ, the very moment I believed? The basis on which the Holy Ghost carries on the *subjective* work in the believer, is the *objective* truth of his eternal completeness in Christ.

Again, "Follow peace with all men, and holiness, without which no man shall see the Lord." (Heb. xii. 14.) Here, is holiness presented as a thing to be "followed after"—to be attained by earnest pursuit—a thing which every true believer will long to cultivate.

May the Lord lead us into the power of these things. May they not dwell as doctrines and dogmas in the region of our intellect, but enter into and abide in the heart, as sacred and powerfully influential realities! May we know the sanctifying power of the truth; (Jno. xvii. 17;) the sanctifying power of faith; (Acts xxvi. 18;) the sanctifying power of the name of Jesus; (1 Cor. i. 30; vi. 11;) the sanctifying of the Holy Ghost; (1 Pet. i. 2;) the sanctifying grace of the Father. (Jude 1.)

And, now, unto the Father, and unto the Son, and unto the Holy Ghost, be honor and glory, might, majesty, and dominion, world without end. Amen.

C. H. M.

FINAL PERSEVERANCE: WHAT IS IT?

Dear friend: The question of final perseverance, though in our judgment a very simple one, has perplexed a great many; and the questions which you introduce to our notice, and the passages of Scripture which you adduce, furnish abundant proof that your own mind is not quite clear or settled on the point.

In seeking, then, to reply to your interesting letter, we have three things to do, namely: first, to establish the doctrine of final perseverance, or, in other words, the eternal security of all Christ's members; secondly, to answer the questions which you have given us, and which we take to be those usually or frequently put by the opposers of the doctrine; and, thirdly, to expound those texts which you have quoted, and in which you seem to find considerable difficulty. May the Holy Spirit be our teacher, and may He give us minds entirely subject to Scripture, so that we may be able to form a sound judgment on the question now before us!

I. And first, as to the doctrine of final perseverance, it seems to us exceedingly clear and simple if only we look at it in immediate connection with Christ Himself. This indeed is the only true way to look at any doctrine. Christ is the soul, centre, and life of all doctrine. A doctrine separated from Christ becomes a lifeless, power-less, worthless dogma — a mere idea in the mind — a mere item in the creed. Hence, therefore, we must look at every truth as it stands connected with Christ. We must make Him our point of view. It is only as we keep near to Him, and look at all points from that one grand point, that we can have a correct view of any point. If for example, I make self my point of view, and look from thence at the subject of final perseverance, I shall be sure to get a false view altogether, inasmuch as it then becomes a question of *my* perseverance, and anything of *mine* must necessarily be doubtful.

But if, on the other hand, I make Christ my viewing-point, and look at the subject from thence, I shall be sure to have a correct view, inasmuch as it then becomes a question of Christ's perseverance, and I am quite sure that He *must* persevere, and that no power of the world, the flesh, or the devil, can ever hinder His final perseverance in the salvation of those whom He has purchased with His own blood, seeing "He is able to save to *the uttermost* them that come unto God by Him." This, surely, is final perseverance. It matters not what the difficulty or what the hostile power may be, "He is able to save to the uttermost." The world, with its ten thousand snares, is against us, but "He is able." Indwelling sin, in its ten thousand workings, is against us, but "He is able." Satan, with his ten thousand devices, is against us, but "He is able." In a word, it is Christ's ability, not ours; it is Christ's faithfulness, not ours; it is Christ's final perseverance, not ours. All depends upon Him as to this weighty matter. He has purchased His sheep, and surely He will keep them to the best of His ability; and, seeing that "*all* power is given unto Him in heaven and on earth," His sheep must be perfectly and forever safe. If aught could touch the life of the feeblest lamb in all the flock of Christ, He could not be said to have "all power."

Thus it is immensely important to consider the question of final perseverance in inseparable connection with Christ. Difficulties vanish. Doubts and fears are chased away. The heart becomes established, the conscience relieved, the understanding enlightened. It is impossible that one who forms a part of Christ's body can ever perish; and the believer is this—"We are members of His body, of His flesh, and of His bones." (Eph. v. 30.) Every member of the body of Christ was written in the book of the slain Lamb before the foundation of the world, nor can anything or any one ever obliterate that writing. Hear what our Lord Jesus Christ saith in reference to those that are His: "My sheep hear my voice, and I know them, and they follow me; and I *give* unto them *eternal* life, and they shall never perish, neither shall *any* (man, devil, or any one else) pluck them out of my hand. My Father, which gave them Me, is greater than all; and no man is able to pluck them out of my Father's hand." (John x. 27-29.)

Here, then, most assuredly, we have final perseverance; and that, moreover, not merely the perseverance of the saints, but of the Father and of the Son and of the Holy Ghost. Yes, dear friend, this is the way we would have you view the matter. It is the final perseverance of the Holy Trinity. It is the perseverance of the Holy Ghost, in opening the ears of the sheep. It is the perseverance of the Son, in receiving all whose ears are thus opened. And, finally, it is the perseverance of the Father, in keeping, through His own name, the blood-bought flock in the hollow of His everlasting hand. This is plain enough. We must either admit the truth—the consolatory and sustaining truth—of final perseverance or succumb to the blasphemous proposition that the enemy of God and man can carry his point against the Holy and Eternal Trinity. We see no middle ground. "Salvation is of the Lord" from first to last. It is a free, unconditional, and everlasting salvation. It reaches down to where the sinner is in all his guilt, ruin, and degradation, and bears him up to where God is in all His holiness, truth, and righteousness; and it endures forever. God the Father is its source, God the Son is its channel, and God the Holy Ghost is the power of application and enjoyment. It is all of God from beginning to end, from foundation to topstone, from everlasting to everlasting. If it were not so, it would be presumptuous folly to speak of final perseverance; but seeing it is so, it would be presumptuous unbelief to think of aught else.

True, there are great and manifold difficulties in the way—difficulties before and difficulties after conversion. There are many and powerful adversaries; but that is the very reason why we must keep the question of final perseverance entirely clear of self and all its belongings, and make it repose simply upon God. It matters not in the least what the difficulties or the adversaries may be, for faith can ever triumphantly inquire, "If God be for us, who can be against us?" And again, "Who shall separate us from the love of Christ? Shall tribulation, or distress, or persecution, or famine, or nakedness, or peril, or sword? As it is written, 'For Thy sake, we are killed all the day long; we are accounted as sheep for the slaughter.' Nay, in all these things we are more than conquerors through Him that loved us. For I am persuaded that neither death, nor life, nor angels, nor principalities, nor powers, nor things present, nor things to come, nor height, nor depth, nor *any other creature*, shall be able to separate us from the love of God, which is in Christ Jesus our Lord." (Rom. viii. 35-39.)

Here, again, we have final perseverance taught, in the clearest and strongest way possible—not any creature shall be able to separate us. Neither self, in all its forms; nor Satan, in all his wiles and machinations; nor the world, in all its alurements, or all its scorn, can ever separate the "us" of Romans viii. 39 from the love of God, which is in Christ Jesus our Lord. No doubt persons may be deceived, and they may deceive others. Spurious cases may arise; counterfeit conversions may take place. Persons may seem to run well for a time, and then break down. The blossoms of spring-time may not be followed by the mellow fruits of autumn. Such things may be; and, moreover, true believers may fail in many things; they may stumble and break down in their course. They may have ample cause for self-judgment and humiliation in the practical details of life. But, allowing the widest possible margin for all these things, the precious doctrine of final perseverance remains unshaken—yea, untouched—upon its own divine and eternal foundation—"I give unto my sheep *eternal* (not temporary or conditional) life, and they shall *never* perish." And again: "Upon this rock I will build my church, and the gates of hell shall not prevail against it." People may argue as they will, and base their arguments on cases which have come under their notice, from time to time, in the history of professing Christians; but, looking at the subject from a divine point of view, and basing our convictions on the sure and unerring Word of God, we maintain that all who belong to the "us" of Romans viii., the "sheep" of John x., and the "church" of Matthew xvi., are as safe as Christ can make them, and this we conceive to be the sum and substance of the doctrine of final perseverance.

II. And now, dear friend, we shall, in the second place, briefly and pointedly reply to the questions which you have put before us:—

1. "Will a believer be saved, no matter into what course of sin he may fall, and die in?" A true believer will, infallibly, be saved; but we consider that salvation includes, not only full deliverance from the future consequences of sin, but from the present power and practice thereof. And, hence, if we find a person living in sin, and yet talking about his assurance of salvation, we look upon him as an antinomian, and not a saved person at all. "If we say that we have fellowship with Him, and walk in darkness, we lie, and do not the truth." The believer may fall, but He will be lifted up; he may be overtaken, but he will be restored; he may wander, but he will be brought back, because Christ is able to save to the uttermost, and not one of His little ones shall perish.

2. "Will the Holy Spirit dwell in a heart where evil and unholy thoughts are *indulged*?" The body of the believer is the temple of the Holy Ghost. (1 Cor. vi. 19.) And this precious truth is the ground of exhortation to purity and holiness of heart and life. We are exhorted not to grieve the Holy Spirit. To "*indulge*" evil and unholy thoughts is not christian walk at all. The Christian may be assaulted, grieved,

and harassed by evil thoughts, and in such a case he has only to look to Christ for victory. Proper christian walk is thus expressed in John's first epistle: "We know that whosoever is born of God sinneth not; but he that is begotten of God keepeth himself, and that wicked one toucheth him not." (Chap. v. 18.) This is the divine side of the question. Alas! we know there is the human side likewise; but we judge the human side by the divine. We do not lower the divine to meet the human, but ever aim at the divine notwithstanding the human. We should never be satisfied with anything lower than 1 John v. 18. It is by keeping up the true standard that we may expect to raise our moral tone. To talk of having the Spirit and yet *"indulge"* in evil and unholy thoughts is, in our judgment, the ancient Nicolaitanism (Rev. ii. 6, 15), or modern antinomianism.

3. "If it be so, then, will not people say, they may live as they like?" Well, how does a true Christian like to live? As like Christ as possible. If one had put this question to Paul, what would have been his answer? 2 Cor. v. 14, 15, and Phil. iii. 7-14, furnish the reply. It is to be feared that the persons who ask such questions know but little of Christ. We can quite understand a person getting entangled in the meshes of a one-sided theological system and being perplexed by the conflicting dogmas of systematic divinity; but we believe that the man who draws a plea from the freedom, sovereignty, and eternal stability of the grace of God to continue in sin, knows nothing of Christianity at all, has neither part nor lot in the matter, but is in a truly awful and dangerous condition.

As to the case which you adduce, of a young man who heard a minister state in his sermon that "once a child, always a child," and who took occasion from that to plunge into and continue in open sin, it is only one of thousands. We believe the minister was right in what he said, but the young man was wrong in what he did. To judge the words of the former by the acts of the latter is utterly false. What should I think of my son, if he were to say, Once a son, always a son, and therefore I may proceed to smash my father's windows and do all sorts of mischief? We judge the minister's statement by the Word of God, and pronounce it true. We judge the young man's conduct by the same rule, and pronounce it false. The matter is quite simple. We have no reason to believe that the unhappy young man ever really tasted the true grace of God; for if he had, he would love and cultivate and exhibit holiness. The Christian has to struggle with sin; but *struggling* with it and *wallowing* in it are two totally different ideas. In the one case we can count on Christ's sympathy and grace; in the other, we are actually blaspheming His name by implying that He is the minister of sin.

We consider it a very serious mistake to set about judging the truth of God by the actings of men. All who do so must reach a false conclusion. The true way is just to reverse the order. Get hold of God's truth first, and then judge everything by that. Set up the divine standard, and test everything thereby. Set up the public scales, and weigh every man's load therein. The scales must not be regulated by each man's load, but each man's load be tested by the scales. If ten thousand professors were to fall away, and live and die in open sin, it would not shake our confidence in the divine doctrine of final perseverance. The selfsame Word that proves the doctrine to be true, proves them to be false. "They went out from us, but they were not of us; for if they had been of us, they would no doubt have continued with us; but they went out, that they might be manifest that they were not all of us." (1 John ii. 19.) "The foundation of God standeth sure, having this seal, The Lord knoweth them that are His. And, let every one that nameth the name of Christ depart from iniquity." (2 Tim. ii. 19.)

III. We shall now proceed to examine the various passages of Scripture which, as you say, are generally adduced by those who seek to overthrow the doctrine of final perseverance. But before doing so, we deem it of importance to lay down the following fundamental principle, which will, in our judgment, be found most helpful in the interpretation of Scripture generally. The principle is very simple. No one passage of Holy Scripture can by any possibility contradict another. If therefore there be a seeming contradiction, it must arise from our want of spiritual intelligence. Thus, for example, if any one were to quote James ii. 24 in defense of the doctrine of justification by works, I might not be able to answer him. It is quite possible that thousands, like Luther, have been sadly perplexed by that passage. They may feel the fullest and clearest assurance that they are justified, and that not by any works that they have done, but simply "by faith of Jesus Christ," and yet be wholly unable to explain these words of James—"Ye see then how that by works a man is justified, and not by faith only."

Now, how is one to meet such a difficulty as this? He really does not understand the apostle James. He is involved in much perplexity by the apparent contradiction between James and Paul. What is he to do? Just to apply the principle above stated. No one passage of Scripture can possibly contradict another. As well might we apprehend a collision between two of the heavenly bodies while moving in their divinely appointed orbits, as that two inspired writers could possibly clash in their statements. Well, then, I read in Rom. iv. 5 such plain words as these: "But to him that *worketh not*, but believeth on Him that justifieth the ungodly, his *faith* is counted for righteousness." Here I find works entirely excluded as a ground of justification, and faith alone recognized. So also in chapter iii. I read, "Therefore we conclude that a man is justified by faith without (or apart from) works of law." And, again, "Being justified by faith, we have peace with God." Exactly similar is the teaching in the epistle to the Galatians, where we read such plain words as these: "*Knowing* that a man is not justified by works of law, but by faith of Jesus Christ, even we (Jews) have believed in Jesus Christ, that we might be justified by faith of Christ, and not by works of law: for by works of law shall no flesh be justified." (Chap. ii. 16.)

In all these passages, and many more which might be quoted, works are sedulously excluded as a ground of justification, and that too in language so plain that a wayfaring man, though a fool, need not err therein. If therefore we cannot explain James ii. 24, we must either deny its inspiration or have recourse to our principle, namely, that no one passage of Holy Scripture can possibly contradict another, and so remain, with unshaken confidence and unruffled repose, rejoicing in the grand foundation truth of justification by faith alone, apart from law-works altogether.

Having called the reader's attention to the famous passage in James ii., it may not be amiss to offer him, in passing, a word or two of exposition which will help him in the understanding of it. There is a little word in verse 14 which will furnish the key to the entire passage. The inspired apostle inquires, "What doth it profit, my brethren, though a man *say* he hath faith?" Had he said, What doth it profit though a man *have* faith? the difficulty would be insuperable, the perplexity hopeless. But the important word "say" quite removes all difficulty, and unfolds in the simplest possible way the point which the apostle has in his mind. We might inquire, What doth it profit though a man *say* he hath ten thousand a year, if he have it not?

Now, we are aware that the word "say" is constantly left out in quoting James ii. 14. Some have even ventured to assert that it is not in the original. But any one who can read Greek has only to look at the passage and he will see the word *legee* (*say*) placed there by the Holy Ghost, and left there by all our leading editors and biblical critics; nor can we well conceive a word of more vital importance in a passage. Its influence, we believe, is felt throughout the entire context in which it occurs. There is no use in a man merely *saying* he has faith; but if he really has it, it "profits" him for time and eternity, inasmuch as it connects him with Christ, and puts him in full and inalienable possession of all that Christ has done and all that He is for us before God.

This leads us to another point, which will greatly tend to clear away the seeming contradiction between the two inspired apostles, Paul and James. There is a very material difference between *law-works* and *life-works*. Paul jealously excludes the former; James as jealously insists on the latter. But be it carefully noted that it is only the former that Paul excludes, as it is only the latter that James insists on. The acts of Abraham and Rahab were not law-works, but life-works. They were the genuine fruits of faith, apart from which they would have possessed no justifying virtue whatever.

It is well worthy of note that with the history of four thousand years before Him, the Holy Ghost, in the apostle, should have fixed upon two such works as that of Abraham in Genesis xxii. and that of Rahab in Joshua ii. He does not adduce some acts of charity or benevolence, though surely He might easily have selected many such from the vast mass of materials which lay before Him. But, as if anticipating the use that the enemy would make of the passage now before us, He takes care to select two such illustrations of His thesis as prove beyond all question that it is life-works and not law-works He is insisting upon, and leaves wholly untouched the priceless doctrine of justification by faith, apart from works of law.

Finally, if any should feel disposed to inquire as to the difference between law-works and life-works, it is simply this: law-works are such as are done in order to get life: life-works are the genuine fruits of life possessed. And how do we get life? By believing on the Son of God. "Verily, verily, I say unto you, He that heareth my words, and believeth on Him that sent Me, *hath* everlasting life." (John v. 24.) We must have life before we can do anything; and we get life, not by "saying" we have faith, but by really having it; and when we have it, we shall manifest the precious fruits thereof, to the glory of God.

Thus, then, we not only implicitly believe that Paul and James *must* harmonize, but we can plainly see that they *do*.

Having thus sought to define and illustrate our principle, we shall leave you, dear friend, to apply it in the various cases of difficulty and perplexity which may come before you in the study of Scripture, while we endeavor to expound, as the Lord may enable us, the important passages of Scripture which you have laid before us.

1. The first quotation is from the second epistle of Peter—"But there were false prophets also among the people, even as there shall be false teachers among you, who privily shall bring in damnable heresies, even denying the Lord that bought them, and bring upon themselves swift destruction." (Chap. ii. 1.) The difficulty of this passage arises, we suppose, from the expression, "denying the Lord that bought them." But there is, in reality, no difficulty whatever in these words. The Lord has a double claim on every man, woman, and child beneath the canopy of heaven. He has a claim founded on creation, and a claim founded on redemption. It is to the latter of these two that the apostle refers. The false teachers will not merely deny the Lord that *made* them, but even the Lord that *bought* them. It is of importance to see this. It will help to clear away many difficulties. The Lord Jesus has a purchased right over every member of the human family. The Father has given Him power over all flesh. Hence the sin of those who deny Him. It would be sin to deny Him as Creator; it is a greater sin to deny Him as Redeemer. It is not at all a question of regeneration. The apostle does not say, Denying the Lord that quickened them. This would indeed be a difficulty; but as the passage stands, it leaves wholly untouched the truth of final perseverance.

2. The second passage occurs at the close of the same chapter (verses 20 and 22)—"For if after they have escaped the pollutions of the world, through the knowledge of the Lord and Saviour Jesus Christ, they are again entangled therein and overcome, the latter end is worse with them than the beginning.... But it is happened unto them according to the true proverb, 'The dog is turned to his own vomit again: and the sow that was washed, to her wallowing in the mire.'" The diffusion of scriptural knowledge and evangelical light may and does frequently exert an amazing influence upon the conduct and character of persons who have known the saving, quickening, emancipating power of the gospel of Christ. Indeed it is hardly possible for an open Bible to be circulated, or a free gospel to be preached, without producing very striking results which, after all, will be found to fall far short of *the* grand result of regeneration. Many gross habits may be abandoned, many "pollutions" laid aside, under the influence of a merely intellectual "knowledge of the Lord and Saviour Jesus Christ"; while, at the same time, the *heart* has never really been savingly reached at all. Now, it will be invariably found that when persons shake off the influence of evangelical light—even though that influence never extended beyond their outward conduct—they are sure to plunge into greater depths of evil, and greater excesses of worldliness and folly than ever; "The latter end is worse with them than the beginning." The devil takes delight in dragging the *quondam* professor through deeper mire than that in which he wallowed in the days of his ignorance and thoughtless folly. Hence the urgent need

of pressing on all with whom we have to do the importance of making sure work of it, so that the knowledge of truth may not merely affect their external conduct, but reach the heart, and impart that life which, when once possessed, can never be lost. There is nothing in this passage to terrify the sheep of Christ, but very much to warn those who, though they may for a time put on the outward appearance of sheep, have never been inwardly aught but as the dog and the sow.

3. Ezekiel xviii. 24, 26—"But when the righteous turneth away from his righteousness, and committeth iniquity, and doeth according to all the abominations that the wicked man doeth, shall he live? All his righteousness that he hath done shall not be mentioned: in his trespass that he hath trespassed, and in his sin that he hath sinned, in them shall he die.... When a righteous man turneth away from his righteousness and committeth iniquity, and dieth in them; for his iniquity, that he hath done, shall he die." With this we may connect your reference to 2 Chronicles xv. 2—"The Lord is with you while ye be with Him: and if ye seek Him, He will be found of you: but if ye forsake Him, He will forsake you." We feel constrained, dear friend, to say that it evidences a sad want of spiritual intelligence to adduce such passages of Scripture as bearing in any way upon the truth of the final perseverance of Christ's members. These, and numberless other scriptures in the Old Testament, as well as many similar passages in the New Testament, unfold to us the deeply important subject of God's moral government. Now, to be merely a subject of God's government is one thing; to be a subject of His unchangeable grace is another. We should never confound them. To elaborate this point, and to refer to the various passages which illustrate and enforce it, would demand a volume: we would here only add our full persuasion that no one can understand the word of God who does not accurately distinguish between man under government and man under grace. In the one case he is looked at as walking down here, in the place of responsibility and danger; in the other, he is looked at as associated with Christ above, in the place of inalienable privilege and eternal security. These two Old Testament scriptures to which you have referred us are entirely governmental, and, as a consequence, have nothing whatever to do with the question of final perseverance.

4. Matthew xii. 45—"Then goeth he and taketh with him seven other spirits more wicked than himself, and they enter in and dwell there: and the last state of that man is worse than the first. Even so shall it be unto this wicked generation." The closing sentence of this passage quite explains the whole context. Our Lord is describing the moral condition of the Jewish people. The spirit of idolatry had gone out of them, but only for a time, and to return again in sevenfold energy and intensity, rendering their last state worse by far than aught that has yet appeared in their most marvelous history. This passage, taken in a secondary way, may be very intelligently applied to an individual who, having undergone a certain moral change, and exhibited a measure of improvement in his outward conduct, afterwards falls back and becomes more openly corrupt and vicious than ever.

5. 2 John i. 8, 9—"Look to yourselves, that we lose not those things which we have wrought, but that we receive a full reward. Whoever transgresseth, and abideth not in the doctrine of Christ, hath not God. He that abideth in the doctrine

of Christ, he hath both the Father and the Son." In verse 8 the apostle exhorts the elect lady and her children to look to themselves, lest by any means he should lose aught of the fruit of his ministry. They were to form part of his reward in the coming day of glory, and he longed to present them faultless in the presence of that glory, that his reward might be full. Verse 9 needs no explanation; it is solemnly plain. If one does not *abide* in the doctrine of Christ, he has got nothing. Let slip the truth as to Christ, and you have no security as to anything. The Christian most assuredly needs to walk watchfully in order to escape the manifold snares and temptations which surround him; but whether is that watchfulness better promoted by placing his feet upon the shifting sand of his own performances or by fixing them firmly upon the rock of God's eternal salvation? Whether am I in a more favorable position for the exercise of watchfulness and prayer while living in perpetual doubt and fear, or reposing in artless confidence in the unchangeable love of my Saviour-God? We think, dear friend, we may very safely anticipate your reply.

6. Rev. iii. 11 — "Behold, I come quickly; hold that fast which thou hast, that no man take thy crown." Two things are here to be considered, namely: first, this is an address to an assembly; and, secondly, it does not say, That no man take thy *life*. A *servant* may lose his *reward*; but a *child* can never lose his eternal *life*. Attention to this would remove a host of difficulties. Sonship is one thing; discipleship is quite another. Security in Christ is one thing; testimony for Christ is quite another. If our security were dependent upon our testimony — our sonship upon our discipleship, where should we be? True, the more I know my security and enjoy my sonship, the more effective will be my testimony and the more faithful my discipleship; but these things must never be confounded.

In conclusion, dear friend, you say that "All those texts which speak of enduring to the end, and overcoming, are thought to mean that, since there is a possibility of our not doing so, we may not be saved in the end." As to this, we would merely add that we shall be most happy at any time to enter with you upon the close examination of every one of those passages to which you in this general way refer,* and to prove, by the grace of God, that not one of them, when rightly interpreted, militates in the smallest degree against the precious truth of final perseverance; but that, on the contrary, each passage contains within itself, or within its immediate context, that which will clearly prove its perfect harmony with the truth of the eternal security of the very feeblest lamb in all the blood-bought flock of Christ.

May the Lord establish our souls, more and more firmly, in His own truth, and preserve us unto His heavenly kingdom, to the glory of His holy name!

C. H. M.

P. S. — Paley observes that "we should never suffer what we know to be disturbed by what we know not." And Butler remarks nearly the same when he says, "If a *truth* be established, *objections* are nothing. The one is founded on our *knowledge*, and the other on our *ignorance*." (See Jay's Autobiography, p. 170.)

A SACRED UNION (POEM)

"'Twixt Jesus and the heavenly race
Subsists a bond of sovereign grace—
A tie which hell's tremendous train
Can ne'er dissolve or rend in twain.

"Life's sacred bond shall never break,
Though earth should to its centre shake:
We rest in hope, assured of this;
For God has pledged His righteousness.

"By Him 'twas counseled, planned, and done,
Wrought in the blood of His dear Son—
The Christ appointed to redeem
All that the Father chose in Him.

"O sacred union, firm and strong!
How great the grace! How sweet the song!
To God alone be all the praise
Of rich, eternal, heavenly grace.

"In spirit one with Him who rose
Victorious o'er His mighty foes;
Who went on high and took His seat,
Pledge of the serpent's full defeat.

"Triumphant thus o'er adverse powers,
(For all He is and has is ours,)
With Him, the Head, we stand or fall—
Our Life, our Surety, and our All.

"Thus saved in Him, a chosen race,
Here may we prove our faithfulness,
And live to Him who for us died,
With whom we shall be glorified."

NOW AND THEN; OR, TIME AND ETERNITY

The principles of truth laid down in Luke xii. are of the most solemn and searching character. Their practical bearing is such as to render them, in a day like the present, of the deepest importance. Worldly-mindedness and carnality cannot live in the light of the truth here set forth. They are withered up by the roots. If one were asked to give a brief and comprehensive title to this most precious section of inspiration, it might be entitled "Time in the light of eternity." The Lord evidently designed to set His disciples in the light of that world where every thing is the direct opposite of that which obtains here—to bring their hearts under the holy influence of unseen things, and their lives under the power and authority of heavenly principles. Such being the faithful purpose of the Divine Teacher, He lays the solid foundation for His superstructure of doctrine with these searching words: "Beware of the leaven of the Pharisees, which is hypocrisy." There must be no undercurrent in the soul. The deep springs of thought must be laid bare. We must allow the pure beams of heaven's light to penetrate to the depths of our moral being. We must not have any discrepancy between the hidden judgment of the soul and the style of our phraseology—between the bent of the life and the profession of the lips. In a word, we specially need the grace of "an honest and a good heart," in order to profit by this wondrous compendium of practical truth.

We are too apt to give an indifferent hearing or a cold assent to *home truth*. We do not like it. We prefer interesting speculations about the mere letter of Scripture, points of doctrine, or questions of prophecy, because we can indulge these in immediate connection with all sorts of worldly-mindedness, covetous practices, and self-indulgence. But ponderous principles of truth, bearing down upon the conscience in all their magnitude and flesh-cutting power, who can bear, save those who, through grace, are seeking to purge themselves from "the leaven of the Pharisees, which is hypocrisy"? This leaven is of a most specious character, takes various shapes, and is therefore most dangerous. Indeed, wherever it exists, there is a most positive and insurmountable barrier placed before the soul in its progress in experimental knowledge and practical holiness. If I do not expose my *whole soul* to the action of divine truth,—if I am closing up some corner or crevice from the light thereof,—if I am cherishing some secret reserve,—if I am dishonestly seeking to accommodate the truth to my own standard of practice, or parry its keen edge from my conscience, then, assuredly, I am defiled by the leaven of hypocrisy, and my growth in likeness to Christ is a moral impossibility. Hence, therefore, it is imperative upon every disciple of Christ to search and see that nothing of this abominable leaven is allowed in the secret chambers of his heart. Let us, by the grace of God, put and keep it far away, so that we may be able on all occasions to say, "Speak, Lord, for Thy servant heareth."[3]

But not only is hypocrisy utterly subversive of spiritual progress, it also fails in attaining the object which it proposes to itself; "for there is nothing covered that shall not be revealed; neither hid, that shall not be known." Every man will find his level, and every thought will be brought to light. What the truth would do *now*, the judgment-seat will do *then*. Every grade and shade of hypocrisy will be unmasked by the light which shall shine forth from the judgment-seat of Christ. Nothing will be allowed to escape. All will be reality *then*, though there is so much fallacy *now*. Moreover, every thing will get its proper name *then*, though it be misnamed *now*. Worldly-mindedness is called prudence; a grasping, covetous spirit is called foresight; and self-indulgence and personal aggrandizement are called judicious management and laudable diligence in business. Thus it is *now*; but *then* it will be quite the reverse. All things will be seen in their true colors, and called by their true names, before the judgment-seat. Wherefore it is the wisdom of the disciple to act in the light of that day, when the secrets of all hearts shall be disclosed. As to this, he is placed on a vantage-ground, for, says the apostle, "we must all [saints and sinners—though not at the same time, nor on the same ground,] be manifested [φανερωθῆναι] before the judgment-seat of Christ.» Should this disturb the disciple›s mind? Assuredly not, if his heart be so purged of the leaven of hypocrisy and his soul so thoroughly grounded, by the teaching of God the Holy Ghost, in the great foundation-truth set forth in this very chapter (2 Cor. v.), namely, that Christ is his life, and Christ his righteousness; that he can say, "We are manifested [πεφανερώμεθα,—an inflection of the same word as is used at verse 10,] unto God, and I trust also are manifested in your consciences."

But if he be deficient in this peace of conscience and transparent honesty of heart, there is no doubt but that the thought of the judgment-seat will disturb his spirit. Hence we see that the Lord, in Luke xii, sets the consciences of His disciples directly in the light of the judgment-seat.—"And I say unto you, *My friends*, Be not afraid of them that kill the body, and after that have no more that they can do. But I will forewarn you whom ye shall fear: Fear Him, which after He hath killed hath power to cast into hell; yea, I say unto you, Fear Him." "The fear of man bringeth a snare," and is closely connected with "the leaven of the Pharisees;" but "the fear of the Lord is the beginning of wisdom," and causes a man always so to carry himself—so to think, speak, and act—as in the full light of Christ's judgment-seat. This would impart immense dignity and elevation to the character, while it would effectually nip, in the earliest bud, the spirit of haughty independence, by keeping the soul under the searching power of divine light, the effect of which is to make every thing and every one manifest.

There is nothing that so tends to rob the disciple of Christ of the proper dignity of his discipleship as walking before the eyes or thoughts of men. So long as we are doing so, we cannot be unshackled followers of our heavenly Master. Moreover,

---

[3] The meaning which is generally attached to hypocrisy is a false profession of religion. It assuredly means this, but it means much more. A tacit assent to principles which do not govern the conduct deserves the appellation of hypocrisy. Looking at the subject in this point of view, we may all find occasion of deep humiliation before the Lord.

the evil of walking before men is morally allied with the evil of seeking to hide our ways from God. Both partake of the "leaven of the Pharisees," and both will find their proper place before the judgment-seat. Why should we fear men? why should we regard their opinions? If their opinions will not bear to be tried in His presence who has power to cast into hell, they are worth nothing; for it is with Him we have to do. "With me it is a very small thing that I should be judged of you, or man's judgment." Man may have a judgment-seat *now*, but he will not have it *then*;—he may set up his tribunal in time, but he will have no tribunal in eternity. Why, therefore, should we shape our way in reference to a tribunal so frail and evanescent? Oh, let us challenge our hearts as to this. God grant us grace to act *now* in reference to *then*—to carry ourselves here with our eye on hereafter—to look at time in the light of eternity.

The poor unbelieving heart may however inquire, If I thus rise above human thoughts and human opinions, how shall I get on in a scene where those very thoughts and opinions prevail? This is a very natural question, but it meets its full and satisfactory answer from the Master's lips; yea, it would even seem as though He had graciously anticipated this rising element of unbelief, when, having carried His disciples above the hazy mists of time, and set them in the clear, searching, powerful light of eternity, He added, "Are not five sparrows sold for two farthings? and not one of them is forgotten before God. But even the very hairs of your head are all numbered. Fear not, therefore; ye are of more value than many sparrows." (Ver. 6, 7.) Here the heart is taught not only to *fear* God, but also to *confide* in Him,—it is not only warned, but also tranquilized. "Fear" and "fear not" may seem a paradox to flesh and blood, but to faith it is no paradox. The man who fears God most will fear circumstances least. The man of faith is at once the most dependent and independent man in the world—dependent upon God, independent upon circumstances. The latter is the consequence of the former.

And mark the ground of the believer's peace. The One who has power to cast into hell, the only One whom he is to fear, has actually taken the trouble to count the hairs of his head. He surely has not taken the trouble for the purpose of letting him perish here or hereafter. The minuteness of our Father's care should silence every doubt that might arise in our hearts. There is nothing too small and there can be nothing too great for Him. The countless orbs that move through infinite space and a falling sparrow are alike to Him. His infinite mind can take in with equal facility the course of everlasting ages and the hairs of our head. This is the stable foundation on which Christ founds His "fear not" and "take no thought." We frequently fail in the practical application of this divine principle. We may admire it as a principle, but it is only in the application of it that its real beauty is seen or felt. If we do not put it in practice, we are but painting sunbeams on canvas, while we famish beneath the chilling influences of our own unbelief.

Now, we find in this scripture before us that bold and uncompromising testimony for Christ is connected with this holy elevation above men's thoughts and this calm reliance upon our Father's minute and tender care. If my heart is lifted above the influence of the fear of man, and sweetly tranquilized by the assurance that God takes account of the hairs of my head, then I am in a condition of soul to confess Christ before men. (See *vv.* 8-10.) Nor need I be careful as to the result of this confession, for so long as God wants me here He will maintain me here. "And when they bring you unto the synagogues, and unto magistrates and powers, take ye no thought how or what thing ye shall answer, or what ye shall say; for the Holy Ghost shall teach you in the same hour what ye ought to say." The only proper ground of testimony for Christ is to be fully delivered from human influence, and established in unqualified confidence in God. So far as I am influenced by or a debtor to men, so far am I disqualified for being a servant of Christ; but I can only be effectually delivered from human influence by a lively faith in God. When God fills the heart, there is no room for the creature; and we may be perfectly sure of this, that no man has ever taken the trouble to count the hairs of our head; we have not even taken that trouble ourselves; but God has, and therefore I can trust God more than any one. God is perfectly sufficient for every exigency, great or small, and we only want to trust Him to know that He is.

True, He may and does use men as instruments; but if we lean on men instead of God,—if we lean on instruments instead of on the hand that uses them, we bring down a curse upon us, for it is written, "Cursed be the man that trusteth in man, and maketh flesh his arm, and whose heart departeth from the Lord." (Jer. xvii. 5.) The Lord used the ravens to feed Elijah, but Elijah never thought of trusting in the ravens. Thus it should be ever. Faith leans on God, counts on Him, clings to Him, trusts in Him, waits for Him, ever leaves a clear stage for Him to act on, does not obstruct His glorious path by any creature-confidence, allows Him to display Himself in all the glorious reality of what He is, leaves every thing to Him; and, moreover, if it gets into deep and rough waters, it will always be seen upon the crest of the loftiest billow, and from thence gazing in perfect repose upon God and His powerful actings. Such is faith—that precious thing—the only thing in this world that gives God and man their respective places.

While the Lord Jesus was in the act of pouring forth these unearthly principles, a true child of earth intrudes upon Him with a question about property.—"And one of the company said unto Him, 'Master, speak to my brother, that he divide the inheritance with me.'" How marvelously little did he know of the true character of that heavenly Man who stood before him! He knew nothing of the profound mystery of His being, or the object of His heavenly mission. He surely had not come from the bosom of the Father to settle lawsuits about property, nor to arbitrate between two covetous men. The spirit of covetousness was manifestly in the whole affair. Both defendant and plaintiff were governed by covetousness. One wanted to grasp and the other wanted to keep; what was this but covetousness? "And he said unto him, 'Man, who made Me a judge or a divider over you?'" It was not a question of which was right or which was wrong as to the property. According to Christ's pure and heavenly doctrine they were both wrong. In the light of eternity a few acres of land were little worth; and as to Christ Himself, He was only teaching principles entirely hostile to all questions of earthly possession; but in His own person and character He set an example of the very opposite. He did not go to law about the inheritance. He was "Heir of all things." The land of Israel, the throne of David, and all creation belonged to Him; but man would not own Him, or give Him possession. "The husbandmen said among themselves, 'This is the heir; come, let us kill him, and seize upon the inheritance.'" To this the Heir submitted in perfect patience, but (eternal homage to His glorious name!) by submitting unto death He crushed the enemy's power, and brought "many sons to glory."

Thus we see in the doctrine and practice of the Heavenly Man the true exhibition of the principles of the kingdom of God. He would not arbitrate, but yet He taught truth which would entirely do away with the need of arbitration. If the principles of the kingdom of God were dominant, there would be no need for courts of law; for inasmuch as people would not be wronged of their rights, they could have no wrongs to be righted. This would be admitted by all. But then the Christian, being in the kingdom, is bound to be governed by the principles of the kingdom, and to carry them out at all cost; for, in the exact proportion that he fails to exhibit those principles, he is robbing his own soul of blessing, and marring his testimony.

Hence, then, a person going to law is not governed, in so doing, by the principles of the kingdom of God, but by the principles of the kingdom of Satan, who is the prince of this world. It is not a question as to his being a Christian, but simply a question as to the principle by which he is governed in the act of going to law under any circumstances.[4] I say nothing of the moral instincts of the divine nature, which would surely lead one to apprehend with accuracy the gross inconsistency of a man who professes to be saved by *grace* going to *law* with a fellow-man—of one who, while he owns that if he had his *right* from the hand of God, he would be burning in hell, nevertheless insists upon exacting his rights from his fellow-man—of one who has been forgiven ten thousand talents, but yet seizes his fellow by the throat for a paltry hundred pence. Upon these things I shall not dwell. I merely look at the question of going to law in the light of the kingdom, in the light of eternity; and if it be true that in the kingdom of God there is no need for courts of law, then I press it solemnly upon my reader's conscience, in the presence of God, that he, as a subject of that kingdom, is totally wrong in going to law. True, it will lead to loss and suffering; but who is "worthy of the kingdom of God" who is not prepared to "suffer for it"? Let those who are governed by the things of *time* go to law; but the Christian is, or ought to be, governed by the things of *eternity*. People go to law *now*, but it will not be so *then*; and the Christian is to act *now* as if it were *then*. He belongs to the kingdom; and it is just because the kingdom of God is not dominant, but the King rejected, that the subjects of the kingdom are called to suffer. Righteousness "suffers" *now*; it will "reign" in the millennium, and it will "dwell" in the new heavens and the new earth. Now, in going to law, the Christian anticipates the millennial age. He is going before his Master in the assertion of his rights. He is called to suffer patiently all sorts of wrongs and injuries. To resent them is to deny the truth of that kingdom to which he professes to belong. I press this principle upon my reader's conscience. I earnestly implore his serious attention thereto. Let it have its full weight upon his conscience. Let him

---

[4] How often, alas! does it happen that people go to law to be *righted* of their *wrongs*, and in the end find themselves *wronged* of their *rights*!

not trifle with its truth. There is nothing which tends so to hinder the freshness and power, growth and prosperity, of the kingdom of God in the heart as the refusal to carry out the principles of that kingdom in the conduct.[5]

But some may say that it is bringing us down from the high ground of the Church, as set forth in Paul's epistles, to press thus the principles of the kingdom. By no means. We belong to the Church, but we are in the kingdom; and while we must never confound the two, it is perfectly plain that the ethics—the moral habits and ways—of the Church can never be below those of the kingdom. If it be contrary to the spirit and principles of the kingdom to assert my rights and go to law, it must, if possible, be still more contrary to the spirit and principles of the Church. This cannot be questioned. The higher my position, the higher should be my code of ethics and tone of character. I fully believe, and desire firmly to hold, experimentally to enter into, and practically to exhibit the truth of the Church as the body and bride of Christ—the possessor of a heavenly standing, and the expectant of heavenly glory, by virtue of her oneness with Christ; but I cannot see how my being a member of that highly privileged body can make my practice lower than if I were merely a subject or member of the kingdom. What is the difference, as regards present conduct and character, between belonging to the body of a rejected Head and belonging to the kingdom of a rejected King? Assuredly it cannot be to lower the tone in the former case. The higher and more intimate my relationship to the rejected One, the more intense should be my separation from that which rejects Him, and the more complete should be my assimilation to His character, and the more precise and accurate my walk in His footsteps in the midst of that scene from which He is rejected.

But the simple fact is, WE WANT CONSCIENCE. Yes, beloved reader, a tender, exercised, honest conscience, which will truly and accurately respond to the appeals of God's pure and holy Word, is, I verily believe, the grand desideratum—

---

[5] The Christian should be governed by the principles of the kingdom in every thing. If he is engaged in business, he should conduct his business as a child of God, and a servant of Christ. He should not have a Christian character on Lord's day and a commercial character on Monday. I should have the Lord with me in my shop, my warehouse, and my counting-house. It is my privilege to depend upon God in my business; but in order to depend upon Him, my business must be of such a nature, and conducted upon such a principle as He can own. If it is not so, I must leave the Lord out, and I am then on the same footing as the men of the world, and left to fall into their ways and manner of doing business.

Of course, everything depends upon the motive which actuates the mind. What, then, is my motive in my daily labor? Is it to provide food and raiment, or is it to lay up treasures upon earth? If the former, God has pleasure in it, and is with it; so that, if you are in the way of His appointment, you have only to depend upon Him.

Faith always puts the soul on a totally different ground from that occupied by the world, no matter where or what our calling may be. Take, for example, David in the valley of Elah. Why did he not fight, like other men? Because he was on the ground of faith. So also Hezekiah. Why did he put on sackcloth when other men put on armor? Because he was on the ground of simple dependence upon God. Just so in the case of a man in trade; he must carry on his trade as a Christian, else he will mar the testimony and rob his own soul of blessing.

the pressing want of the present moment. It is not so much principles we want, as the grace, the energy, the holy decision, that will carry them out, cost what it may. We admit the truth of principles which most plainly cut at the very things which we ourselves are either directly or indirectly doing,—we admit the principle of grace, and yet we live by the strict maintenance of righteousness. For example, how often does it happen that persons are preaching, teaching, and professing to enjoy grace, while at the very moment they are insisting upon their rights in reference to their tenants; and, either directly themselves or indirectly by means of their agents, dispossessing poor people, unroofing their houses, and sending them out, in destitution and misery, upon a cold, heartless world! This is a plain, palpable case, of which, alas! there have been too many painful illustrations in the world within the last ten years.

And why put cases? Because one finds such melancholy deficiency in sensibility of conscience at the present day, that unless the thing is brought home plainly to one's self it will not be understood. Like David, our indignation is wrought up to the highest pitch by a picture of moral turpitude, so long as we do not see *self* in that picture. It needs some Nathan to sound in our ears, "Thou art the man," in order to prostrate us in the dust, with a smitten conscience, and true self-abhorrence. Thus, at the present day, eloquent sermons are preached, eloquent lectures delivered, and elaborate treatises written about the principles of grace, and yet the courts of law are frequented, attorneys, lawyers, sheriffs, agents, and sub-agents are called into requisition, with all their terrible machinery, in order to assert our rights; but we feel it not, because we are not present to witness the distress, and hear the groans and execrations of houseless mothers and children. Need we wonder, therefore, that true practical Christianity is at a low ebb amongst us? Is it any marvel that leanness, barrenness, drought and poverty, coldness and deadness, darkness, ignorance, and spiritual depression should be found amongst us? What else could be expected, when the principles of the kingdom of God are openly violated?

But is it unrighteous to seek to get our own, and to make use of the machinery within our reach in order to do so? Surely not. What is here maintained is, that no matter how well defined and clearly established the right may be, the assertion thereof is diametrically opposed to the kingdom of God. The servant in Matthew xviii. was called "a wicked servant," and "delivered to the tormentors," not because he acted unrighteously in enforcing the payment of a lawful debt, but because he did not act in grace and remit that debt. Well, therefore, might the Lord Jesus sound in His disciples' ears this warning voice, "Take heed and beware of covetousness; for a man's life consisteth not in the abundance of the things which he possesseth."

But how difficult to define this "covetousness"! how hard to bring it home to the conscience! It is, as some one has said of worldliness, "shaded off gradually from white to jet black;" so that it is only as we are imbued with the spirit and mind of heaven, and thoroughly schooled in the principles of eternity, that we shall be able to detect its working. And not only so, but our hearts must, in this also, be purged from the leaven of the Pharisees, which is hypocrisy. The Pharisees were covetous, and could only turn Christ's doctrine into ridicule (see Luke xvi. 14); and so will it be with all those who are tainted by their leaven. They *will* not see the just application of truth, either as to covetousness or any thing else. They will seek to define it in such a way as will suit themselves. They will interpret, modify, pare down, accommodate, until they have fully succeeded in getting their conscience from under the edge of God's truth; and thus they get into the power and under the influence of the enemy. I must either be governed by the pure truth of the Word or by the impure principles of the world, which, as we very well know, are forged in Satan's workshop, and brought into the world to be used in doing his work.

In the parable of the rich man, which the Lord here puts forth in illustration of covetousness, we see a character which the world respects and admires. But in this, as in every thing else brought forward in this searching chapter, we see the difference between *now* and *then*—between "time and eternity." All depends upon the light in which you look at men and things. If you merely look at them *now*, it may be all very well to get on in trade, and enlarge one's concerns, and make provision for the future. The man who does this is counted wise *now*, but he will be a "fool" *then*. But, my reader, let us remember that we must make God's *then* to be our *now*; we must look at the things of time in the light of eternity—the things of earth in the light of heaven. This is true wisdom, which does not confine the heart to that system of things which obtains "under the sun," but conducts it into the light, and leaves it under the power of "that world" where the principles of the kingdom of God bear sway. What should we think of courts of law and insurance offices if we look at them in the light of eternity?[6] These things do very well for men who are only governed by *now*, but the disciple of Christ is to be governed by *then*. This makes all the difference; and truly it is a serious difference.

"The ground of a certain rich man brought forth plentifully." What sin is there in being a successful agriculturist or merchant? If God bless a man's labor, should he not rejoice? Truly so; but mark the moral progress of a covetous heart. "He thought *within himself*." He did not think in the presence of God,—he did not think under the mighty influences of the eternal world; no, "he thought within himself"—within the narrow compass of his selfish heart. Such was his range; and therefore we need not marvel at his practical conclusion. "What shall I do, because

---

[6] It should be a serious question with a child of God, ere he avails himself of an assurance company, whether in the matter of fire or life, "Am I hereby distrusting God? or am I seeking by human agency to counteract divine visitations?" There is something sadly anomalous in a Christian's insuring his life. He professes to be *dead*, and that Christ is his *life*; why then talk of insuring his life? But many will say, "We cannot bring Christianity into such things." I ask, Where are we to leave it? Is Christianity a convenient sort of garment, which we put on on Lord's day, and at the close of that day take it off, fold it carefully up, and lay it on the shelf till the following Lord's day? It is too often thus. People have two characters; and what is this but the leaven of the Pharisees, which is hypocrisy? Insurance offices are all very well for the men of this world, who should certainly avail themselves of them, inasmuch as every thing around and within is so uncertain. But to the child of God *all is sure.* God has insured his life forever, and hence he should regard insurance offices as so many depots of unbelief.

I have no room where to bestow my fruits?" What! Was there no way of using his resources with a view to God's future? Alas! no. Man has a future (or thinks he has) on which he counts, and for which he makes provision; but self is the only object which figures in that future,—self, whether in my own person or that of my wife or child, which is morally the same thing.

The grand object in God's future is Christ; and true wisdom will lead us to fix our eye on Him, and make Him our undivided object for time and eternity—*now* and *then*. But this, in the judgment of a worldly man, is nonsense. Yes, Heaven's wisdom is nonsense in the judgment of earth. Hearken to the wisdom of earth, and the wisdom of those who are under the influence of earthly maxims and habits. "And he said, 'This will I do: I will pull down my barns, and build greater; and *there* will I bestow *all* my fruits and my goods.'" Thus we have what he "thought," what he "said," and what he "did;" and there is a melancholy consistency between his thoughts, his words, and his acts. "*There*," in my self-built storehouse, "will I bestow *all*." Miserable treasure-house to contain the "all" of an immortal soul! God was not an item in the catalogue. God was neither his treasury nor his treasure. This is plain; and it is always thus with a mere man of the world. "And I will say to my soul, Soul, thou hast much goods laid up for many years; take thine ease, eat, drink, and be merry." Thus we see that a worldly man's provision is only "for many years." Make the best of it, it cannot go beyond that narrow limit. It cannot, even in his own thought about it, reach into that boundless eternity which stretches beyond this contracted span of time. And this provision he offers to his never-dying soul as the basis of its "ease and merriment." Miserable fatuity! Senseless calculation!

How different is the address which a believer may present to his soul! He too may say to his soul, "Soul, take thine ease; eat, drink, and be merry;—eat of the fatness of God's storehouse, and drink of the river of His pleasures, and of the wine of His kingdom; and be glad in His accomplished salvation; for thou hast much goods, yea, unsearchable riches, untold wealth, laid up, not merely for many years, but for eternity. Christ's finished work is the ground of thine eternal peace, and His coming glory the sure and certain object of thy hope." This is a different character of address, my reader. This shows the difference between *now* and *then*. It is a fatal mistake not to make Christ the Crucified, Christ the Risen, Christ the Glorified, the Alpha and Omega of all our calculations. To paint a future, and not to place Christ in the foreground, is extravagance of the wildest character; for the moment God enters the scene, the picture is hopelessly marred.

"But God said unto him, 'Thou fool! this night thy soul shall be required of thee: THEN whose shall those things be which thou hast provided?'" And then mark the moral of all this. "So is he," no matter who—saint or sinner, "that layeth up *treasure for himself*, and is not rich toward God." The man who hoards up is virtually making a god of his hoard. His mind is tranquilized as to the future when he thinks of his hoard, for if he had not that hoard he would be uneasy. It is sufficient to put a natural man entirely out of his reason to give him naught but God to depend upon. Any thing but that for him. Give him old pieces of parchment in the shape of title-deeds, in which some clever lawyer will finally pick a hole, and prove worthless. He will lean on them—yea, die in peace, if he can leave such to his heirs. Give him an insurance policy,—any thing, in short, but God for the natural heart. ALL IS REALITY SAVE THE ONLY REALITY, in the judgment of nature. This proves what nature's true condition is. It cannot trust God. It *talks* about Him, but it cannot *trust* Him. The very basis of man's moral constitution is distrust of God; and one of the fairest fruits of regeneration is the capacity to confide in God for every thing. "They that know Thy name will put their trust in Thee." None else can.

However, my main object in this paper is to deal with Christian consciences. I ask the Christian reader, therefore, in plain terms, is it in keeping with Christ's doctrine, as set forth in the gospel, for His disciples to lay up for themselves treasure on the earth? It seems almost an absurdity to put such a question, in the face of Luke xii. and parallel scriptures. "Lay not up for yourselves treasure on the earth, where moth and rust doth corrupt, and where thieves break through and steal; but lay up for yourselves treasure in heaven, where neither moth nor rust doth corrupt, and where thieves do not break through and steal." This is plain enough, and only wants an honest conscience to apply it, in order to produce its proper results. It is directly contrary to the doctrine of the kingdom of God, and perfectly incompatible with true discipleship, to lay up "treasure," in any shape or form, "on the earth." In this, as in the matter of going to law, we have only to remember that we are in the kingdom of God, in order to know how we should act. The principles of that kingdom are eternal and binding upon every disciple of Christ.

"And He said unto His disciples, 'Therefore I say unto you, Take no thought for your life, what ye shall eat; neither for the body, what ye shall put on. The life is more than meat, and the body is more than raiment.'" "Be careful for nothing," says the Spirit by the apostle. Why? Because God is caring for you. There is no use in two thinking about the same thing, when One can do every thing and the other can do nothing. "In every thing by prayer and supplication with thanksgiving let your requests be made known to God. And the peace of God, which passeth all understanding, shall garrison [φρουρήδει] your hearts and minds through Christ Jesus.» This is the solid foundation of peace of heart, which so few really enjoy. Many have gotten peace of conscience through faith in the sufficiency of Christ›s work, who do not enjoy peace of heart through faith in the sufficiency of God's care. And oftentimes we go to pray about our difficulties and trials, and we rise from our knees as troubled as we knelt down. We profess to put our affairs into the hands of God, but we have no notion of *leaving them*, there; and consequently we do not enjoy peace of heart. Thus it was with Jacob, in Genesis xxxii. He asked God to deliver him from the hand of Esau; but no sooner did he rise from his knees than he set forth the real ground of his soul's dependence, by saying, "I will appease him by a present." It is clear he had much more confidence in the "present" than in God. This is a common error amongst the children of God. We profess to be looking to the Eternal Fountain; but the eye of the soul is askance upon some creature-stream. Thus God is practically shut out; our souls are not delivered, and we have not got peace of heart.

The apostle then goes on, in Philippians iv. 8, to give a catalogue of those things about which we ought to think; and we find that *self* or its affairs is not once alluded to. "Whatsoever things are true, whatsoever things are venerable [σεμνά], whatsoever things are just, whatsoever things are pure, whatsoever things are lovely, whatsoever things are of good report; if there be any virtue, and if there be any praise, think on these things.... And the God of peace shall be with you." Thus, when I know and believe that God is thinking about me, I have *"the peace of God;"* and when I am thinking about Him and the things belonging to Him, I have *"the God of peace."* This, as might be expected, harmonizes precisely with Christ's doctrine in Luke xii. After relieving the minds of His disciples in reference to present supplies and future treasure, He says, "But rather seek ye the kingdom of God, and all these things shall be added unto you." That is, I am not to seek the kingdom with the latent thought in my mind that my wants will be supplied in consequence. That would not be true discipleship. A true disciple never thinks of aught but the Master and His kingdom; and the Master will assuredly think of him and his wants. Thus it stands, my beloved reader, between a faithful servant and an all-powerful and all-gracious Master. That servant may therefore be free, perfectly free, from care.

But there is another ground on which we are exhorted to be free from care, and that is, the utter worthlessness of that care. "Which of you, with taking thought, can add to his stature one cubit? If ye then be not able to do that thing which is least, why take ye thought for the rest?" We gain nothing by our care; and by indulging therein we only unfit ourselves for seeking the kingdom of God, and place a barrier, by our unbelief, in the way of His acting for us. It is always true in reference to us, "He could there do no mighty work, because of their unbelief." Unbelief is the great hindrance to the display of God's mighty works on our behalf. If we take our affairs into our own hands, it is clear that we do not want God. Thus we are left to the depressing influence of our own perplexing thoughts, and finally we take refuge in some human resource, and make shipwreck of faith.

It is important to understand that we are either leaning on God or on circumstances. It will not do, by any means, to say that we are leaning on God *and* circumstances. It must be God *only*, or not at all. It is all very well to talk of faith when our hearts are, in reality, leaning on the creature in some shape or form. We should sift and try our ways closely as to this; for inasmuch as absolute dependence upon God is one of the special characteristics of the divine life, and one of the fundamental principles of the kingdom, it surely becomes us to look well to it that we are not presenting any barrier to our progress in that heavenly quality. True, it is most trying to flesh and blood to have no settled thing to lean upon. The heart will quiver as we stand upon the shore of circumstances, and look forth upon that unknown ocean—unknown to all but faith, and where naught but simple faith can live for an hour. We may feel disposed, like Lot, to cry out, "Is it not a little one? and my soul shall live." The heart longs for some shred of the creature, some plank from the raft of circumstances,—any thing but absolute dependence upon God. But oh! let God only be known, and He must be trusted; let Him be trusted, and He must be known.

Still the poor heart will yearn after something settled, something tangible. If it be a question of maintenance, it will earnestly desire some settled income, a certain sum in the funds, a certain amount of landed property, or a fixed jointure or annuity of some kind or other. Then, if it be a question of public testimony or ministry of any kind, it will be the same thing. If a man is going to preach or lecture, he will like to have something to lean upon; if not a written sermon, at least some notes, or some kind of previous preparation,—any thing but unqualified, self-emptied dependence upon God. Hence it is that worldliness prevails to such a fearful extent amongst Christians. Faith alone can overcome the world and purify the heart. It brings the soul from under the influence of time, and keeps it habitually in the light of eternity. It is occupied not with now, but with *then*,—not with *here*, but *hereafter*,—not with earth, but with heaven. Thus it overcomes the world and purifies the heart. It hears and believes Christ's word, "Fear not, little flock, for it is your Father's good pleasure to give you the kingdom." Now, if "the kingdom" fills my soul's vision, I have no room for aught beside. I can let go present shadows, in the prospect of future realities; I can give up an evanescent *now*, in the prospect of an eternal *then*.

Wherefore the Lord immediately adds, "Sell that ye have, and give alms: provide yourselves bags which wax not old, a treasure in the heavens that fadeth not, where no thief approacheth, neither moth corrupteth. For where your treasure is, there will the heart be also." If I have treasure on earth, no matter in what shape, my *heart* will be there also, and I shall be a downright worldly man. How shall I most effectually empty my heart of the world? By getting it filled with Christ. He is the true treasure which neither the world's "bags" nor its "storehouses" can contain. The world has its "barns" and its "bags," in which it hoards its "goods;" but its barns will fall and its bags will wax old: and then, what will become of the treasure? Truly "they build too low that build beneath the skies."

Yet people will build and hoard up, if not for themselves, at least for their children, or in other words, their second selves. If I hoard for my children, I am hoarding for myself; and not only so, but in numberless cases, the hoard, in place of proving a blessing, proves a positive curse to the child, by taking him off the proper ground appointed for him, as well as for all, in God's moral government, namely, "working with his hands the thing which is good, that he may have [not to hoard up for himself, or for his second self, but] to give to him that needeth." This is God's appointed ground for every man; and therefore if I hoard for my child, I am taking both myself and him off the divine ground, and the consequence will be a forfeiture of blessing. Do I taste the surpassing sweetness of obedience to and dependence upon God, and shall I deprive my child thereof? Shall I rob him, virtually, and so far as in me lies, of God, and give him, as a substitute, a few "old bags," an insurance policy, or some musty parchments?

But why need I hoard up for my children? If I can trust God for myself, why not trust Him for them likewise? Cannot the One who has fed and clothed me feed and clothe them also? Let not the truth be misunderstood or misinterpreted. I am bound, by the powerful obligations of the word and example of God, to provide for my own; for, "if any provide not for his own, and especially for those of his own house, he hath denied the faith, and is worse than an infidel." (1 Tim. v. 8.) This is plain enough. And, moreover, I am bound to fit my children, so far as God's principles admit, and my province extends, for any service to which He may be graciously pleased to call them. But I am no where instructed in the Word of God to give my children a hoard in place of an honest occupation, with simple dependence upon a heavenly Father. As a matter of actual fact, few children ever thank their fathers for inherited wealth; whereas they will ever remember, with gratitude and veneration, having been led, by parental care and management, into a godly course of action for themselves.

I do not, however, forget a passage which has often been used, or rather abused, to defend the worldly, unbelieving practice of hoarding up. I allude to 2 Corinthians xii. 14.—"Behold, the third time I am ready to come to you; and I will not be burdensome to you: for I seek not yours, but you: for the children ought not to lay up for the parents, but the parents for the children." How glad people are when they get a semblance of Scripture-authority for their worldliness! In this passage it is but a semblance of authority; for the apostle is certainly not teaching Christians to hoard up—he is not teaching heavenly men to lay up treasure upon the earth, for any object. He simple refers to a common practice *in the world*, and to a common feeling *in nature*, in order to illustrate his own mode of dealing with the Corinthians, who were his children in the faith. He had not burdened them, and he would not burden them, for he was the parent. Now, if the saints of God are satisfied to go back to the world and its maxims, to nature and its ways, then let them hoard up with all diligence—let them "heap treasure together for the last days;" but let them remember that the moth, the canker-worm, and the rust will be the end of it all. Oh for a heart to value those immortal "bags" in which faith lays up its "unfading treasure," those heavenly storehouses where faith "bestows all its fruits and its goods"! Then shall we pursue a holy and elevated path through this present evil world—then, too, shall we be lifted upon faith's vigorous pinion above the dark atmosphere which inwraps this Christ-rejecting, God-hating world, and which is impregnated and polluted by those two elements, namely, *hatred of God, and love of gold.*

I shall only add, ere closing this paper, that the Lord Jesus—the Adorable, the Divine, the Heavenly Teacher, having sought to raise, by His unearthly principles, the thoughts and affections of His disciples to their proper centre and level, gives them two things to do; and these two things may be expressed in the words of the Holy Ghost—"To serve the living and true God, and wait for His Son from heaven." The entire of the teaching of Luke xii, from verse 35 to the end, may be ranged under the above comprehensive heads, to which I call the Christian reader's prayerful attention. We have no one else to serve but "the living God", and nothing to wait for—nothing worth waiting for but "His Son." May the Holy Ghost clothe His own Word with heavenly power, so that it may come home to the heart and conscience, and tell upon the life of every child of God, that the name of the Lord Christ may be magnified, and His truth vindicated in the conduct of those that belong to Him. May the grace of an honest heart, and a tender, upright, well-adjusted conscience, be largely ministered to each and all of us, so that we may be like a well-tuned instrument, yielding a true tone when touched by the Master's hand, and harmonizing with His heavenly voice.

Finally, if this paper should fall into the hands of one who has not yet found rest of conscience in the perfected atonement of the Son of God, I would say to such an one, You will surely lay this paper down and say, "This is a hard saying, who can hear it?" You may be disposed to ask, "What would the world come to, if such principles were universally dominant?" I reply, It would cease to be governed by Satan, and would be "the kingdom of God." But let me ask you, my friend, "To which kingdom do you belong? Which is it—*now*, or *then*—with you? Are you living for time, or eternity,—earth, or heaven,—Satan, or Christ?" Do, I affectionately implore of you, be thoroughly honest with yourself in the presence of God. Remember, "there is *nothing* covered that shall not be revealed." The judgment-seat will bring *all* to light. Therefore I say, Be honest with yourself, and now ask your heart, "Where am I? How do I stand? What is the ground of my peace? What are my prospects for eternity?" Do not imagine that God wants *you* to buy heaven with a surrender of earth. No; He points you to Christ, who, by bearing sin in His own body on the cross, has opened the way for the believing sinner to come into the presence of God in the power of divine righteousness. You are not asked to do or to be any thing; but the gospel tells you what Jesus is, and what He has done; and if you believe this in your heart, and confess it with your mouth, you shall be saved. Christ—God's Eternal Son—God manifest in the flesh—co-equal with the Father, being conceived by the Holy Ghost, was born of a woman, took upon Him a body prepared by the power of the Highest, and thus became a REAL MAN— very God and very man,—He, having lived a life of perfect obedience, died upon the cross, being made sin and a curse, and having exhausted the cup of Jehovah's righteous wrath, endured the sting of death, spoiled the grave of its victory, and destroyed him that had the power of death, He went up into heaven, and took His seat at the right hand of God. Such is the infinite merit of His perfect sacrifice, that all who believe are justified from ALL THINGS—yea, are accepted in Him—stand in His acceptableness before God, and can never come into condemnation, but have passed from death into life. This is the gospel!—the glad tidings of salvation, which God the Holy Ghost came down from heaven to preach to every creature. My reader, let me exhort you, in this concluding line, to "behold the Lamb of God that taketh away the sin of the world." BELIEVE AND LIVE!

C. H. M.

THE ALL-SUFFICIENCY OF CHRIST

PART I

When once the soul has been brought to feel the reality of its condition before God—the depth of its ruin, guilt, and misery—its utter and hopeless bankruptcy, there can be no rest until the Holy Spirit reveals a full and an all-sufficient Christ to the heart. The only possible answer to our total ruin is God's perfect remedy.

This is a very simple, but a most important truth; and we may say, with all possible assurance, the more deeply and thoroughly the reader learns it for himself the better. The true secret of peace is, to get to the very end of a guilty, ruined, helpless, worthless self, and there find an all-sufficient Christ as God's provision for our very deepest need. This truly is rest—a rest which can never be disturbed. There may be sorrow, pressure, conflict, exercise of soul, heaviness through manifold temptations, ups and downs, all sorts of trials and difficulties; but we feel persuaded that when a soul is really brought by God's Spirit to see the end of self, and to rest in a full Christ, it finds a peace which can never be interrupted.

The unsettled state of so many of God's dear people is the result of not having received into their hearts a full Christ, as God's very own provision for them. No doubt this sad and painful result may be brought about by various contributing causes, such as a legal mind, a morbid conscience, a self-occupied heart, bad teaching, a secret hankering after this present world, some little reserve in the heart as to the claims of God, of Christ, and of eternity. But whatever may be the producing cause, we believe it will be found, in almost every case, that the lack of settled peace, so common amongst the Lord's people, is the result of not seeing, not believing, what God has made His Christ to be to them and for them, and that forever.

Now, what we propose in this paper is, to show the anxious reader, from the precious pages of the Word of God, that there is treasured up for him in Christ all he can possibly need, whether it be to meet the claims of his conscience, the cravings of his heart, or the exigencies of his path. We shall seek, by the grace of God, to prove that the *work* of Christ is the only true resting-place for the *conscience*; His *Person*, the only true object for the *heart*; His *Word*, the only true guide for the *path*.

And first, then, let us dwell for a little upon

THE WORK OF CHRIST AS THE ONLY RESTING-PLACE FOR THE CONSCIENCE.

In considering this great subject, two things claim our attention; first, what

Christ has done for us; secondly, what He is doing for us. In the former, we have atonement; in the latter, advocacy. He died for us on the cross: He lives for us on the throne. By His precious atoning death He has met our entire condition as sinners. He has borne our sins, and put them away forever. He stood charged with all our sins—the sins of all who believe in His name. "Jehovah laid on Him the iniquity of us all." (Isa. liii.) And again, "For Christ also hath once suffered for sins, the just for the unjust, that He might bring us to God." (1 Pet. iii. 18.)

This is a grand and all-important truth for the anxious soul—a truth which lies at the very foundation of the whole Christian position. It is impossible that any truly awakened soul, any spiritually enlightened conscience, can enjoy divinely settled peace until this most precious truth is laid hold of in simple faith. I must know, upon divine authority, that all my sins are put away forever out of God's sight; that He Himself has disposed of them in such a manner as to satisfy all the claims of His throne and all the attributes of His nature; that He has glorified Himself in the putting away of my sins, in a far higher and more wonderful manner than if He had sent me to an everlasting hell on account of them.

Yes, He Himself has done it. This is the very gist and marrow—the heart's core of the whole matter. God has laid our sins on Jesus, and He tells us so in His holy Word, so that we may know it upon divine authority—an authority that cannot lie. God planned it; God did it; God says it. It is all of God, from first to last, and we have simply to rest in it like a little child. How do I know that Jesus bore my sins in His own body on the tree? By the very same authority which tells me I had sins to be borne. God, in His marvelous and matchless love, assures me, a poor guilty, hell-deserving sinner, that He has Himself undertaken the whole matter of my sins, and disposed of it in such a manner as to bring a rich harvest of glory to His own eternal name, throughout the wide universe, in presence of all created intelligence.

The living faith of this must tranquilize the conscience. If God has satisfied Himself about my sins, I may well be satisfied also. I know I am a sinner—it may be, the chief of sinners. I know my sins are more in number than the hairs of my head; that they are black as midnight—black as hell itself. I know that any one of these sins, the very least, deserves the eternal flames of hell. I know—because God's Word tells me—that a single speck of sin can never enter His holy presence; and hence, so far as I am concerned, there was no possible issue save eternal separation from God. All this I know, upon the clear and unquestionable authority of that Word which is settled forever in heaven.

But, oh, the profound mystery of the cross!—the glorious mystery of redeeming love! I see God Himself taking all my sins—the black and terrible category—all my sins, as He knew and estimated them. I see Him laying them all upon the head of my blessed Substitute, and dealing with Him about them. I see all the billows and waves of God's righteous wrath—His wrath against my sins—His wrath which should have consumed me, soul and body, in hell, throughout a dreary eternity,—I see them all rolling over the Man who stood in my stead, who represented me before God, who bore all that was due to me, with whom a holy God dealt as He should have dealt with me. I see inflexible justice, holiness, truth, and righteousness dealing with my sins, and making a clear and eternal riddance of them. Not one of them is suffered to pass! There is no connivance, no palliation, no slurring over, no indifference. This could not possibly be, once God Himself took the matter in hand. His glory was at stake; His unsullied holiness, His eternal majesty, the lofty claims of His government.

All these had to be provided for in such wise as to glorify Himself in view of angels, men, and devils. He might have sent me to hell—righteously, justly, sent me to hell—because of my sins. I deserved nothing else. My whole moral being, from its profoundest depths, owns this—must own it. I have not a word to say in excuse for a single sinful thought, to say nothing of a sin-stained life from first to last—yes, a life of deliberate, rebellious, high-handed sin.

Others may reason as they please as to the injustice of an eternity of punishment for a life of sin—the utter want of proportion between a few years of wrong-doing and endless ages of torment in the lake of fire. They may reason, but I thoroughly believe, and unreservedly confess, that for a single sin against such a Being as the God whom I see at the cross, I richly deserved everlasting punishment in the deep, dark, and dismal pit of hell.

I am not writing as a theologian; if I were, it would be a very easy task indeed to bring an unanswerable array of Scripture evidence in proof of the solemn truth of eternal punishment. But no; I am writing as one who has been divinely taught the true desert of sin, and that desert, I calmly, deliberately, and solemnly declare, is, and can be, nothing less than eternal exclusion from the presence of God and the Lamb—eternal torment in the lake that burneth with fire and brimstone.

But—eternal halleluiahs to the God of all grace!—instead of sending us to hell because of our sins, He sent His Son to be the propitiation for those sins. And in the unfolding of the marvelous plan of redemption, we see a holy God dealing with the question of our sins, and executing judgment upon them in the Person of His well-beloved, eternal, and co-equal Son, in order that the full flood-tide of His love might flow down into our hearts. "Herein is love, not that we loved God, but that He loved us, and sent His Son to be the propitiation for our sins." (1 John iv. 10.)

Now, this must give peace to the conscience, if only it be received in the simplicity of faith. How is it possible for a person to believe that God has satisfied Himself as to his sins and not have peace? If God says to us, "Your sins and iniquities I will remember no more," what could we desire further as a basis of peace for our conscience? If God assures me that all my sins are blotted out as a thick cloud—that they are cast behind His back—forever gone from His sight, should I not have peace? If He shows me the Man who bore my sins on the cross, now crowned at the right hand of the Majesty in the heavens, ought not my soul to enter into perfect rest as to the question of my sins? Most assuredly.

For how, let me ask, did Christ reach the place which He now fills on the throne of God? Was it as God over all, blessed forever? No; for He was always that. Was it as the eternal Son of the Father? No; He was ever that—ever in the bosom of the Father—the object of the Father's eternal and ineffable delight. Was it as a spotless, holy, perfect Man—One whose nature was absolutely pure, perfectly free from sin? No; for in that character, and on that ground, He could at any moment, between the manger and the cross, have claimed a place at the right hand of God. How was it, then? Eternal praise to the God of all grace! it was as the One who had by His death accomplished the glorious work of redemption—the One who had stood charged with the full weight of our sins—the One who had perfectly satisfied all the righteous claims of that throne on which He now sits.

This is a grand, cardinal point for the anxious reader to seize. It cannot fail to emancipate the heart and tranquilize the conscience. We cannot possibly behold, by faith, the Man who was nailed to the tree, now crowned on the throne, and not have peace with God. The Lord Jesus Christ having taken upon Himself our sins, and the judgment due to them, He could not be where He now is if a single one of those sins remained unatoned for. To see the Sin-bearer crowned with glory is to see our sins gone forever from the divine presence. Where are our sins? They are all obliterated. How do we know this? The One who took them all upon Himself has passed through the heavens to the very highest pinnacle of glory. Eternal justice has wreathed His blessed brow with a diadem of glory, as the Accomplisher of our redemption—the Bearer of our sins; thus proving, beyond all question, or possibility of a question, that our sins are all put away out of God's sight forever. A crowned Christ and a clear conscience are, in the blessed economy of grace, inseparably linked together. Wondrous fact! Well may we chant, with all our ransomed powers, the praises of redeeming love.

But let us see how this most consolatory truth is set forth in holy Scripture. In Romans iii. we read, "But now the righteousness of God without law [χωρὶς νόμου] is manifested, being witnessed by the law and the prophets; even the righteousness of God by faith of Jesus Christ unto all and upon all them that believe; for there is no difference: for all have sinned, and come short of the glory of God; being justified freely by His grace through the redemption that is in Christ Jesus: *whom God hath set forth* a propitiation through faith in His blood, to declare His righteousness for the remission [or passing over] of sins that are past [in time gone by], through the forbearance of God; to declare at this time His righteousness; that He might be just and the justifier of him which believeth in Jesus."

Again, in chapter iv, speaking of Abraham's faith being counted to him for righteousness, the apostle adds, "Now it was not written for his sake alone, that it was imputed to him; but for us also, to whom it shall be imputed, if we *believe on Him that raised up Jesus our Lord from the dead; who was delivered for our offenses, and raised again for our justification.*" Here we have God introduced to our souls as the One who raised from the dead the Bearer of our sins. Why did He do so? Because the One who had been delivered for our offenses had perfectly glorified Him respecting those offenses, and put them away forever. God not only sent His only begotten Son into the world, but He bruised Him for our iniquities, and raised Him from the dead, in order that we might know and believe that our iniquities are all disposed of in such a manner as to glorify Him infinitely and everlastingly. Eternal and universal homage to His name!

But we have further testimony on this grand fundamental truth. In Hebrews i. we read such soul-stirring words as these: "God, who at sundry times and in divers manners [or in divers measures and modes] spake in time past unto the fathers by the prophets, hath in these last days spoken unto us by [His] Son, whom He hath appointed heir of all things, by whom also He made the worlds; who being the brightness of His glory, and the express image of His Person, and upholding all things by the word of His power, *when He had by Himself purged our sins*, sat down on the right hand of the Majesty on high." Our Lord Christ, blessed be His name! would not take His seat on the throne of God until He had, by the offering of Himself on the cross, purged our sins. Hence, a risen Christ at God's right hand is the glorious and unanswerable proof that our sins are all gone, for He could not be where He now is if a single one of those sins remained. God raised from the dead the self-same Man on whom He Himself had laid the full weight of our sins. Thus all is settled—divinely, eternally settled. It is as impossible that a single sin can be found on the very weakest believer in Jesus as on Jesus Himself. This is a wonderful thing to be able to say, but it is the solid truth of God, established in manifold places in holy Scripture, and the soul that believes it must possess a peace which the world can neither give nor take away.

PART II

Thus far, we have been occupied with that aspect of the work of Christ which bears upon the question of the forgiveness of sins, and we earnestly trust that the reader is thoroughly clear and settled on this grand point. It is assuredly his happy privilege so to be, if only he will take God at His word. "Christ hath once suffered for sins, the just for the unjust, that He might bring us to God."

If, then, Christ hath suffered for our sins, should we not know the deep blessedness of being eternally delivered from the burden of those sins? Can it be according to the mind and heart of God that one for whom Christ suffered should remain in perpetual bondage, tied and bound with the chain of his sins, and crying out, from week to week, month to month, and year to year, that the burden of his sins is intolerable?

If such utterances are true and proper for the Christian, then what has Christ done for us? Can it be true that Christ has put away our sins and yet that we are tied and bound with the chain of them? Is it true that He bore the heavy burden of our sins and yet that we are still crushed beneath the intolerable weight thereof?

Some would fain persuade us that it is not possible to know that our sins are forgiven—that we must go on to the end of our life in a state of complete uncertainty on this most vital and important question. If this be so, what has become of the precious gospel of the grace of God—the glad tidings of salvation? In the view of such miserable teaching as this, what mean those glowing words of the blessed apostle Paul in the synagogue of Antioch?—"Be it known unto you therefore, men and brethren, that through this Man [Jesus Christ, dead and risen] is preached [not promised as a future thing, but proclaimed now] the forgiveness of sins; and by Him all who believe *are* [not shall be, or hope to be] justified from *all things*, from which ye could not be justified by the law of Moses." (Acts xiii. 38, 39.)

If we were resting on the law of Moses, on our keeping the commandments, on our doing our duty, on our feeling as we ought, on our valuing Christ and loving God as we ought, reason would that we should be in doubt and dark uncertainty, seeing we could have no possible ground of assurance. If we had so much as the movement of an eyelash to do in the matter, then, verily, it would be the very height of presumption on our part to think of being certain.

But on the other hand, when we hear the voice of the living God, who cannot lie, proclaiming in our ears the glad tidings that through His own beloved Son, who died on the cross, was buried in the grave, raised from the dead, and seated in the glory—that through Him alone—through Him, without any thing whatever of ours—through His one offering of Himself once and forever, full and everlasting remission of sins is preached, as a present reality, to be enjoyed now by every soul who simply believes the precious record of God, how is it possible for any one to continue in doubt and uncertainty? Is Christ's work finished? He said it was. What did He do? He put away our sins. Are they, then, put away, or are they still on us?—which?

Reader, say which? where are thy sins? Are they blotted out as a thick cloud? or are they still lying as a heavy load of guilt, in condemning power, on thy conscience? If they were not put away by the atoning death of Christ, they will never be put away; if He did not bear them on the cross, you will have to bear them in the tormenting flames of hell forever and ever and ever. Yes; be assured of it, there is no other way of disposing of this most weighty and momentous question. If Christ did not settle the matter on the cross, you must settle it in hell. It must be so, if God's Word be true.

But glory be to God, His own testimony assures us that Christ hath once suffered for sins, the just for the unjust, that He might bring us to God; not merely bring us to heaven when we die, but bring us to God *now*. How does He bring us to God? Tied and bound with the chain of our sins? with an intolerable burden of guilt on our souls? Nay, verily; He brings us to God without spot or stain or charge. He brings us to God in all His own acceptableness. Is there any guilt on Him? No. There was, blessed be His name, when He stood in our stead, but it is gone—gone forever—cast as lead into the unfathomable waters of divine forgetfulness. He was charged with our sins on the cross. God laid on Him all our iniquities, and dealt with Him about them. The whole question of our sins, according to God's estimate thereof, was fully gone into and definitively, because divinely, settled between God and Christ, amid the awful shadows of Calvary. Yes, it was all done, once and forever, there. How do we know it? By the authority of the only true God. His Word assures us that *we have* redemption through the blood of Christ, the remission of sins, according to the riches of His grace. He declares to us, in accents of sweetest, richest, deepest mercy, that our sins and our iniquities He will remember no more. Is not this enough? Shall we still continue to cry out that we are tied and bound with the chain of our sins? Shall we thus cast a slur upon the perfect work of Christ? Shall we thus tarnish the lustre of divine grace, and give the lie to the testimony of the Holy Ghost in the Scripture of truth? Far be the thought! It must not be so. Let us rather hail with thanksgiving the blessed boon so freely conferred upon us by love divine, through the precious blood of Christ. It is the joy of the heart of God to forgive us our sins. Yes, God delights in pardoning iniquity and transgression. It gratifies and glorifies Him to pour into the broken and contrite heart the precious balm of His own pardoning love and mercy. He spared not His own Son, but delivered Him up, and bruised Him on the cursed tree, in order that He might be able, in perfect righteousness, to let the rich streams of grace flow forth from His large, loving heart, to the poor, guilty, self-destroyed, conscience-smitten sinner.

But should it be that the reader still feels disposed to inquire how he may have the assurance that this blessed remission of sins—this fruit of Christ's atoning work—applies to him, let him hearken to those magnificent words which flowed from the lips of the risen Saviour as He commissioned the earliest heralds of His grace.—"And He said unto them, 'Thus it is written, and thus *it was necessary* for Christ to suffer, and to rise from the dead the third day; and that repentance and remission of sins should be preached in His name among all nations, beginning at Jerusalem.'" (Luke xxiv. 46, 47.)

Here we have the great and glorious commission—its basis, its authority, its sphere. Christ has suffered. This is the meritorious ground of remission of sins. Without shedding of blood there is no remission of sins; but by the shedding of blood, *and by it alone*, there is remission of sins—a remission as full and complete as the precious blood of Christ is fitted to effect.

But where is the authority? *"It is written."* Blessed, indisputable authority! Nothing can ever shake it. I know, on the solid authority of the Word of God, that my sins are all forgiven, all blotted out, all gone forever, all cast behind God's back, so that they can never, by any possibility, rise against me.

Finally, as to the sphere. It is, "all nations." This includes me, beyond all question. There is no sort of exception, condition, or qualification. The blessed tidings were to be wafted, on the wings of love, to all nations—to all the world—to every creature under heaven. How could I exclude myself from this world-wide commission? Do I question, for a moment, that the beams of God's sun are intended for me? Surely not. And why should I question the precious fact that remission of sins is for me? Not for a single instant. It is for me as surely as though I were the only sinner beneath the canopy of God's heaven. The universality of its aspect precludes all question as to its being designed for me.

And surely, if any further encouragement were needed, it is found in the fact that the blessed ambassadors were to "begin at Jerusalem"—the very guiltiest spot on the face of the earth. They were to make the earliest offer of pardon to the very murderers of the Son of God. This the apostle Peter does in those words of marvelous and transcendent grace, "Unto you first God, having raised up His Son, sent Him to bless you, by turning away every one of you from your iniquities." (Acts iii. 26.)

It is not possible to conceive any thing richer or fuller or more magnificent than this. The grace that could reach the murderers of the Son of God can reach any one: the blood that could cleanse the guilt of such a crime can cleanse the vilest sinner outside the precincts of hell.

Anxious reader, do you, can you, still hesitate as to the forgiveness of your sins? Christ has suffered for sins. God preaches remission of sins. He pledges His own Word on the point. "To Him give all the prophets witness, that through His name whosoever believeth in Him shall receive remission of sins." What more would you have? How can you any longer doubt or delay? What are you waiting for? You have Christ's finished work and God's faithful word. Surely these ought to satisfy your heart and tranquilize your mind. Do, then, let us entreat you to accept the full and everlasting remission of all your sins. Receive into your heart the sweet tidings of divine love and mercy, and go on your way rejoicing. Hear the voice of a risen Saviour, speaking from the throne of the Majesty in the heavens, and assuring you that your sins are all forgiven. Let those soothing accents, from the very mouth of God Himself, fall, in their enfranchising power, upon your troubled spirit,—"Your sins and iniquities will I remember no more." If God thus speaks to me, if He assures me that He will no more remember my sins, should I not be fully and forever satisfied? Why should I go on doubting and reasoning when God has spoken? What can give certainty but the Word of God, that liveth and abideth forever? It is the only ground of certainty; and no power of earth or hell—human or diabolical—can ever shake it. The finished work of Christ and the faithful Word of God are the basis and the authority of full forgiveness of sins.

But, blessed forever be the God of all grace, it is not only remission of *sins* which is announced to us through the atoning death of Christ. This in itself would be a boon and a blessing of the very highest order; and, as we have seen, we enjoy it according to the largeness of the heart of God, and according to the value and efficacy of the death of Christ, as God estimates it. But besides the full and perfect remission of sins, we have also

ENTIRE DELIVERANCE FROM THE PRESENT POWER OF SIN.

This is a grand point for every true lover of holiness. According to the glorious economy of grace, the same work which secures the complete remission of *sins* has broken forever the power of *sin*. It is not only that the *sins of the life* are blotted out, but the *sin of the nature* is condemned. The believer is privileged to regard himself as dead to sin. He can sing, with a glad heart,

> "For me, Lord Jesus, Thou hast died,
> And I have died in Thee;
> Thou'rt risen, my bands are all untied,
> And now Thou livest in me.
> The Father's face of radiant grace
> Shines now in light on me."

This is the proper breathing of a Christian. "I am crucified with Christ, nevertheless I live; yet not I, but Christ liveth in me." This is Christianity. The old "I" crucified, and Christ living in me. The Christian is a new creation. Old things are passed away. The death of Christ has closed forever the history of the old "I;" and hence, though sin dwells in the believer, its power is broken and gone forever. Not only is its guilt canceled, but its terrible dominion completely overthrown.

This is the glorious doctrine of Romans vi.-viii. The thoughtful student of this most magnificent epistle will observe that from chapter iii. 21 to chapter v. 11 we have the work of Christ applied to the question of *sins*; and from chapter v. 12 to the end of chapter viii. we have another aspect of that work, namely, its application to the question of *sin*—"our old man"—"the body of *sin*"—"*sin* in the flesh." There is no such thing in Scripture as the forgiveness of sin. God has condemned sin, not forgiven it—an immensely important distinction. God has set forth His eternal abhorrence of sin in the cross of Christ. He has expressed and executed His judgment upon it, and now the believer can see himself as linked and identified with the One who died on the cross and is raised from the dead. He has passed out of the sphere of sin's dominion into that new and blessed sphere where grace reigns through righteousness. "God be thanked," says the apostle, "that ye *were* [once, but now no longer are to be] the servants of sin, but ye have obeyed from the heart that type of doctrine to which ye were delivered. (Margin.) Being then made *free from sin* [not merely sins forgiven], ye became the servants of righteousness. I speak after the manner of men, because of the infirmity of your flesh; for as ye have yielded your members servants to uncleanness and to iniquity unto iniquity, even so now yield your members servants to righteousness unto holiness. For when ye *were* the servants of sin, ye were free from righteousness. What fruit had ye then in those things whereof ye are now ashamed? for the end of those things is death. But now being made *free from sin*, and become servants to God, ye have your fruit unto holiness, and the end everlasting life." (Rom. vi. 17-22.)

Here lies the precious secret of holy living. We are dead to sin; alive to God. The reign of sin is over. What has sin to do with a dead man? Nothing. Well, then, the believer has died with Christ; he was buried with Christ; he is risen with Christ, to walk in newness of life. He lives under the precious reign of grace, and he has his fruit unto holiness. The man who draws a plea from the abundance of divine grace to live in sin, denies the very foundation of Christianity. "How shall we that have died to sin, live any longer therein?" Impossible. It would be a denial of the whole Christian standing. To imagine the Christian as one who is to go on, from day to day, week to week, month to month, and year to year, sinning and repenting, sinning and repenting, is to degrade Christianity and falsify the whole Christian position. To say that a Christian *must* go on sinning because he has the flesh in him is to ignore the death of Christ in one of its grand aspects, and to give the lie to the whole of the apostle's teaching in Romans vi.-viii. Thank God, there is no necessity whatever why the believer should commit sin. "My little children, these things write I unto you that ye sin not." We should not justify ourselves in a single sinful thought. It is our sweet privilege to walk in the light, as God is in the light; and most surely, when we are walking in the light, we are not committing sin. Alas! we get out of the light and commit sin; but the normal, the true, the divine idea of a Christian is, walking in the light, and not committing sin. A sinful thought is foreign to the true genius of Christianity. We have sin in us, and shall have it so long as we are in the body; but if we walk in the Spirit, the sin in our nature will not show itself in the life. To say that *we need not sin* is to state a Christian privilege; to say that *we cannot sin* is a deceit and a delusion.

PART III

From what has already passed before as, we learn that the grand result of the work of Christ in the past is to give us a divinely perfect standing before God. "He has perfected forever them that are sanctified." He has introduced us into the Divine Presence, in all His own perfect acceptability, in the full credit and virtue of His name, of His Person, and of His work; so that, as the apostle John declares, "as He is, so are we in this world." (1 John iv. 17.)

Such is the settled standing of the very feeblest lamb in all the blood-bought flock of Christ. Nor could it possibly be otherwise. It must be either this or eternal perdition. There is not the breadth of a hair between this standing of absolute perfectness before God and a condition of guilt and ruin. We are either in our sins or in a risen Christ. There is no middle ground. We are either covered with guilt or complete in Christ. But the believer is declared, by the authoritative voice of the Holy Ghost in Scripture, to be "complete in Christ"—"perfect, as pertaining to his conscience"—"perfected in perpetuity"—"clean every whit"—"accepted in the Beloved"—"made [or become] the righteousness of God in Christ."

And all this through the sacrifice of the cross. That precious atoning death of Christ forms the solid and irrefragable foundation of the Christian's standing. "This Man, after He had offered one sacrifice for sins, forever sat down on the right hand of God." A seated Christ is the glorious proof and the perfect definition of the believer's place in the presence of God. Our Lord Christ, having glorified God about our sins, and borne His judgment on our entire condition as sinners, has conducted us, in living association with Himself, into a place, not only of forgiveness, acceptance, and peace, but of complete deliverance from the dominion of sin—a place of assured victory over every thing that could possibly be against us, whether indwelling sin, the fear of Satan, the law, or this present evil world.

Such, we repeat, is the absolutely settled standing of the believer, if we are to be taught by holy Scripture. And we earnestly entreat the Christian reader not to be satisfied with any thing less than this. Let him not any longer accept the muddled teachings of christendom's creeds, and its liturgical services, which only drive the soul back into the darkness, distance, and bondage of Judaism—that system which God found fault with, and which He has forever abolished, because it did not meet His holy mind, or satisfy His loving heart, in giving the worshiper perfect peace, perfect liberty, perfect nearness to Himself, and that forever.

We solemnly call upon all the Lord's people, throughout the various sections of the professing church, to consider where they are, and to see how far they understand and enjoy the true Christian position, as set forth in the various passages of Scripture which we have quoted, and which might easily be multiplied a hundredfold. Let them diligently and faithfully compare the teachings of christendom with the Word of God, and see how far they agree. In this way they will find how completely the professing Christianity of the present day stands in contrast with the living teachings of the New Testament; and as a consequence, souls are robbed of the precious privileges which belong to them as Christians, and they are kept in the moral distance which characterized the Mosaic economy.

All this is most deplorable. It grieves the Holy Spirit, wounds the heart of

Christ, dishonors the grace of God, and contradicts the plainest statements of holy Scripture. We are most thoroughly persuaded that the condition of thousands of precious souls at this moment is enough to make the heart bleed; and all this, to a large extent, is traceable to christendom's teachings, its creeds and its formularies. Where will you find, amid the ordinary ranks of Christian profession, a person in the enjoyment of a perfectly purged conscience, of peace with God, of the Spirit of adoption? Is it not true that people are publicly and systematically taught that it is the height of presumption for any one to say that his sins *are* all forgiven—that he *has* eternal life—that he *is* justified from all things—that he *is* accepted in the Beloved—that he *is* sealed with the Holy Ghost—that he cannot be lost, because he is actually united to Christ by the indwelling Spirit? Are not all these Christian privileges practically denied and ignored in christendom? Are not people taught that it is dangerous to be too confident—that it is morally safer to live in doubt and fear—that the very utmost we can look for is the hope of getting to heaven when we die? Where are souls taught the glorious truths connected with the new creation? Where are they rooted and grounded in the knowledge of their standing in a risen and glorified Head in the heavens? Where are they led into the enjoyment of those things which are freely given of God to His beloved people?

Alas! alas! we grieve to think of the only true answer which can be given to such inquiries. The flock of Christ is scattered upon the dark mountains and desolate moors. The souls of God's people are left in the dim distance which characterized the Jewish system. They know not the meaning of the rent vail, of nearness to God, of conscious acceptance in the Beloved. The very table of the Lord is shrouded with the dark and chilling mists of superstition, and surrounded by the repulsive barriers of a dark and depressing legality. Accomplished redemption, full remission of sins, perfect justification before God, acceptance in a risen Christ, the Spirit of adoption, the bright and blessed hope of the coming of the Bridegroom,—all these grand and glorious realities—these chartered privileges of the Church of God are practically set aside by christendom's teachings and religious machinery.

Some, perhaps, may think we have drawn too gloomy a picture. We can only say—and we say it with all sincerity—Would to God it were so! We fear the picture is far too true—yea, the reality is far more appalling than the picture. We are deeply and painfully impressed with the fact that the condition, not merely of the professing church, but of thousands of the true sheep of the flock of Christ, is such, that if we only realized it as God sees it, it would break our hearts.

However, we must pursue our subject, and by so doing, furnish the very best remedy that can possibly be suggested for the deplorable condition of so many of the Lord's people.

We have dwelt upon that precious work which our Lord Jesus Christ has accomplished for us, in the putting away of all our *sins*, and in the condemnation of *sin*, securing for us perfect remission of the former, and entire deliverance from the latter, as a ruling power. The Christian is one who is not only forgiven, but delivered. Christ has died for him, and he has died in Christ. Hence he is free, as one who is raised from the dead and alive unto God, through Jesus Christ our Lord. He is a new creation. He has passed from death unto life. Death and judgment are behind him, and nothing but glory before him. He possesses an unblotted title and an unclouded prospect.

Now, if all this be indeed true of every child of God—and Scripture says it is—what more do we want? Nothing, as to title; nothing, as to standing; nothing, as to hope. As to all these, we have absolute, divine perfection; but then our *state* is not perfect, our *walk* is not perfect. We are still in the body, compassed about with manifold infirmities, exposed to manifold temptations, liable to stumble, to fall, and to wander. We are unable of ourselves to think a right thought, or to keep ourselves for one moment in the blessed position into which grace has introduced us. True it is, we have everlasting life, and we are linked to the living Head in heaven, by the Holy Ghost sent down to earth, so that we are eternally secure. Nothing can ever touch our life, inasmuch as it is "hid with Christ in God."

But while nothing can touch our life, or interfere with our standing, yet, seeing that our state is imperfect and our walk imperfect, our communion is liable to be interrupted, and hence it is that we need

THE PRESENT WORK OF CHRIST FOR US.

Jesus lives at the right hand of God for us. His active intervention on our behalf never ceases for a single moment. He has passed through the heavens, in virtue of accomplished atonement, and there He ever carries on His perfect advocacy for us before our God. He is there as our subsisting righteousness, to maintain us ever in the divine integrity of the position and relationship into which His atoning death has introduced us. Thus we read, in Romans v. 10, "If, while we were enemies, we were reconciled to God by the death of His Son, much more, being reconciled, we shall be saved by His life." So also in Hebrews iv. we read, "Seeing then that we have a great High-Priest that has passed through the heavens, Jesus the Son of God, let us hold fast the confession. For we have not a High-Priest which cannot be touched with the feeling of our infirmities; but was in all points tempted, in like manner, without sin. Let us therefore come boldly unto the throne of grace, that we may obtain mercy, and find grace to help in time of need." Again, in chapter vii.—"But this Man, because He continueth forever, hath an unchangeable priesthood. Wherefore He is able also to save them to the uttermost that come unto God by Him, seeing He ever liveth to make intercession for them." And in chapter ix.—"For Christ is not entered into the holy places made with hands, which are the figures of the true; but into heaven itself, now to appear in the presence of God for us."

Then, in the first epistle of John, we have the same great subject presented under a somewhat different aspect.—"My little children, these things write I unto you, that ye sin not. And if any one sin, we have an Advocate with the Father, Jesus Christ the righteous: and He is the propitiation for our sins; and not our sins only, but also for the whole world."

How precious is all this to the true-hearted Christian, who is ever conscious— deeply and painfully conscious—of his weakness, need, infirmity, and failure! How, we may lawfully inquire, is it possible for any one, with his eye resting on such passages as we have just quoted, to say nothing of his own self-consciousness—the sense of his own imperfect state and walk, to call in question the Christian's need of the unceasing ministry of Christ on his behalf? Is it not marvelous that any reader of the epistle to the Hebrews, any observer of the state and walk of the most advanced believer, should be found denying the application of Christ's priesthood and advocacy to Christians now?

For whom, let us ask, is Christ now living and acting at the right hand of God? Is it for the world? Clearly not; for He says, in John xvii, "I pray not for the world, but for them which Thou hast given Me; for they are Thine." And who are these? are they the Jewish remnant? Nay; that remnant is yet to appear on the scene. Who are they, then? Believers—children of God—Christians, who are now passing through this sinful world, liable to fail and to contract defilement every step of the way. These are the subjects of Christ's priestly ministry. He died to make them clean: He lives to keep them clean. By His death He expiated our guilt, and by His life He cleanses us, through the action of the Word by the power of the Holy Ghost. "This is He that came by water and blood; not by water only, but by water and blood." We have expiation and cleansing through a crucified Saviour. The double stream emanated from the pierced side of Christ, dead for us. All praise to His name!

We have all, in virtue of the precious death of Christ. Is it a question of our guilt? It is canceled by the blood of atonement. Is it a question of our daily short-comings? We have an Advocate with the Father—a great High-Priest with God. "If any man sin." He does not say, If any man repent. No doubt there is, and must be, repentance and self-judgment; but how are they produced? whence do they proceed? Here it is: "We have an Advocate with the Father." It is His all-prevailing intercession that procures for the sinning one the grace of repentance, self-judgment, and confession.

It is of the very utmost importance for the Christian reader to be thoroughly clear as to this great cardinal truth of the advocacy or priesthood of Christ. We sometimes erroneously think that when we fail in our work, something has to be done on our part to set matters straight between our souls and God. We forget that ere we are even conscious of the failure—before our conscience becomes really cognizant of the fact, our blessed Advocate has been to the Father about it; and it is to His intercession we are indebted for the grace of repentance, confession, and restoration. "If any man sin, we have"—what? The blood to return to? No; mark carefully what the Holy Ghost declares.—"We have an Advocate with the Father, Jesus Christ the righteous." Why does He say, "the righteous"? why not the gracious, the merciful, the sympathizing? Is He not all this? Most surely; but not any one of these attributes would be in place here, inasmuch as the blessed apostle is putting before us the consolatory truth that in all our errors, our sins, and our failures, we have "a righteous" representative ever before the righteous God, the holy Father, so that our affairs can never fall through. "He *ever* liveth to make intercession for us;" and because He ever liveth, "He is able to save *to the uttermost*"—right through to the very end—"them that come unto God by Him."

What solid comfort is here for the people of God! and how needful for our souls to be established in the knowledge and sense of it! Some there are who have an imperfect sense of the true *standing* of a Christian, because they do not see what Christ has done for them in the past; others, on the contrary, have such an entirely one-sided view of the *state* of the Christian that they do not see our need of what Christ is doing for us now. Both must be corrected. The former are ignorant of the extent and value of the atonement; the latter are ignorant of the place and application of the advocacy. Such is the perfection of our *standing*, that the apostle can say, "As He is, so are we in this world." If this were all, we should certainly have no need of priesthood or advocacy; but then, such is our *state*, that the apostle has to say, "If any man sin." This proves our continual need of the Advocate. And, blessed be God, we have Him continually; we have him *ever living for us*. He lives and serves on high. He is our subsisting righteousness before our God. He lives to keep us always right in heaven, and to set us right when we go wrong upon earth. He is the divine and indissoluble link between Our souls and God.

PART IV

Having, in the three preceding papers of this series, sought to unfold the grand foundation-truths connected with the work of Christ for us—His work in the past and His work in the present—His atonement and His advocacy, we shall now seek, by the gracious aid of the Spirit of God, to present to the reader something of what the Scriptures teach us as to the second branch of our subject, namely,—

CHRIST AS AN OBJECT FOR THE HEART.

It is a wonderfully blessed thing to be able to say, "I have found an object which perfectly satisfies my heart—I have found Christ." It is this which gives true elevation above the world. It renders us thoroughly independent of the resources to which the unconverted heart ever betakes itself. It gives *settled rest*. It imparts a calmness and quietness to the spirit which the world cannot comprehend. The poor votary of the world may think the life of the true Christian a very slow, dull, stupid affair indeed. He may marvel how such an one can manage to get on without what he calls amusement, recreation, and pleasure;—no theatres, no balls or parties, no concerts, no cards or billiards, no hunts or races, no club or news-room, no cricket or croquet parties.

To deprive the unconverted man of such things would almost drive him to despair or lunacy; but the Christian does not want such things—would not have them. They would be a perfect weariness to him. We speak, of course, of the true Christian, of one who is not merely a Christian in name, but in reality. Alas! alas! many profess to be Christians, and take very high ground in their profession, who are, nevertheless, to be found mixed up in all the vain and frivolous pursuits of the men of this world. They may be seen at the communion-table on the Lord's day, and at a theatre or a concert on Monday: they may be found assaying to take part in some one or other of the many branches of Christian work on Sunday, and during the week you may see them in the ball-room, at the race-course, or some such scene of folly and vanity.

It is very evident that such persons know nothing of Christ as an object for the heart. Indeed, it is very questionable how any one with a single spark of divine life in the soul can find pleasure in the wretched pursuits of a godless world. The true and earnest Christian turns away from such things—turns away instinctively; and this, not merely because of the positive wrong and evil of them—though most surely he feels them to be wrong and evil—but because he has no taste for them, and because he has found something infinitely superior, something which perfectly satisfies all the desires of the new nature. Could we imagine an angel from heaven taking pleasure at a ball, a theatre, or a race-course? The bare thought is supremely ridiculous. All such scenes are perfectly foreign to a heavenly being.

And what is a Christian? He is a heavenly man; he is a partaker of the divine nature. He is dead to the world—dead to sin—alive to God. He has not a single link with the world: he belongs to heaven. He is no more of the world than Christ his Lord. Could Christ take part in the amusements, gayeties, and follies of the world? The very idea were blasphemy. Well, then, what of the Christian? Is he to be found where his Lord could not be? Can he consistently take part in things which he knows in his heart are contrary to Christ? Can he go into places and scenes and circumstances in which, he must admit, his Saviour and Lord can take no part? Can he go and have fellowship with a world which hates the One to whom he professes to owe every thing?

It may perhaps seem to some of our readers that we are taking too high ground. We would ask such, What ground are we to take? Surely, Christian ground, if we are Christians. Well, then, if we are to take Christian ground, how are we to know what that ground really is? Assuredly, from the New Testament. And what does it teach? Does it afford any warrant for the Christian to mix himself, in any shape or form, with the amusements and vain pursuits of this present evil world? Let us hearken to the weighty words of our blessed Lord in John xvii. Let us hear from His lips the truth as to our portion, our position, and our path in this world. He says, addressing the Father, "I have given them Thy Word; and the world hath hated them, because *they are not of the world, even as I am not of the world. I* pray not that Thou shouldest take them out of the world, but that Thou shouldest keep them from the evil. *They are not of the world, even as I am not of the world.* Sanctify them through Thy truth; Thy Word is truth. As Thou hast sent Me into the world, even so have I also sent them into the world." (Ver. 14-18.)

Is it possible to conceive a closer measure of identification than that set before us in these words? Twice over, in this brief passage, our Lord declares that we are not of the world, even as He is not. What has our blessed Lord to do with the world? Nothing. The world has utterly rejected Him and cast Him out. It nailed Him to a shameful cross, between two malefactors. The world lies as fully and as freshly under the charge of all this as though the act of the crucifixion took place yesterday, at the very centre of its civilization, and with the unanimous consent of all. There is not so much as a single moral link between Christ and the world. Yea, the world is stained with His murder, and will have to answer to God for the crime.

How solemn is this! What a serious consideration for Christians! We are passing through a world that crucified our Lord and Master, and He declares that we are not of that world, even as He is not of it. Hence it follows that in so far as we have any fellowship with the world, we are false to Christ. What should we think of a wife who could sit and laugh and joke with a set of men who had murdered her husband? and yet this is precisely what professing Christians do when they mix themselves up with this present evil world, and make themselves part and parcel of it.

It will perhaps be said, What are we to do? are we to go out of the world? By no means. Our Lord expressly says, "I pray not that Thou shouldest take them out of the world, but that Thou shouldest keep them from the evil." In it, but not of it, is the true principle for the Christian. To use a figure, the Christian in the world is like a diver. He is in the midst of an element which would destroy him, were he not protected from its action, and sustained by unbroken communication with the scene above.

And what is the Christian to do in the world? what is his mission? Here it is: "As Thou hast sent Me into the world, even so have I sent them into the world." And again, in John xx. 21 — "As My Father hath sent Me, even so send I you."

Such is the Christian's mission. He is not to shut himself within the walls of a monastery or convent. Christianity does not consist in joining a brotherhood or a sisterhood. Nothing of the kind. We are called to move up and down in the varied relations of life, and to act in our divinely appointed spheres, to the glory of God. It is not a question of what we are doing, but of how we do it. All depends upon the object which governs our hearts. If Christ be the commanding and absorbing object of the heart, all will be right; if He be not, nothing is right. Two persons may sit down at the same table to eat; the one eats to gratify his appetite, the other eats to the glory of God—eats simply to keep his body in proper working order as God's vessel, the temple of the Holy Ghost, the instrument for Christ's service.

So in every thing. It is our sweet privilege to set the Lord always before us. He is our model. As He was sent into the world, so are we. What did He come to do? To glorify God. How did He live? By the Father. "As the living Father hath sent Me, and I live by the Father, so he that eateth Me, even he shall live by Me." (John vi. 57.)

This makes it all so simple. Christ is the standard and touchstone for every thing. It is no longer a question of mere right and wrong according to human rules; it is simply a question of what is worthy of Christ. Would He do this or that? would He go here or there? "He left us an example, that we should follow *His* steps;" and most assuredly, we should not go where we cannot trace His blessed footsteps. If we go hither and thither to please ourselves, we are not treading in His steps, and we cannot expect to enjoy His blessed presence.

Christian reader, here lies the real secret of the whole matter. The grand question is just this: Is Christ my one object? what am I living for? Can I say, "The life that I live in the flesh, I live by the faith of the Son of God, who loved me, and gave Himself for me"? Nothing less than this is worthy of a Christian. It is a poor miserable thing to be content with being saved, and then to go on with the world, and live for self-pleasing and self-interest—to accept salvation as the fruit of Christ's toil and passion, and then live at a distance from Himself. What should we think of a child who only cared about the good things provided by his father's hand, and never sought his father's company—yea, preferred the company of strangers? We should justly despise him; but how much more despicable is the Christian who owes his present and his eternal all to the work of Christ and yet is content to live at a cold distance from His blessed Person, caring not for the furtherance of His cause—the promotion of His glory!

PART V

If the reader has been enabled, through grace, to make his own of what has passed before our minds in this series of papers, he will have a perfect remedy for all uneasiness of conscience and all restlessness of heart. The work of Christ, if only it be laid hold of by an artless faith, must, of blessed necessity, meet the former; and the Person of Christ, if only He be contemplated with a single eye, must perfectly meet the latter. If, therefore, we are not in the enjoyment of peace of conscience, it can only be because we are not resting on the finished work of Christ; and if the heart is not at ease, it proves that we are not satisfied with Christ Himself.

And yet, alas! how few, even of the Lord's beloved people, know either the one or the other. How rare it is to find a person in the enjoyment of true peace of conscience and rest of heart! In general, Christians are not a whit in advance of the condition of Old-Testament saints. They do not know the blessedness of an accomplished redemption; they are not in the enjoyment of a purged conscience; they cannot draw nigh with a true heart, in full assurance of faith, having the heart sprinkled from an evil conscience, and the body washed with pure water; they do not apprehend the grand truth of the indwelling of the Holy Ghost, enabling them to cry, "Abba, Father;" they are, as to their experience, under law; they have never really entered into the deep blessedness of being under the reign of grace. They have life. It is impossible to doubt this. They love divine things; their tastes, their habits, their aspirations—yea, their very exercises, their conflicts, their anxieties, doubts, and fears all go to prove the existence of divine life. They are, in a way, separated from the world, but their separation is rather negative than positive. It is more because they see the utter vanity of the world, and its inability to satisfy their hearts, than because they have found an object in Christ. They have lost their taste for the things of the world, but they have not found their place and their portion in the Son of God where He now is at the right hand of God. The things of the world cannot satisfy them, and they are not in the enjoyment of their proper heavenly standing, object, and hope; hence they are in an anomalous condition altogether; they have no certainty, no rest, no fixedness of purpose; they are not happy; they do not know their true bearings; they are neither one thing nor the other.

Is it thus with the reader? We fondly hope not. We trust he is one of those who, through infinite grace, "know the things that are freely given them of God;" who know that they have passed from death unto life—that they have eternal life; who enjoy the precious witness of the Spirit; who realize their association with a risen and glorified Head in the heavens, with whom they are linked by the Holy Ghost, who dwells in them; who have found their object in the Person of that blessed One whose finished work is the divine and eternal basis of their salvation and peace; and who are earnestly looking for the blessed moment when Jesus shall come to receive them to Himself, that where He is, they may be also, to go no more out forever.

This is Christianity. Nothing else deserves the name. It stands out in bold and striking contrast with the spurious religiousness of the day, which is neither pure Judaism on the one hand, nor pure Christianity on the other, but a wretched mixture, composed of some of the elements of each, which unconverted people can adopt and go on with, because it sanctions the lusts of the flesh, and allows them to enjoy the pleasures and vanities of the world to their heart's content. The archenemy of Christ and of souls has succeeded in producing an awful system of religion, half Jewish, half Christian, combining, in the most artful manner, the world and the flesh, with a certain amount of Scripture, so used as to destroy its moral force and hinder its just application. In the meshes of this system souls are hopelessly entangled. Unconverted people are deceived into the notion that they are very good Christians indeed, and going on all right to heaven; and on the other hand, the Lord's dear people are robbed of their proper place and privileges, and dragged down by the dark and depressing influence of the religious atmosphere which surrounds and almost suffocates them.

It lies not, we believe, within the compass of human language to set forth the appalling consequences of this mingling of the people of God with the people of the world in one common system of religiousness and theological belief. Its effect upon the former is to blind their eyes to the true moral glories of Christianity as set forth in the pages of the New Testament; and this to such an extent, that if any one attempts to unfold these glories to their view, he is regarded as a visionary enthusiast, or a dangerous heretic: its effect upon the latter is to deceive them altogether as to their true condition, character, and destiny. Both classes repeat the same formularies, subscribe the same creed, say the same prayers, are members of the same community, partake of the same sacrament, are, in short, ecclesiastically, theologically, religiously one.

It will perhaps be said in reply to all this, that our Lord, in His wonderful discourse in Matthew xiii, distinctly teaches that the wheat and the tares are to grow together. Yes; but where? in the *Church*? Nay; but "in the field;" and He tells us that *"the field is the world."* To confound these things is to falsify the whole Christian position, and to do away with all godly discipline in the assembly. It is to place the teaching of our Lord in Matthew xiii. in opposition to the teaching of the Holy Ghost in 1 Corinthians v.

However, we shall not pursue this subject further just now. It is far too important and too extensive to be disposed of in a brief article like the present. We may perhaps discuss it more fully on some future occasion. That it demands the serious consideration of the Christian reader we are most thoroughly convinced; bearing, as it does, so manifestly on the glory of Christ, on the true interests of His people, on the progress of the gospel, on the integrity of Christian testimony and service, it would be quite impossible to overestimate its importance. But we must leave it for the present, and draw this paper to a close by a brief reference to the third and last branch of our subject, namely,

THE WORD OF CHRIST AS THE ALL-SUFFICIENT GUIDE FOR OUR PATH.

If Christ's work suffices for the conscience, if His blessed Person suffices for the heart, then, most assuredly, His precious Word suffices for the path. We may assert, with all possible confidence, that we possess in the divine volume of holy Scripture all we can ever need, not only to meet all the exigencies of our individual path, but also the varied necessities of the Church of God, in the most minute details of her history in this world.

We are quite aware that in making this assertion we lay ourselves open to much scorn and opposition, in more quarters than one. We shall be met on the one hand by the advocates of tradition, and on the other by those who contend for the supremacy of man's reason and will; but this gives us very little concern indeed. We regard the traditions of men, whether fathers, brothers, or doctors, *if presented as an authority*, as the small dust of the balance; and as to human reason, it can only be compared to a bat in the sunshine, dazzled by the brightness, and blindly dashing itself against objects which it cannot see.

It is the deepest joy of the Christian's heart to retire from the conflicting traditions and doctrines of men into the calm light of holy Scripture; and when encountered by the impudent reasonings of the infidel, the rationalist, and the skeptic, to bow down his whole moral being to the authority and power of holy Scripture. He thankfully recognizes in the Word of God the only perfect standard for doctrine, for morals, for every thing. "All Scripture is given by inspiration of God, and is profitable for doctrine, for reproof, for correction, for instruction in righteousness; that the man of God may be *perfect* [αρτιος], *throughly furnished unto all good works.*"

What more can we need? Nothing. If Scripture can make a child "wise unto salvation," and if it can make a man "perfect," and furnish him "throughly to all good works," what do we want of human tradition or human reasonings? If God has written a volume for us, if He has graciously condescended to give us a revelation of His mind, as to all we ought to know and think and feel and believe and do, shall we turn to a poor fellow-mortal—be he ritualist or rationalist—to help us? Far away be the thought! As well might we turn to our fellow-man to add something to the finished work of Christ, in order to render it sufficient for our conscience, or to supply some deficiency in the Person of Christ, in order to render Him a sufficient object for the heart, as to betake ourselves to human tradition or human reason to supply some deficiency in divine revelation.

All praise and thanks to our God, it is not so. He has given us in His own beloved Son all we want for the conscience, for the heart, for the path—for time, with all its changing scenes—for eternity, with its countless ages. We can say,—

> "Thou, O Christ, art all we want;
> More than all in Thee we find."

There is, there could be, no lack in the Christ of God. His atonement and advocacy must satisfy all the cravings of the most deeply exercised conscience. The moral glories—the powerful attractions of His divine Person must satisfy the most intense aspirations and longings of the heart. And His peerless revelation—that priceless volume—contains within its covers all we can possibly need, from the starting-post to the goal of our Christian career.

Christian reader, are not these things so? Dost thou not, from the very centre of thy renewed moral being, own the truth of them? If so, art thou resting, in calm repose, on Christ's work? art thou delighting in His Person? art thou submitting, in all things, to the authority of His Word? God grant it may be so with thee, and with all who profess His name! May there be a fuller, clearer, and more decided testimony to "the all-sufficiency of Christ," till "that day."

C. H. M.

JOB AND HIS FRIENDS

The book of Job occupies a very peculiar place in the volume of God. It possesses a character entirely its own, and teaches lessons which are not to be learnt in any other section of inspiration. It is not by any means our purpose to enter upon a line of argument to prove the genuineness, or establish the fact of the divine inspiration, of this precious book. We take these things for granted; being fully persuaded of them as established facts, we leave the proofs to abler hands. We receive the book of Job as part of the Holy Scriptures given of God for the profit and blessing of His people. We need no proofs of this for ourselves, nor do we attempt to offer any to our reader.

And we may further add that we have no thought of entering upon the field of inquiry as to the authorship of this book. This, howsoever interesting it may be in itself, is to us entirely secondary. We receive the book from God. This is enough for us. We heartily own it to be an inspired document, and we do not feel it to be our province to discuss the question as to where, when, or by whom it was penned. In short, we purpose, with the Lord's help, to offer a few plain and practical remarks on a book which we consider needs to be more closely studied, that it may be more fully understood. May the Eternal Spirit, who indited the book, expound and apply it to our souls!

The opening page of this remarkable book furnishes us with a view of the patriarch Job, surrounded by every thing that could make the world agreeable to him, and make him of importance in the world. "There was a man in the land of Uz whose name was Job; and that man was perfect and upright, and one that feared God and eschewed evil." Thus much as to *what he was*. Let us now see *what he had*.

"And there were born unto him seven sons and three daughters. His substance also was seven thousand sheep, and three thousand camels, and five hundred yoke of oxen, and five hundred she-asses, and a very great household; so that this man was the greatest of all the children of the east. And his sons went and feasted in their houses every one his day; and sent and called for their three sisters, to eat and to drink with them." Then, to complete the picture, we have the record of *what he did*.

"And it was so, when the days of their feasting were gone about, that Job sent and sanctified them, and rose up early in the morning, and offered burnt-offerings according to the number of them all; for Job said, 'It may be that my sons have sinned, and cursed God in their hearts.' Thus did Job continually."

Here, then, we have a very rare specimen of a man. He was perfect, upright,

God-fearing, and eschewed evil. Moreover, the hand of God had hedged him round about on every side, and strewed his path with richest mercies. He had all that heart could wish,—children and wealth in abundance,—honor and distinction from all around. In short, we may almost say, his cup of earthly bliss was full.

But Job needed to be tested. There was a deep moral root in his heart which had to be laid bare. There was self-righteousness which had to be brought to the surface and judged. Indeed, we may discern this root in the very words which we have just quoted. He says, "It may be that my sons have sinned." He does not seem to contemplate the possibility of sinning himself. A soul really self-judged, thoroughly broken before God, truly sensible of its own state, tendencies, and capabilities, would think of his own sins, and his own need of a burnt-offering.

Now, let the reader distinctly understand that Job was a real saint of God,—a divinely quickened soul,—a possessor of divine and eternal life. We cannot too strongly insist upon this. He was just as truly a man of God in the first chapter as he was in the forty-second. If we do not see this, we shall miss one of the grand lessons of the book. The eighth verse of chap. i. establishes this point beyond all question. "And the Lord said unto Satan, 'Hast thou considered *My servant* Job, that there is none like him in the earth,—a perfect and an upright man, one that feareth God and escheweth evil?'"

But, with all this, Job had never sounded the depths of his own heart. He did not know himself. He had never really grasped the truth of his own utter ruin and total depravity. He had never learnt to say, "I know that in me, that is in my flesh, dwelleth no good thing." This point must be seized, or the book of Job will not be understood. We shall not see the specific object of all those deep and painful exercises through which Job was called to pass unless we lay hold of the solemn fact that his conscience had never been really in the divine presence,—that he had never seen himself in the light,—never measured himself by a divine standard,—never weighed himself in the balances of the sanctuary.

If the reader will turn for a moment to chap. xxix., he will find a striking proof of what we assert. He will there see distinctly what a strong and deep root of self-complacency there was in the heart of this dear and valued servant of God, and how this root was nourished by the very tokens of divine favor with which he was surrounded. This chapter is a pathetic lament over the faded light of other days; and the very tone and character of the lament prove how necessary it was that Job should be stripped of every thing, in order that he might learn himself in the searching light of the divine presence.

Let us hearken to his words.

"Oh that I were as in months past, as in the days when God preserved me; when His candle shined upon my head, and when by His light I walked through darkness; as I was in the days of my youth, when the secret of God was upon my tabernacle; when the Almighty was yet with me, when my children were about me; when I washed my steps with butter, and the rock poured me out rivers of oil; when I went out to the gate through the city; when I prepared my seat in the street! The young men saw me and hid themselves, and the aged arose and stood up. The princes refrained talking, and laid their hand on their mouth. The nobles held their peace, and their tongue cleaved to the roof of their mouth. When the ear heard me, then it blessed me; and when the eye saw me, it gave witness to me: because I delivered the poor that cried, and the fatherless, and him that had none to help him. The blessing of him that was ready to perish came upon me, and I caused the widow's heart to sing for joy. I put on righteousness, and it clothed me: my judgment was as a robe and a diadem. I was eyes to the blind, and feet was I to the lame. I was a father to the poor, and the cause which I knew not I searched out. And I brake the jaws of the wicked, and plucked the spoil out of his teeth. Then I said, 'I shall die in my nest, and I shall multiply my days as the sand.' My root was spread out by the waters, and the dew lay all night upon my branch. My glory was fresh in me, and my bow was renewed in my hand. Unto me men gave ear, and waited, and kept silence at my counsel. After my words they spake not again, and my speech dropped upon them. And they waited for me as for the rain, and they opened their mouth wide as for the latter rain. If I laughed on them, they believed it not; and the light of my countenance they cast not down. I chose out their way, and sat chief, and dwelt as a king in the army, as one that comforteth the mourners. But now, they that are younger than I have me in derision, whose fathers I would have disdained to have set with the dogs of my flock."

This, truly, is a most remarkable utterance. We look in vain for any breathings of a broken and a contrite spirit here. There are no evidences of self-loathing, or even of self-distrust. We cannot find so much as a single expression of conscious weakness and nothingness. In the course of this single chapter, Job refers to himself more than forty times, while the references to God are but five. It reminds us of the seventh of Romans, by the predominance of "I;" but there is this immense difference, that, in the seventh of Romans, "I" is a poor, weak, good-for-nothing, wretched creature in the presence of the holy law of God; whereas, in Job xxix., "I" is a most important, influential personage, admired and almost worshiped by his fellows.

Now Job had to be stripped of all this; and when we compare chap. xxix. with chap. xxx. we can form some idea of how painful the process of stripping must have been. There is peculiar emphasis in the words, *But now*." Job draws a most striking contrast between his past and his present. In chap. xxx. he is still occupied with himself. It is still "I;" but ah, how changed! The very men who flattered him in the day of his prosperity, treat him with contempt in the day of his adversity. Thus it is ever in this poor, false, deceitful world, and it is well to be made to prove it. All must, sooner or later, find out the hollowness of the world,—the fickleness of those who are ready to cry out "hosanna" to-day, and "crucify Him" to-mor-row. Man is not to be trusted. It is all very well while the sun shines; but wait till the nipping blasts of winter come, and then you will see how far nature's fair promises and professions can be trusted. When the prodigal had plenty to spend, he found plenty to share his portion; but when he began to be in want, "no man gave unto him."

Thus it was with Job in chap. xxx. But be it well remembered that there is very much more needed than the stripping of self, and the discovery of the hollowness and deceitfulness of the world. One may go through all these, and the result be merely chagrin and disappointment. Indeed, it can be nothing more if God be not reached. If the heart be not brought to find its all-satisfying portion in God, then a reverse of fortune leaves it desolate; and the discovery of the fickleness and hollowness of men fills it with bitterness. This will account for Job's language in chap. xxx.: "But now they that are younger than I have me in derision, whose fathers I would have disdained to have set with the dogs of my flock." Was this the spirit of Christ? Would Job have spoken thus at the close of the book? He would not. Ah, no, reader; when once Job got into God's presence, there was an end the egotism of chap. xxix. and the bitterness of chap. xxx.[7]

But hear Job's further outpourings. "They were children of fools, yea, children of base men; they were viler than the earth. And now am I their song, yea, I am their by-word. They abhor me, they flee far from me, and spare not to spit in my face. Because He hath loosed my cord, and afflicted me, they also let loose the bridle before me. Upon my right hand rise the youth; they push away my feet, and they raise up against me the ways of their destruction. They mar my path, they set forward my calamity, they have no helper. They came upon me as a wide breaking in of waters: in the desolation they rolled themselves upon me."

Now, all this, we may truly say, is very far short of the mark. Lamentations over departed greatness, and bitter invectives against our fellow-men, will not do the heart much good; neither do they display aught of the spirit and mind of Christ, nor bring glory to His holy name. When we turn our eyes toward the blessed Lord Jesus we see something wholly different. That meek and lowly One met all the rebuffs of this world, all the disappointments in the midst of His people Israel, all the unbelief and folly of His disciples, with an, "Even so, Father." He was able to retire from the rebuffs of men into His resources in God, and then to come forth with those balmy words, "Come unto Me ... and I will give you rest." No chagrin, no bitterness, no harsh invectives, nothing rough or unkind, from that gracious Saviour who came down into this cold and heartless world to manifest the perfect love of God, and who pursued His path of service spite of all man's perfect hatred.

But the fairest and best of men must retire into the shade when tested by the perfect standard of the life of Christ. The light of His moral glory makes manifest the defects and blemishes of even the most perfect of the sons of men. "In all things He must have the pre-eminence." He stands out in vivid contrast with even a Job or a Jeremiah in the matter of patient submission to all that He was called upon to endure. Job completely breaks down under his heavy trials. He not only pours forth a torrent of bitter invective upon his fellows, but actually curses the day of his birth. "After this opened Job his mouth and cursed his day. And Job spake and said, 'Let the day perish wherein I was born, and the night in which it was said, There is a man-child conceived'" (chap. iii. 1-3).

We notice the selfsame thing in Jeremiah — that blessed man of God. He, too, gave way beneath the heavy pressure of his varied and accumulated sorrows, and

[7] The reader will bear in mind that, while it is the Holy Ghost who records what Job and his friends said, yet we are not to suppose that they *spoke* by inspiration.

gave vent to his feelings in the following bitter accents: "Cursed be the day where-in I was born; let not the day wherein my mother bare me be blessed. Cursed be the man who brought tidings to my father, saying, 'A man-child is born unto thee;' making him very glad. And let that man be as the cities which the Lord overthrew, and repented not; and let him hear the cry in the morning, and the shouting at noontide. *Because He slew me not from the womb*; or that my mother might have been my grave, and her womb to be always great with me. Wherefore came I forth out of the womb to see labor and sorrow, that my days should be consumed with shame?" (Jer. xx. 14-18.)

What language is here! Only think of cursing the man that brought tidings of his birth! cursing him because he had not slain him! All this, both in the prophet and the patriarch, contrasts strongly with the meek and lowly Jesus of Nazareth. That spotless One passed through deeper sorrows and more in number than all His servants put together; but not one murmuring word ever escaped His lips. He patiently submitted to all; and met the darkest hour with such words as these, "The cup which My Father hath given Me, shall I not drink it?" Blessed Lord Jesus, Son of the Father, we adore Thee! We bow down at Thy feet, lost in wonder, love, and praise, and own Thee Lord of all!—the fairest among ten thousand, and the altogether lovely.

There is no more fruitful field of study than that which is opened before us in the history of God's dealings with souls. It is full of interest, and abounds in instruction and profit. One grand object in those dealings is to produce real brokenness and humility—to strip us of all false righteousness, empty us of all self-confidence, and teach us to lean wholly upon Christ. All have to pass through what may be called the process of stripping and emptying. With some this process precedes, with others it follows, conversion or the new birth. Many are brought to Christ through deep plowings and painful exercises of heart and conscience— exercises extending over years, often over the whole lifetime. Others, on the contrary, are brought with comparatively little exercise of soul. They lay hold, speedily, of the glad tidings of forgiveness of sins through the atoning death of Christ, and are made happy at once. But the stripping and emptying come afterward, and, in many cases, cause the soul to totter on its foundation, and almost to doubt its conversion.

This is very painful, but very needful. The fact is, self must be learnt and judged, sooner or later. If it be not learnt in communion with God, it must be learnt by bitter experience in failures and falls. "No flesh shall glory in His presence;" and we must all learn our utter powerlessness, in every respect, in order that we may taste the sweetness and comfort of the truth, that Christ is made of God unto us wisdom, righteousness, sanctification, and redemption. God will have *broken material*. Let us remember this. It is a solemn and necessary truth, "Thus saith the high and lofty One that inhabiteth eternity, whose name is Holy: I dwell in the high and holy place, with him also that is of a contrite and humble spirit, to revive the spirit of the humble, and to revive the heart of the contrite ones." And again, "Thus saith the Lord, 'The heaven is My throne, and the earth is My footstool: where is the house that ye build unto Me? and where is the place of My rest? For all those things hath Mine hand made, and all those things have been, saith the Lord: but to this man will I look, even to him that is poor and of a contrite spirit, and trembleth at My word.'" (Is. lvii. 15; lxvi. 1, 2.)

These are seasonable words for all of us. One special want of the present moment is brokenness of spirit. Nine-tenths of our trouble and difficulty may be traced to this want. It is marvelous how we get on from day to day, —in the family, in the assembly, in the world, in our entire practical life, when *self* is subdued and mortified. A thousand things which else would prove more than a match for our hearts are esteemed as nothing, when our souls are in a truly contrite state. We are enabled to bear reproach and insult, to overlook slights and affronts, to trample upon our crotchets, predilections, and prejudices, to yield to others where weighty principle is not involved, to be ready to every good work, to exhibit a genial large-heartedness in all our dealings, and an elasticity in all our moral movements which so greatly tend to adorn the doctrine of God our Saviour. How often, alas! it is otherwise with us. We exhibit a stiff, unyielding temper; we stand up for our rights; we maintain our interests; we look after our own things; we contend for our own notions. All this proves, very clearly, that self is not habitually measured and judged in the presence of God.

But we repeat—and with emphasis—God will have broken material. He loves us too well to leave us in hardness and unsubduedness; and hence it is that He sees fit to pass us through all sorts of exercises in order to bring us into a condition of soul in which He can use us for His own glory. The will must be broken; self-confidence, self-complacency, and self-importance must be cut up by the roots. God will make use of the scenes and circumstances through which we have to pass, the people with whom we are associated in daily life, to discipline the heart and subdue the will. And further, He will deal with us directly Himself, in order to bring about these great practical results.

All this comes out with great distinctness in the book of Job, and gives a wonderful interest and charm to its pages. It is very evident that Job needed a severe sifting. Had he not needed it, we may rest assured the gracious, loving Lord would not have passed him through it. It was not for nothing that He let Satan loose upon His dear servant. We may say, with fullest confidence, that nothing but the most stern necessity would have led Him to adopt such a line of action. God loved Job with a perfect love; but it was a wise and faithful love; a love that could take account of every thing, and, looking below the surface, could see the deep moral roots in the heart of His servant—roots which Job had never seen, and, therefore, never judged. What a mercy to have to do with such a God! to be in the hands of One who will spare no pains in order to subdue every thing in us which is contrary to Himself, and to bring out in us His own blessed image!

But, beloved reader, is there not something profoundly interesting in the fact that God can even make use of Satan as an instrument in the discipline of His people? We see this in the case of the apostle Peter, as well as in that of the patriarch Job. Peter had to be sifted, and Satan was used to do the work. "Simon, Simon, behold Satan hath desired to have you, that he may sift you as wheat." Here, too, there was a stern necessity. There was a deep root to be reached in Peter's heart—

the root of self-confidence; and his faithful Lord saw it absolutely needful to pass him through a most severe and painful process in order that this root should be exposed and judged; and therefore Satan was permitted to sift him thoroughly, so that he might never again trust his own heart, but walk softly all his days. God will have broken material, whether it be in a patriarch or an apostle. All must be mellowed and subdued in order that the divine glory may shine forth with an ever brightening lustre.

Had Job understood this great principle—had he apprehended the divine object,—how differently he would have carried himself! But, like ourselves, he had to learn his lesson; and the Holy Ghost has furnished us with the record of the mode in which the lesson was learnt, so that we may profit by it also.

Let us pursue the narrative.

"Now there was a day when the sons of God came to present themselves before the Lord, and Satan came also among them. And the Lord said unto Satan, 'Whence comest thou?' Then Satan answered the Lord and said, 'From going to and fro in the earth, and from walking up and down in it.' And the Lord said unto Satan, 'Hast thou considered my servant Job, that there is none like him in the earth, a perfect and an upright man, one that feareth God and escheweth evil?' Then Satan answered the Lord, and said, 'Doth Job fear God for naught? Hast not Thou made a hedge about him, and about his house, and about all that he hath on every side? Thou hast blest the work of his hands, and his substance is increased in the land. But put forth Thine hand now, and touch all that he hath, and he will curse Thee to Thy face.'" What a view we have here of Satan's malignity! What a striking proof of the way in which he watches and considers the ways and works of God's people! What insight into human character! What an intimate knowledge of man's mental and moral constitution! What a terrible thing to fall into his hands! He is ever on the watch; ever ready, if permitted of God, to put forth all his malignant energy against the Christian.

The thought of this is most solemn, and should lead us to walk humbly and watchfully through a scene where Satan rules. He has no power whatever over a soul who abides in the place of dependence and obedience; and, blessed be God, he cannot, in any case, go one hair's breadth beyond the limit prescribed by divine command. Thus, in Job's case, "The Lord said unto Satan, 'Behold, all that he hath is in thy power; only upon himself put not forth thine hand.'"

Here Satan was permitted to lay his hand on Job's possessions—to bereave him of his children, and despoil him of all his wealth. And truly he lost no time in despatching his business. With marvelous rapidity he executed his commission. Blow after blow fell, in quick succession, on the devoted head of the patriarch. Hardly had one messenger told his melancholy tale, ere another arrived with still heavier tidings, until, at length, the afflicted servant of God "arose and rent his mantle, and shaved his head, and fell down upon the ground, and worshiped, and said, 'Naked came I out of my mother's womb, and naked shall I return thither: the Lord gave, and the Lord hath taken away; blessed be the name of the Lord.' In all this, Job sinned not, nor charged God foolishly" (chap. i. 20-22).

All this is deeply touching. To speak after the manner of men, it was enough to make reason totter, to be thus, in a moment, bereft of his ten children, and reduced from princely wealth to absolute penury. What a striking contrast between the opening and the closing lines of our first chapter! In the former, we see Job surrounded by a numerous family, and in the enjoyment of vast possessions; in the latter, we see him left alone, in poverty and nakedness. And to think of Satan's being allowed — yea, commissioned of God — to bring about all this! And for what? For the deep and permanent profit of Job's precious soul. God saw that His servant needed to be taught a lesson; and, moreover, that, in no other way, by no other means, could this lesson be taught than by passing him through an ordeal the bare record of which fills the mind with solemn awe. God *will* teach His children, even though it be by stripping them of all that the heart clings to in this world.

But we must follow our patriarch into still deeper waters.

"Again there was a day when the sons of God came to present themselves before the Lord, and Satan came also among them to present himself before the Lord. And the Lord said unto Satan, 'From whence comest thou?' And Satan answered the Lord, and said, 'From going to and fro in the earth, and from walking up and down in it.' And the Lord said unto Satan, 'Hast thou considered My servant Job, that there is none like him in the earth, a perfect and an upright man, one that feareth God and escheweth evil? and still he holdeth fast his integrity, although thou movedst Me against him, to destroy him without cause.' And Satan answered the Lord, and said, 'Skin for skin, yea, all that a man hath will he give for his life. But put forth Thine hand now, and touch his bone and His flesh, and he will curse Thee to Thy face.' And the Lord said unto Satan, 'Behold, he is in thy hand; but save his life.' So went Satan forth from the presence of the Lord, and smote Job with sore boils from the sole of his foot unto his crown. And he took him a potsherd to scrape himself withal; and he sat down among the ashes. Then said his wife unto him, 'Dost thou still retain thine integrity? curse God, and die.' But he said unto her, 'Thou speakest as one of the foolish women speaketh. What? shall we receive good at the hand of God, and shall we not receive evil?' In all this did not Job sin with his lips" (chap. ii. 1-10).

This is a very remarkable passage. It instructs us as to the place which Satan occupies in respect to God's government. He is a mere instrument, and, though ever ready to accuse the Lord's people, can do nothing save as he is allowed of God. So far as Job was concerned, the efforts of Satan proved abortive; and having done his utmost, he goes away, and we hear nothing more of his actings, whatever may have been his inward temptations. Job was enabled to hold fast his integrity; and, had matters ended here, his patient endurance would only have strengthened the platform of his righteousness, and ministered to his self-complacency. "Ye have heard," says James, "of the patience of Job." And what then? "Ye have seen *the end of the Lord*; that the Lord is very pitiful, and of tender mercy." Had it been simply a question of Job's patience, it would have proved an additional ground of self-confidence, and thus "the end of the Lord" would not have been reached. For, be it ever remembered, the Lord's pity and tender mercy can only be tasted by those who are truly penitent and broken-hearted. Now Job was not this, even when he lay amid the ashes. He was not yet thoroughly broken down before God. He was still the great man—great in his misfortunes as he had been in his prosperity—great beneath the keen and withering blasts of adversity as he had been in the sunshine of brighter and better days. Job's heart was still unreached. He was not yet prepared to cry out, "Behold, I am vile." He had not yet learnt to "abhor" himself, "and repent in dust and ashes."

We are anxious that the reader should distinctly seize this point. It is, to a very great extent, the key to the entire book of Job. The divine object was to expose to Job's view the depths of his own heart, in order that he might learn to delight in the grace and mercy of God, and not in his own goodness, which was as a morning cloud and the early dew, that passeth away. Job was a true saint of God; and all Satan's accusations were flung back in his face; but, all the while, Job was unbroken material, and therefore unprepared for "the end of the Lord"—that blessed end for every contrite heart—that end which is marked by "pity and tender mercy." God, blessed and praised be His name! will not suffer Satan to accuse us; but He will expose us to ourselves, so that we may judge ourselves, and thus learn to mistrust our own hearts, and rest in the eternal stability of His grace.

Thus far, then, we see Job "holding fast his integrity." He meets with calmness all the heavy afflictions which Satan is allowed to bring upon him; and, moreover, he refuses the foolish counsel of his wife. In a word, he accepts all as from the hand of God, and bows his head in the presence of His mysterious dispensations.

All this is well. But the arrival of Job's three friends produces a marked change. Their very presence—the bare fact of their being eye-witnesses of his trouble—affects him in a very remarkable manner. "Now when Job's three friends heard of all this evil that was come upon him, they came every one from his own place,—Eliphaz the Temanite, and Bildad the Shuhite, and Zophar the Naamathite; for they had made an appointment together to come to mourn with him and to comfort him. And when they lifted up their eyes afar off, and knew him not, they lifted up their voices and wept; and they rent every one his mantle, and sprinkled dust upon their heads toward heaven. So they sat down with him upon the ground seven days and seven nights, and none spake a word unto him; for they saw that his grief was very great." (Chap. ii. 11-13.)

Now, we can fully believe that those three men were governed, in the main, by kindly feelings toward Job; and it was no small sacrifice on their part to leave their homes and come to condole with their bereaved and afflicted friend. All this we can easily believe. But it is very evident that their presence had the effect of stirring up feelings and thoughts in his heart and mind which had hitherto lain dormant. He had borne submissively the loss of children, property, and of bodily health. Satan had been dismissed, and the wife's counsel rejected; but the presence of his friends caused Job to break down completely. "After this, Job opened his mouth, and cursed his day."

This is very remarkable. It does not appear that the friends had spoken a single sentence. They sat in total silence, with rent garments, and covered with dust, gazing on a grief too profound for them to reach. It was Job himself who first broke silence; and the whole of the third chapter is an outpouring of the most bitter lamentation, affording melancholy evidence of an unsubdued spirit. It is, we may confidently assert, impossible that any one who had learnt, in any little measure, to say, "Thy will be done," could ever curse his day, or use the language contained in the third chapter of Job. It may doubtless be said, "It is easy for those to speak who have never been called to endure Job's heavy trials." This is quite true; and it may further be added that no other man would have done one whit better under the circumstances. All this we can fully understand; but it in no wise touches the great moral of the book of Job—a moral which it is our privilege to seize. Job was a true saint of God; but he needed to learn himself, as we all do. He needed to have the roots of his moral being laid bare in his own sight, so that he might really abhor himself, and repent in dust and ashes. And furthermore, he needed a truer and deeper sense of what God was, so that he might trust Him and justify Him under all circumstances.

But we look in vain for aught of this in Job's opening address. "Job spake and said, 'Let the day perish wherein I was born, and the night in which it was said, There is a man-child conceived.... Why died I not from the womb?'" These are not the accents of a broken and a contrite spirit, or of one who had learnt to say, "Even so, Father, for so it seemed good in Thy sight." It is a grand point in the soul's history when one is enabled to bow with meekness to all the dispensations of our Father's hand. A broken will is a rich and rare endowment. It is a high attainment in the school of Christ to be able to say, "I have learnt, in whatsoever state I am, to be content." (Phil. iv. 11.) Paul had to *learn* this. It was not natural to him; and, most surely, he never learnt it at the feet of Gamaliel. He had to be thoroughly broken down at the feet of Jesus of Nazareth, ere he could say from his heart, "I am content." He had to ponder the meaning of those words, "My grace is sufficient for thee" ere he could "take pleasure in infirmities." The man who could use such language was standing at the very antipodes of the man who could curse his day, and say, "Why died I not from the womb?" Only think of a saint of God, and heir of glory, saying, "Why died I not from the womb?" Ah! if Job had been in the presence of God he never could have uttered such words. He would have known full well why he had not died. He would have had a soul-satisfying sense of what God had in store for him. He would have justified God in all things. But Job was not in the presence of God, but in the presence of his friends; who proved, very distinctly, that they understood little or nothing of the character of God or the real object of His dealings with His dear servant Job.

It is not, by any means, our purpose to enter minutely into the lengthened discussion between Job and his friends—a discussion extending over twenty-nine chapters. We shall merely quote a few sentences from the opening address of each of the friends which will enable the reader to form an idea of the real ground occupied by these mistaken men.

Eliphaz was the first speaker. "Then Eliphaz the Temanite answered and said, 'If we essay to commune with thee wilt thou be grieved? but who can withhold himself from speaking? Behold, thou hast instructed many, and thou hast strengthened the weak hands. Thy words have upholden him that was falling, and thou hast strengthened the feeble knees. But now it is come upon thee, and thou faintest; it toucheth thee, and thou art troubled. Is not this thy fear, thy confidence, thy hope, and the uprightness of thy ways? Remember, I pray thee, who ever perished, being innocent? or where were the righteous cut off? *Even as I have seen,* they that plow iniquity, and sow wickedness, reap the same'" (chap. iv. 1-8). And again, "*I have seen* the foolish taking root; but suddenly I cursed his habitation" (chap. v. 3; see also chap. xv. 17).

From these sentences it seems very evident that Eliphaz belonged to that class of people who argue very much from their own experience. His motto was, "As I have seen." Now, what we have seen may be all true enough, so far as we are concerned. But it is a total mistake to found a general rule upon individual *experience*, and yet it is a mistake to which thousands are prone. What, for instance, had the experience of Eliphaz to do with Job? It may be he had never met a case exactly similar; and if there should happen to be a single feature of dissimilarity between the two cases, then the whole argument based on experience must go for nothing. And that it went for nothing in Job's case is evident, for no sooner had Eliphaz ceased speaking, than, without the slightest attention to his words, Job proceeded with the tale of his own sorrows, intermingled with much self-vindication and bitter complaints against the divine dealings (chap. vi. 7).

Bildad is the next speaker. He takes quite different ground from that occupied by Eliphaz. He never once refers to his own experience, or to what had come under his own observation. He appeals to antiquity. "Inquire, I pray thee, of *the former age,* and prepare thyself to the search of their *fathers.* (For we are but of yesterday, and know nothing, because our days upon earth are a shadow.) Shall not they teach thee, and tell thee, and utter words out of their heart?" (Chap. viii.-x.)

Now, it must be admitted that Bildad conducts us into a much wider field than that of Eliphaz. The authority of a number of "fathers" has much more weight and respectability than the experience of a single individual. Moreover, it would argue much more modesty to be guided by the voice of a number of wise and learned men than by the light of one's own experience. But the fact is that neither experience nor tradition will do. The former may be true so far as it goes, but you can hardly get two men whose experience will exactly correspond; and as to the latter, it is a mass of confusion,—for one father differs from another; and nothing can be more slippery or uncertain than the voice of tradition—the authority of the fathers.

Hence, as might be expected, Bildad's words had no more weight with Job than those of Eliphaz. The one was as far from the truth as the other. Had they appealed to divine revelation it would have been a different matter altogether. *The truth of God* is the only standard—the one grand authority. By that, all must be measured; to that all must, sooner or later, bow down. No man has any right to lay down his own experience as a rule for his fellows; and if no man has a right, neither have any number of men. In other words, it is not the voice of man, but the voice of God which must govern us all. It is not experience or tradition which shall judge at the last day, but the word of God. Solemn and weighty fact! May we consider it! Had Bildad and Eliphaz understood it, their words would have had much more weight with their afflicted friend.

Let us now very briefly refer to the opening address of Zophar the Naamathite.

He says, "Oh, that God would speak, and open His lips against thee, and that He would show thee the secrets of wisdom, that they are double to that which is! Know, therefore, that God exacteth of thee less than thine iniquity deserveth." And again, "*If* thou prepare thy heart, and stretch out thy hands toward Him; if iniquity be in thy hand, put it far away, and let not wickedness dwell in thy tabernacles. For then shalt thou lift up thy face without spot: yea, thou shalt be stedfast, and shalt not fear." (Chap. xi. 5, 6, 13-15.)

These words savor strongly of *legality*. They prove very distinctly that Zophar had no right sense of the divine character. He did not know God. No one possessing a true knowledge of God could speak of Him as opening His lips against a poor afflicted sinner, or as exacting aught from a needy, helpless creature. God is not against us, but for us, blessed forever be His name! He is not a legal exactor, but a liberal giver. Then, again, Zophar says, "If thou prepare thy heart." But if not, what then? No doubt a man ought to prepare his heart,—and if he were right, he would; but then, he is not right, and hence, when he sets about preparing his heart, he finds nothing there but evil. He finds himself perfectly powerless. What is he to do? Zophar cannot tell. No; nor can any of his school. How can they? They only know God as a stern exactor—as One who, if He opens His lips, can only speak against the sinner.

Need we marvel, therefore, that Zophar was as far from convincing Job as either of his two companions? They were all wrong. Legality, tradition, experience, were alike defective, one-sided, false. Not any one of them, or all of them put together, could meet Job's case. They only darkened counsel by words without knowledge. Not one of the three friends understood Job; and what is more, they did not know God's character or His object in dealing with His dear servant. They were wholly mistaken. They knew not how to present God to Job; and, as a consequence, they knew not how to lead Job's conscience into the presence of God. In place of leading him to self-judgment, they only ministered to a spirit of self-vindication. They did not introduce God into the scene. They said some *true things*, but they had not *the truth*. They brought in experience, tradition, legality, but not the truth.

Hence the three friends failed to convince Job. Their ministry was one-sided, and instead of silencing Job, they only led him forth into a field of discussion which seemed almost boundless. He gives them word for word, and far more. "No doubt," he says, "but ye are the people, and wisdom shall die with you. But *I have understanding as well as you; I am not inferior to you*: yea, who knoweth not such things as these?" "What ye know, the same do I know also; I am not inferior to you." "Ye are forgers of lies, ye are all physicians of no value. Oh that ye would altogether hold your peace! and it should be your wisdom." "I have heard many such things: miserable comforters are ye all. Shall vain words have an end? or what emboldeneth thee that thou answerest? I also could speak as ye do: if your soul were in my soul's stead, I could heap up words against you, and shake my head at you." "How long will ye vex my soul, and break me in pieces with words? These ten times have ye reproached me; ye are not ashamed that ye make yourselves strange to me." "Have pity upon me, have pity upon me, O ye my friends; for the hand of God hath touched me."

All these utterances prove how far Job was from that true brokenness of spirit and humility of mind which ever flow from being in the divine presence. No doubt the friends were wrong—quite wrong in their notions about God, wrong in their method of dealing with Job; but their being wrong did not make him right. Had Job's conscience been in the presence of God, he would have made no reply to his friends, even though they had been a thousand times more mistaken and severe in their treatment. He would have meekly bowed his head, and allowed the tide of reproof and accusation to roll over him. He would have turned the very severity of his friends to profitable account, by viewing it as a wholesome moral discipline for his heart. But no; Job had not yet reached the end of himself. He was full of self-vindication, full of invective against his fellows, full of mistaken thoughts about God. It needed another ministry to bring him into a right attitude of soul.

The more closely we study the lengthened discussion between Job and his three friends, the more clearly we must see the utter impossibility of their ever coming to an understanding. He was bent upon vindicating himself; and they were bent upon the very reverse. He was unbroken and unsubdued, and their mistaken course of treatment only tended to render him more so. Had they changed sides, they would have reached a different issue altogether. If Job had condemned himself, had he taken a low place, had he owned himself nothing and nobody, he would have left his friends nothing to say. And, on the other hand, had they spoken softly, tenderly, and soothingly to him, they would have been far more likely to melt him down. As it was, the case was hopeless. He could see nothing wrong in himself; and they could see nothing right. He was determined to maintain his integrity; and they were quite as determined to pick holes and find out flaws. There was no point of contact whatever—no common ground of understanding. He had no penitential breathings for them, and they had no tender compassions for him. They were traveling in entirely opposite directions, and never could meet. In a word, there was a demand for another kind of ministry altogether, and that ministry is introduced in the person of Elihu.

"So these three men ceased to answer Job [high time they should], because he was righteous in his own eyes. Then was kindled the wrath of Elihu, the son of Barachel the Buzite, of the kindred of Ram: against Job was his wrath kindled, because he justified himself rather than God. Also against his three friends was his wrath kindled, because they had found no answer, and yet had condemned Job." (Chap. xxxii. 1-3.)

Here Elihu, with remarkable force and clearness, seizes upon the very root of the matter on each side. He condenses, in two brief sentences, the whole of the elaborate discussion contained in twenty-nine chapters. Job justified himself instead of justifying God: and they had condemned Job, instead of leading him to condemn himself.

It is of the very last moral importance to see that whenever we justify ourselves, we condemn God; and on the other hand, when we condemn ourselves, we justify God. "Wisdom is justified of all her children." This is a grand point. The truly broken and contrite heart will vindicate God at all cost. "Let God be true, but every man a liar; as it is written, That thou mightest be justified in thy sayings, and mightest overcome when thou art judged." (Rom. iii. 4.) God must have the upper hand in the end; and it is the path of true wisdom to give Him the upper hand now. The very moment the soul is broken down in true self-judgment, God rises before it in all the majesty of His grace as a Justifier. But so long as we are ruled by a spirit of self-vindication or self-complacency, we must be total strangers to the deep blessedness of the man to whom God imputeth righteousness without works. The greatest folly that any one can be guilty of is to justify himself; inasmuch as God must then impute sin. But the truest wisdom is to condemn one's self utterly; for in that case God becomes the Justifier.

But Job had not yet learnt to tread this marvelously blessed path. He was still built up in his own goodness, still clothed in his own righteousness, still full of self-complacency. Hence the wrath of Elihu was kindled against him. Wrath must assuredly fall upon self-righteousness. It cannot be otherwise. The only true ground for a sinner to occupy is the ground of genuine repentance. Here there is naught but that pure and precious grace that reigns through righteousness by Jesus Christ our Lord. Thus it stands ever. There is nothing but wrath for the self-righteous—nothing but grace for the self-judged.

Reader, remember this. Pause for a moment, and consider it. On what ground dost thou, at this moment, stand? Hast thou bowed before God in true repentance? Hast thou ever really measured thyself in His holy presence? Or, art thou on the ground of self-righteousness, self-vindication, and self-complacency? Do, we entreat you, weigh these solemn questions. Do not put them aside. We are most anxious to deal with the heart and conscience of the reader. We do not write merely for the understanding, for the mind, for the intelligence. No doubt it is well to seek to enlighten the understanding, by the word of God; but we should exceedingly regret if our work were to end here. There is far more than this. God wants to deal with the heart, with the moral being, with the inward man. He will have us real before Him. It is of no possible use to build ourselves up in self-opinionativeness; for nothing is surer than that every thing of that kind must be broken up. The day of the Lord will be against every thing high and lifted up; and hence it is our wisdom now to be low and broken down; for it is from the low place that we get the very best view of God and His salvation. May the reader be led by God's Spirit into the reality of all this! May we all remember that God delights in a broken and contrite spirit—that He ever finds His abode with such; but the proud He knoweth afar off.

Thus, then, we may understand why Elihu's wrath was kindled against Job. He was entirely on God's side. Job was not. We hear nothing of Elihu until chap. xxxii., though it is very evident that he had been an attentive listener to the whole discussion. He had given a patient hearing to both sides, and he found that both were wrong. Job was wrong in seeking to defend himself; and the friends were wrong in seeking to condemn him.

How often is this the case in our discussions and controversies! And oh, what sorrowful work it is! In ninety-nine cases out of a hundred in the which persons are at issue, it will be found to be very much as it was with Job and his friends. A little brokenness on one side, or a little softness on the other, would go a great way toward settling the question. We speak not, of course, of cases in which the truth of God is concerned. There, one must be bold, decided, and unyielding. To yield where the truth of God or the glory of Christ is concerned, would be disloyalty to the One to whom we owe every thing. Plain decision and unflinching firmness alone become us in all cases in which it is a question of the claims of that blessed One who, when our interests were concerned, surrendered every thing, even life itself, in order to secure them. God forbid we should drop a sentence or pen a line which might have the effect of relaxing our grasp of truth, or abating our ardor in contending earnestly for the faith once delivered to the saints. Ah, no, reader, this is not the moment for ungirding the loins, laying aside the harness, or lowering the standard. Quite the reverse. Never was there more urgent need of having the loins girt about with truth, of having firm footing, and of maintaining the standard of divine principle in all its integrity. We say this advisedly. We say it in view of all the efforts of the enemy to drive us off the platform of pure truth by referring us to those who have failed in the maintenance of pure morals. Alas! alas! there is failure—sad, humiliating failure. We do not deny it. Who could? It is too patent—too flagrant—too gross. The heart bleeds as we think of it. Man fails always and every where. His history, from Eden to the present hour, is stamped with failure.

All this is undeniable. But, blessed be God! His foundation standeth sure, nor can human failure ever touch it. God is faithful. He knoweth them that are His; and let every one that nameth the name of Christ depart from iniquity. We have yet to learn that the way to improve *our* morals is to lower God's standard. We do not and cannot believe it. Let us humble ourselves in view of our failure; but never surrender the precious truth of God.

But all this is a digression into which we have allowed ourselves to be drawn in order to guard against the thought that, in urging upon the reader the importance of cultivating a broken, yielding spirit, we would have him to yield a single jot or tittle of divine revelation. We must now return to our subject.

There is something peculiarly marked and striking in the ministry of Elihu. He stands in vivid contrast with the three friends. His name signifies "God is he," and no doubt we may view him as a type of our Lord Jesus Christ. He brings God into the scene, and puts a complete stop to the weary strife and contention between Job and his friends. Elihu argues not on the ground of experience; he appeals not to tradition; he breathes not the accents of legality; he brings in God. This is the only way of putting a stop to controversy, of hushing strife, of ending a war of words. Let us hearken to the words of this remarkable personage.

"Now Elihu had waited till Job had spoken, because they were elder than he. When Elihu saw that there was no answer in the mouth of these three men, then his wrath was kindled." Note this: *"There was no answer."* In all their reasonings, in all their arguments, in all their references to experience, tradition, and legality, there was "no answer." This is very instructive. Job's friends had traveled over a very wide range, had said many true things, had attempted many replies; but, be it carefully noted, they found "no answer." It is not in the range of earth or of nature to find an answer for a self-righteous heart. God alone can answer it, as we shall see in the sequel. To all else but God the unbroken heart can find a ready reply. This is most strikingly proved in the history now before us. Job's three friends found no answer. "And Elihu, the son of Barachel the Buzite, answered and said, 'I am young, and ye are very old; wherefore I was afraid, and durst not show mine opinion. I said, Days should speak [but, alas! they either do not speak at all or they speak a quantity of error and folly], and multitude of years should teach wisdom. But there is a spirit in man, and the inspiration of the Almighty giveth him understanding." Here divine light, the light of inspiration, begins to stream in upon the scene, and to roll away the thick clouds of dust raised by the strife of tongues. We are conscious of moral power and weight the very moment this blessed servant opens his lips. We feel we are listening to a man who speaks as the oracles of God—a man who is sensibly standing in the divine presence. It is not a man drawing from the meagre store of his own narrow and one-sided experience; nor yet a man appealing to hoary antiquity, or to a bewildering tradition, or the ever-conflicting voices of the fathers. No; we have before us now a man who introduces us at once into the very presence of "the inspiration of the Almighty."

This is the only sure authority—the only unerring standard. "'Great men are not always wise, neither do the aged understand judgment.[8] Therefore I said, Hearken to me; I also will show mine opinion. Behold, I waited for your words; I gave ear to your reasons, whilst ye searched out what to say. Yea, I attended unto you, and, behold, there was none of you that convinced Job, or that answered his words: lest ye should say, We have found out wisdom: God thrusteth him down, not man. Now he hath not directed his words against me, neither will I answer him with your speeches.' They were amazed; they answered no more; they left off speaking." Experience, tradition, and legality are all swept off the platform to leave room for the "inspiration of the Almighty"—for the direct and powerful ministry of the Spirit of God.

The ministry of Elihu breaks upon the soul with peculiar power and fullness. It stands in vivid contrast with the one-sided and most defective ministry of the three friends. Indeed, it is quite a relief to reach the close of a controversy which seemed likely to prove interminable—a controversy between intense egotism on the one hand and experience, tradition, and legality on the other,—a controversy barren of any good, so far as Job was concerned, and leaving all parties at the close very much where they were at the beginning.

---

[8] What would Elihu have said to the recent dogma of the infallibility of a man—a dogma accepted by over five hundred rational beings sitting in solemn conclave?

And this is to be henceforth part and parcel of the faith of Christians! Not long since, men were called upon to believe in *an immaculate woman*; now they are called upon to believe in *an infallible man*! What is to come next? Surely the "strong delusion" must soon set in, when men will be compelled, by God's judicial dealings, to believe a lie, because they *would* not believe the truth. May the eternal Spirit put forth His mighty energy in the conversion of precious souls ere the day of vengeance sets in!

Still, however, the controversy is not without its value and interest to us. It teaches us very distinctly that when two parties join issue, they never can reach an understanding unless there be a little brokenness and subduedness on one side or the other. This is a valuable lesson, and one to which we all need to give attention. There is a vast amount of headiness and high-mindedness abroad, not only in the world, but in the Church. There is a great deal of self-occupation—a quantity of "I, I, I"—and that, too, even where we least suspect it, and where it is, most of all, unsightly, namely, in connection with the holy service of Christ. Never, we may safely assert, is egotism more truly detestable than when it shows itself in the service of that blessed One who made Himself of no reputation—whose whole course was one of perfect self-surrender, from first to last—who never sought His own glory in any thing, never maintained His own interest, never pleased Himself.

And yet, for all that, reader, is there not a most deplorable amount of hateful, unsubdued self displayed on the platform of Christian profession and Christian service? Alas! we cannot deny it. We are disposed to marvel, as the eye scans the record of the remarkable discussion between Job and his friends; we are amazed to find close upon a hundred references to himself in Job xxix.-xxxi. alone. In short, it is all "I" from beginning to end.

But, let us look to ourselves. Let us judge our own hearts in their deeper workings. Let us review our ways in the light of the divine presence. Let us bring all our work and service, and have it weighed in the holy balances of the sanctuary of God. Then shall we discover how much of hateful self is insinuated, like a dark and defiling tissue, into the whole web of our Christian life and service. How, for example, comes it to pass that we are so ready to mount the high horse when self is touched, even in the most remote degree? Why are we so impatient of reproof, be it clothed in language ever so refined and gentle? Why so ready to take offense at the slightest disparagement of self? And, further, why is it that we find our sympathies and our regards and our predilections going out, with special energy, after those who think well of us,—who value our ministry, agree with our opinions, and adopt our *cue*?

Do not all these things tell a tale? Do they not prove to us that, ere we condemn the egotism of our ancient patriarch, we should seek to get rid of a vast amount of our own? It is not, surely, that he was right; but we are far more wrong. It is far less to be wondered at that a man, amid the dim twilight of the far-back patriarchal age, was entangled in the snare of self-occupation, than that we, in the full blaze of Christianity, should fall thereinto. Christ had not come. No prophetic voice had fallen on the ear. Even the law had not been given when Job lived and spoke and thought. We can form a very poor conception indeed of the tiny ray of light by which men had to walk in the days of Job. But to us pertain the high privilege and holy responsibility of walking in the very meridian light of a full-orbed Christianity. Christ has come. He has lived, died, risen, and gone back to heaven. He has sent down the Holy Ghost to dwell in our hearts, as the witness of His glory, the seal of accomplished redemption, and the earnest of the inheritance, until the redemption of the purchased possession. The canon of Scripture is closed. The circle of revelation is complete. The Word of God is filled up. We have before us the divine record of the self-emptied One who went about doing good—the marvelous story of what He did, and how He did it, of what He said, and how He said it, of who He was and what He was. We know that He died for our sins according to the Scriptures; that He condemned sin and put it away; that our old nature—that odious thing called self, sin, the flesh—has been crucified and buried out of God's sight—made an end of forever, so far as its power over us is concerned. Moreover, we are made partakers of the divine nature; we have the holy Ghost dwelling in us; we are members of Christ's body, of His flesh, and of His bones; we are called to walk, even as He walked; we are heirs of glory—heirs of God and joint-heirs with Christ.

What did Job know of all this? Nothing. How could he know what was not revealed till fifteen centuries after his time? The full extent of Job's knowledge is poured upon us in those few glowing and impassioned words at the close of chap xix. "Oh, that my words were now written! Oh, that they were printed in a book! That they were graven with an iron pen and lead in the rock forever! For I know that my Redeemer liveth, and that He shall stand at the latter day upon the earth. And though, after my skin worms destroy this body yet in my flesh shall I see God: whom I shall see for myself, and my eyes shall behold, and not another; though my reins be consumed within me."

This was Job's knowledge—this was his creed. There was a great deal in it, in one sense; but very little indeed when compared with the mighty circle of truths in the midst of which we are privileged to move. Job looked forward, through the dim twilight, to something that was to be done in the far-off future. We look back, from amid the full flood-tide of divine revelation, to something that has been done. Job could say of his Redeemer that "He *shall* stand in the latter day upon the *earth*." We know that our Redeemer sitteth on the throne of the Majesty in the heavens, after having lived and labored and died on the earth.

In short, the measure of Job's light and privilege admits of no comparison with that which we enjoy; and for this reason it is the less excusable in us to indulge in the varied forms of egotism and self-occupation. Our self-abnegation should be in proportion to the measure of our spiritual privilege. But alas! it is not so. We profess the very highest truths; but our character is not formed, nor is our conduct governed, by them. We speak of the heavenly calling; but our ways are earthly, sometimes sensual, or worse. We profess to enjoy the very highest standing; but our state does not comport therewith. Our real condition does not answer to our assumed position. We are high-minded, touchy, tenacious, and easily provoked. We are quite as ready to embark in the business of self-vindication as was our patriarch Job.

And then, on the other hand, when we feel called upon to approach another in the attitude and tone of reproof, with what rudeness, coarseness, and harshness we discharge the necessary work! How little softness of tone or delicacy of touch! How little of the tender and the soothing! How little of the "excellent oil!" How little of the broken heart and weeping eye! What slender ability to bring our erring brother down into the dust! Why is this? Simply because we are not habitually in the dust ourselves. If, on the one hand, we fail quite as much as Job in the matter of egotism and self-vindication, so on the other, we prove ourselves fully as incompetent as Job's friends to produce self-judgment in our brother. For example, how often do we parade our own experience, like Eliphaz; or indulge in a legal spirit, like Zophar; or introduce human authority, like Bildad! How little of the spirit and mind of Christ! How little of the power of the Holy Ghost, or the authority of the Word of God!

It is not pleasant to write thus. Quite the contrary. But it is pressed upon us, and we must write. We feel most solemnly, the growing laxity and indifference of the day in which we live. There is something perfectly appalling in the disproportion between our profession and practice. The highest truths are professed in immediate connection with gross worldliness and self-indulgence. Indeed, it would appear as though, in some cases, the higher the doctrines professed, the lower the walk. There is a wide diffusion of truth in our midst; but where is its formative power? Floods of light are poured upon the intelligence; but where are the profound exercises of heart and conscience in the presence of God? The rigid rule of precise and accurate statement is attended to; but where is the true practical result? Sound doctrine is unfolded in the letter; but where is the spirit? There is the form of words; but where is the living exponent?

Is it that we do not prize sound doctrine and accurate statement? Is it that we undervalue the wide diffusion of precious truth, in its very highest forms? Far, far away be the thought! Human language would utterly fail to set forth our estimate of these things. God forbid we should pen a line which might tend in any wise to lower in the mind of the reader the sense of the unspeakable value and importance of a lofty—yea, the very loftiest—standard of truth and sound doctrine. We are most thoroughly convinced that we shall never improve our morals by lowering, the breadth of a hair, the standard of principle.

But, Christian reader, we would lovingly and solemnly ask you, Does it not strike you that there is in our midst a most melancholy lack of the tender conscience and the exercised heart? Does our practical piety keep pace with our profession of principle? Is the standard of morals at all up to the standard of doctrine?

Ah! we anticipate the reply of the grave and thoughtful reader. We know too well the terms in which that reply must be couched. It is but too plain that the truth does not act on the conscience—that the doctrine does not shine in the life—that the practice does not correspond with the profession.

We speak for ourselves. As God is our witness, we pen these lines, in His presence, in a spirit of self-judgment. It is our hearty desire that the knife should enter into our own soul, and reach the deep roots of things there. The Lord knows how much we should prefer laying the ax to the root of self and there leave it to do its work. But we feel we have a sacred duty to discharge to the individual reader and to the Church of God; and, moreover, we feel that that duty would not be discharged were we merely to set forth the precious and the beautiful and the true. We are convinced that God would have us not only to be exercised in heart and conscience ourselves, but also to seek to exercise the hearts and consciences of all with whom we have to do.

True it is (a truth often stated and proved) that worldliness and carnality, and self-indulgence in all its phases,—in the wardrobe, the library, the equipage, and the table,—that fashion and style, folly and vanity, pride of *caste*, of intellect, and of purse,—none of these things can be talked down, written, lectured, or scolded down. This we fully believe. But must not conscience be addressed? Must not the voice of holy exhortation fall on the ear? Shall we suffer laxity, indifferentism, and Laodicean lukewarmness to pave the way for a universal skepticism, infidelity, and practical atheism, and not be roused in conscience ourselves, and seek to rouse others? God forbid! No doubt, the higher and the better way is to have the evil expelled by the good, to have the flesh subdued by the Spirit, to have self displaced by Christ, to have the love of the world supplanted by the love of the Father:—all this we fully feel and freely admit; but, while feeling and admitting all this, we must still press upon our own conscience and that of the reader the urgent demand for solemn and searching review—for deep searchings of heart in the secret of the presence of God—for profound self-judgment, in reference to our whole career. Blessed be God! we can carry on these exercises before the throne of grace, the precious mercy-seat. "Grace reigns." Precious consoling sentence! Should it prevent exercise of soul? Nay, it should only impart the right tone and character thereto. We have to do with victorious grace, not that we may indulge self, but mortify it all the more thoroughly.

May the Lord make us really humble, earnest, and devoted! May the deep utterance of the heart both of the writer and the reader be, "Lord, I am Thine—Thine only, Thine wholly, Thine forever!"

This may seem to some a digression from our special theme; but we trust the digression may not be in vain, but that, by the grace of God, it will yield something for the heart and conscience of both the writer and the reader; and thus we shall be better prepared to understand and appreciate the powerful ministry of Elihu, to which we shall now turn our attention, in dependence upon divine guidance.

The reader cannot fail to notice the double bearing of this remarkable ministry,—its bearing upon our patriarch and its bearing upon his friends. This is only what we might expect. Elihu, as we have already remarked, had patiently listened to the arguments on both sides. He had, as we say, heard both parties out. He had allowed them to exhaust themselves—to say all they had to say: "Elihu had waited till Job had spoken, because they were older than he." This is in lovely moral order. It was, most surely, the way of the Spirit of God. Modesty in a young man is most graceful. Would there were more of it in our midst! Nothing is more attractive in the young than a quiet, retiring spirit. When real worth lies concealed beneath a modest and humble exterior, it is sure to draw the heart with irresistible power. But on the other hand, nothing is more repulsive than the bold self-confidence, the pushing forwardness, and self-conceit of many of the young men of the present day. All such persons would do well to study the opening words of Elihu, and to imitate his example.

"And Elihu, the son of Barachel the Buzite, answered and said, 'I am young, and ye are very old; wherefore I was afraid, and durst not show you mine opinion. I said, Days should speak, and multitude of years should teach wisdom.'" This is the natural order. We expect hoary heads to contain wisdom; and hence it is but right and comely for young men to be swift to hear, slow to speak, in the presence of their elders. We may set it down as an almost fixed principle that a forward young man is not led by the Spirit of God—that he has never measured himself in the divine presence—that he has never been thoroughly broken down before God.

No doubt it may often happen, as in the case of Job and his friends, that old men give utterance to very foolish things. Gray hairs and wisdom do not always go together; and it not unfrequently happens that aged men, relying upon the mere fact of their years, assume a place for which they have no sort of power, either moral, intellectual, or spiritual. All this is perfectly true, and it has to be considered by those whom it may concern. But it leaves wholly untouched the fine moral sentiment contained in Elihu's opening address: "I am young, and ye are very old; wherefore I was afraid, and durst not show you mine opinion." This is always right. It is always comely for a young man to be afraid to show his opinion. We may rest assured that a man who possesses inward moral power—who, as we say, *has it in him*—is never in haste to push himself forward; but yet, when he does come forward, he is sure to be heard with respect and attention. The union of modesty and moral power imparts an irresistible charm to the character; but the most splendid abilities are marred by a self-confident style.

"But," continues Elihu, "there is a spirit in man; and the inspiration of the Almighty giveth him understanding." This introduces another element altogether. The moment the Spirit of God enters the scene, it ceases to be a question of youth or old age, inasmuch as he can speak by old or young. "Not by might or by power; but by My Spirit, saith the Lord of hosts." This holds good always. It was true for the patriarchs; true for the prophets; true for apostles; true for us; true for all. It is not by human might or power, but by the eternal Spirit.

Here lay the deep secret of Elihu's quiet power. He was filled with the Spirit, and hence we forget his youth, while hearkening to the words of spiritual weight and heavenly wisdom that proceed out of his mouth; and we are reminded of Him who spake as one having authority, and not as the scribes. There is a striking difference between a man who speaks as an oracle of God, and one who speaks in mere official routine—between one who speaks from the heart, by the Spirit's holy unction, and one who speaks from the intellect by human authority. Who can duly estimate the difference between these two? None but those who possess and exercise the mind of Christ.

But let us proceed with Elihu's address.

"Great men," he tells us, "are not always wise." How true! "Neither do the aged understand judgment. Therefore I said, Hearken to me; I also will show mine opinion. Behold, I waited for your words; I gave ear to your reasons, whilst ye searched out what to say. Yea, I attended unto you, and, behold, there was none of you that convinced Job, or that answered his words."

Let us specially note this. "There was none of you that convinced Job." This was clear enough. Job was just as far from being convinced at the close of the discussion as he was at the commencement. Indeed we may say that each fresh argument drawn from the treasury of experience, tradition, and legality only served to stir some fresh and deeper depth of Job's unjudged, unsubdued, unmortified nature. This is a grand moral truth, illustrated on every page of the book which lies open before us.

But how instructive the reason for all this! "Lest ye should say, We have found out wisdom; God thrusteth him down, not man." No flesh shall glory in the presence of God. It may boast itself outside. It may put forth its pretensions, and glory in its resources, and be proud of its undertakings, so long as God is not thought of. But only introduce Him, and all the vauntings, the boastings, the vain-gloryings, the lofty pretensions, and the self-complacency, and the self-conceit will be withered up in a moment.

Reader, let us remember this. "Boasting is excluded." Yes; all boasting—the boasting of Job, the boasting of his friends. If Job had succeeded in establishing his cause, he would have boasted. If, on the other hand, his friends had succeeded in silencing him, they might have boasted. But no; "God thrusteth him down, not man."

Thus it was; thus it is; and thus it must ever be. God knows how to humble the proud heart and subdue the stubborn will. It is utterly vain for any one to set himself up; for we may rest assured that every one who is set up must, sooner or later, be upset. The moral government of God has so ordered and enacted that all that is high and lifted up must come down. This is a salutary truth for us all; but especially for the young, the ardent, and the aspiring. The humble, retired, shady path is, unquestionably, the safest, the happiest, and the best. May we ever be found treading it, until we reach that bright and blessed scene where pride and ambition are unknown?

The effect of Elihu's opening words upon Job's three friends was most striking. "They were amazed; they answered no more; they left off speaking. When I had waited—for they spake not, but stood still, and answered no more—I said, I will answer also my part; I also will show mine opinion." And then, lest any should suppose that he was speaking his own words, he adds, "For I am full of matter; the spirit within me constraineth me." This is the true spring and power of all ministry, in all ages. It must be "the inspiration of the Almighty," or it is worth absolutely nothing.

We repeat, this is the only true source of ministry, at all times and in all places. And in saying this, we do not forget that a mighty change took place when our Lord Christ ascended to heaven and took His seat at the right hand of God, in virtue of accomplished redemption. To this glorious truth we have often referred the readers of our magazine, *Things New and Old*; and hence shall not now permit ourselves to dwell upon it. We merely touch upon it in this place, lest the reader might imagine that, when we speak of the true source of ministry in all ages, we were forgetting what is marked and distinctive in the Church of God now, in consequence of the death and resurrection of Christ, the presence and indwelling of the Holy Ghost, in the individual believer, and in the Church, which is the body of Christ on earth. Far from it. Thanks and praise be to God! we have too deep a sense of the value, importance, and practical weight of that grand and glorious truth ever to lose sight of it for a moment. Indeed, it is just this deep sense, together with the remembrance of Satan's ceaseless effort to ignore the truth of the presence of the Holy Ghost in the Church, that leads us to pen this cautionary paragraph.

Still, Elihu's principle must ever hold good. If any man is to speak with power and practical effect, he must be able, in some measure, to say, "I am full of matter; the spirit within me constraineth me.[9] Behold, my belly is as wine which hath no vent; it is ready to burst like new bottles. I will speak, that I may be refreshed: I will open my lips and answer." Thus it must ever be, in measure at least, with all who will speak with real power and effect to the hearts and consciences of their fellows. We are forcibly reminded, by Elihu's glowing words, of that memorable passage in the seventh of John, "He that believeth on Me, as the Scripture hath said, out of his belly shall flow rivers of living water." True it is that Elihu knew not the glorious truth set forth in these words of our Lord, inasmuch as they were not made good till fifteen centuries after his time. But then he knew the principle—he possessed the germ of what was afterward to come out in full blow and rich mellow fruit. He knew that a man, if he is to speak with point, pungency, and power, must speak by the inspiration of the Almighty. He had listened till he was tired to men talking a quantity of powerless matter—saying some truisms—drawing from their own experience, or from the musty stores of human tradition. He was wellnigh wearied out with all this, and he rises, in the mighty energy of the Spirit, to address his hearers as one fitted to speak like an oracle of God.

Here lies the deep and blessed secret of ministerial power and success. "If any man speak," says Peter, "let him speak as the oracles of God." It is not, be it carefully observed, merely speaking according to Scripture—an all-important and essential matter, most surely. It is more. A man may rise and address his fellows for an hour, and, from beginning to end of his discourse, he may not utter so much as a single unscriptural sentence; and all the while, he may not have been God's oracle at the time,—he may not have been God's mouthpiece, or the present exponent of His mind to the souls before him.

This is peculiarly solemn, and demands the grave consideration of all who are called to open their lips in the midst of God's people. It is one thing to utter a certain amount of true sentiment, and quite another to be the living channel of communication between the very heart of God and the souls of God's people. It is

---

[9] Let the reader distinctly understand that Elihu, in the above quotation, speaks, not of the indwelling of the Holy Ghost, as believers now know it. This was wholly unknown to saints in Old-Testament times, and was the direct result of accomplished redemption—the special fruit of the glorification of Christ at the right hand of the Majesty in the heavens. This important truth has been repeatedly referred to and dwelt upon at other times, and hence we shall not go into it now; but we would request the reader to turn to Jno. vii. 39 and xvi. 7, and meditate upon the doctrine there taught, apart from all preconceived thoughts of his own, and irrespective of all the opinions of men. From these scriptures, he will see distinctly that the Holy Ghost did not and could not come until Jesus was glorified. This is not a mere speculation—a human theory—the dogma of a certain school. It is a grand foundation-truth of Christianity, to be reverently received, tenaciously held, and faithfully confessed by every true Christian. May all the Lord's people be led to see and believe it!

this latter, and this alone, that constitutes true ministry. A man who speaks as an oracle of God will bring the conscience of the hearer so into the very light of the divine presence that every chamber of the heart is laid open, and every moral spring touched. This is true ministry. All else is powerless, valueless, fruitless. Nothing is more deplorable and humiliating than to listen to a man who is evidently drawing from his own poor and scanty resources, or trafficking in second-hand truth—in borrowed thoughts. Better far for such to be silent—better for their hearers, better for themselves. Nor this only. We may often hear a man giving forth to his fellows that on which his own mind has been dwelling in private with much interest and profit. He may utter truth, and important truth; but it is not *the* truth for the souls of the people—*the* truth for the moment. He has spoken according to Scripture so far as his matter is concerned, but he has not spoken as an oracle of God.

Thus, then, may all learn a valuable lesson from Elihu; and, most surely, it is a needed lesson. Some may feel disposed to say it is a difficult lesson—a hard saying. But no; if we only live in the Lord's presence, in the abiding sense of our own nothingness and of His all-sufficiency, we shall know the precious secret of all effective ministry; we shall know how to lean upon God alone, and thus be independent of men, in the right sense; we shall be able to enter into the meaning and force of Elihu's further words, "Let me not, I pray you, accept any man's person; neither let me give flattering titles unto man. For I know not to give flattering titles; in so doing, my Maker would soon take me away." (Job xxxii. 21, 22.)

In studying the ministry of Elihu, we find in it two grand elements, namely, "grace and truth." Both these were essential in dealing with Job; and, consequently, we find both coming out with extraordinary power. He tells Job and his friends very distinctly that he knows not how to give flattering titles unto man. Here the voice of "truth" falls with great clearness on the ear. Truth puts every one in his right place; and, just because it does so, it cannot bestow titles of flattery upon a poor guilty mortal, however much that mortal might be gratified by them. Man must be brought to know himself, to see his true condition, to confess what he really is. This was precisely what Job needed. He did not know himself, and his friends could not give him that knowledge. He needed to be led down into the depths; but his friends could not conduct him thither. He needed self-judgment; but his friends were wholly unable to produce it.

But Elihu begins by telling Job the truth. He introduces God into the scene in His true character. This was just what the three friends had failed to do. No doubt they had referred to God; but their references were cloudy, distorted, and false. This is plain from chap. xlii. 7, 8, where we are told that "the Lord said to Eliphaz the Temanite, My wrath is kindled against thee, and against thy two friends; for *ye have not spoken of Me the thing* that is right, as My servant Job hath. Therefore take unto you now seven bullocks and seven rams, and go to my servant Job, and offer up for yourselves a burnt-offering; and my servant Job shall pray for you, for him will I accept: lest I deal with you after your folly, in that ye have not spoken of Me the thing which is right, like My servant Job."[10] They had utterly failed to bring

---

[10] The reader will bear in mind that the above words were spoken after Job's repentance. It is of the very last importance to see this.

God before the soul of their friend, and there they failed in producing the needed self-judgment.

Not so Elihu. He pursues a totally different line of things. He brings the light of "truth" to bear upon Job's conscience; and at the same time he administers the precious balm of "grace" to his heart. Let us quote his further sayings, "Wherefore, Job, I pray thee, hear my speeches, and hearken to all my words. Behold, now I have opened my mouth, my tongue hath spoken in my mouth. My words shall be of the uprightness of my heart, and my lips shall utter knowledge clearly. The Spirit of God hath made me, and the breath of the Almighty hath given me life. If thou canst answer me, set thy words in order before me, stand up. Behold, I am according to thy wish in God's stead: I am also formed out of clay. Behold, my terror shall not make thee afraid, neither shall my hand be heavy upon thee."

In these accents, the ministry of "grace" unfolds itself, sweetly and powerfully, to the heart of Job. Of this most excellent ingredient there was a total absence in the ministry of the three friends. They showed themselves only too ready to bear down upon Job with "a heavy hand." They were stern judges, severe censors, false interpreters. They could fix their cold, gray eye upon the wounds of their poor afflicted friend, and wonder how they came there. They looked on the crumbling ruins of his house, and drew the harsh inference that the ruin was but the result of his bad behavior. They beheld his fallen fortunes, and, with unmitigated severity, concluded that those fortunes had fallen because of his faults. They had proved themselves to be entirely one-sided judges. They had wholly misunderstood the dealings of God. They had never seized the full moral force of that one weighty sentence, "*God trieth the righteous.*" In a word, they were utterly astray. Their standpoint was false, and hence their whole range of vision was defective. There was neither "grace" nor "truth" in their ministry, and therefore they failed to convince Job. They condemned him without convincing him, whereas they ought to have convinced him and made him condemn himself.

Here it is that Elihu stands out in vivid contrast. He tells Job the truth; but he lays no heavy hand upon him. Elihu has learnt the mighty mysterious power of "the still small voice"—the soul-subduing, heart-melting virtue of grace. Job had given utterance to a quantity of false notions about himself, and those notions had sprouted from a root to which the sharp ax of "truth" had to be applied. "Surely," says Elihu, "thou hast spoken in my hearing, and I have heard the voice of thy words, saying, 'I am clean without transgression, I am innocent; neither is there iniquity in me.'"

What words for any poor sinful mortal to utter! Surely, though "the true light" in which we may walk had not shone on the soul of this patriarch, we may well marvel at such language. And yet, mark what follows. Although he was so clean, so innocent, so free from iniquity, he nevertheless says of God, that "He findeth occasions, he counteth me for His enemy. He putteth my feet in the stocks, He marketh all my paths." Here is a palpable discrepancy. How could a holy, just, and righteous Being count a pure and innocent man His enemy? Impossible. Either Job was self-deceived, or God was unrighteous; and Elihu, as the minister of truth, is not long in pronouncing a judgment, and telling us which is which. "Behold, in this thou art not just: I will answer thee, that God is greater than man." What a simple truth! And yet how little understood! If God is greater than man, then obviously He, and not man, must be the judge of what is right. This, the infidel heart refuses; and hence the constant tendency to sit in judgment upon the works and ways and word of God—upon God Himself. Man, in his impious and infidel folly, undertakes to pronounce judgment upon what is and what is not worthy of God; to decide upon what God ought and what He ought not to say and to do. He proves himself utterly ignorant of that most simple, obvious necessary truth, that "God is greater than man."

Now, it is when the heart bows under the weight of this great moral truth, that we are in a fit attitude to understand to object of God's dealings with us. Assuredly He must have the upper hand. "Why dost thou strive against Him? for He giveth not account of any of His matters. For God speaketh once, yea, twice, yet man perceiveth it not. In a dream, in a vision of the night, when deep sleep falleth upon men, in slumberings upon the bed; then He openeth the ears of men, and sealeth their instruction, *that He may withdraw man from his purpose, and hide pride from man. He keepeth back* his soul from the pit, and his life from perishing by the sword."

The real secret of all Job's false reasoning is to be found in the fact that he did not understand the character of God, or the object of all His dealings. He did not see that God was trying him, that He was behind the scenes and using various agents for the accomplishment of His wise and gracious ends. Even Satan himself was a mere instrument in the hand of God; nor could he move the breadth of a hair beyond the divinely prescribed limit; and moreover, when he had executed his appointed business, he was dismissed, and we hear no more about him. God was dealing with Job. He was trying him in order that He might instruct him, withdraw him from his purpose, and hide pride from him. Had Job seized this grand point, it would have saved him a world of strife and contention. Instead of getting angry with people and things, with individuals and influences, he would have judged himself and bowed low before the Lord in meekness and brokenness and true contrition.

This is immensely important for us all. We are all of us prone to forget the weighty fact that "God trieth the righteous." "He withdraweth not His eyes from them." We are in His hands, and under His eye continually. We are the objects of His deep, tender, and unchanging love; but we are also the subjects of His wise moral government. His dealings with us are varied. They are sometimes preventive; sometimes corrective; always instructive. We may be bent on some course of our own, the end of which would be moral ruin. He intervenes and withdraws us from our purpose. He dashes into fragments our air-built castles, dissipates our golden dreams, and interrupts many a darling scheme on which our hearts were bent, and which would have proved to be certain destruction. "Lo, all these things worketh God oftentimes with man, to bring back his soul from the pit, *to be enlightened with the light of the living.*"

If the reader will turn for a moment to Hebrews xii. 3-12, he will find much precious instruction on the subject of God's dealings with His people. We do not attempt to dwell upon it, but would merely remark that it presents three distinct ways in which we may meet the chastening of our Father's hand. We may "*despise*" it, as though His hand and His voice were not in it; we may "*faint*" under it, as though it were intolerable, and not the precious fruit of His love; or, lastly, we may be "*exercised* by it," and thus reap in due time, "the peaceable fruits of righteousness."

Now if our patriarch had only seized the great fact that God was dealing with him; that He was trying him for his ultimate good; that He was using circumstances, people, the Sabeans, Satan himself, as His instruments; that all his trials, his losses, his bereavements, his sufferings, were but God's marvelous agency in bringing about His wise and gracious end; that He would assuredly perfect that which concerned His dear and much-loved servant, because His mercy endureth forever; in a word, had Job only lost sight of all second causes, and fixed his thoughts upon the living God alone, and accepted all from His loving hand, he would have more speedily reached the divine solution of all his difficulties.

But it is precisely here that we are all apt to break down. We get occupied with men and things; we view them in reference to ourselves. We do not walk with God through, or rather above, the circumstances; but on the contrary, we allow the circumstances to get power over us. In place of keeping God between us and our circumstances, we permit these latter to get between us and God. Thus we lose the sense of His presence, the light of His countenance, the holy calmness of being in His loving hand, and under His fatherly eye. We become fretful, impatient, irritable, fault-finding. We get far away from God, out of communion, thoroughly astray, judging every one except ourselves, until at length God takes us in hand, and by His own direct and powerful ministry, brings us back to Himself in true brokenness of heart and humbleness of mind. This is "the end of the Lord."

We must, however, draw this paper to a close. Gladly would we expatiate further on Elihu's remarkable ministry; with pleasure and profit could we quote his further appeals to Job's heart and conscience, his pungent arguments, his pointed questions. But we must forbear, and leave the reader to go through the remaining chapters for himself. In so doing, we will find that when Elihu closes his ministry, God Himself begins to deal directly with the soul of His servant (chap. xxxviii.-xli.). He appeals to His works in creation as the display of a power and wisdom which ought assuredly to make Job feel his own littleness. We do not attempt to cull passages from one of the most magnificent and sublime sections of the inspired canon. It must be read as a whole. It needs no comment. The human finger could but tarnish its lustre. Its plainness is only equaled by its moral grandeur. All we shall attempt to do is to call attention to the powerful effect produced upon the heart of Job by this the most marvelous ministry surely under which mortal man was ever called to sit—the immediate ministry of the living God Himself.

This effect was threefold. It had reference to God, to himself, and to his friends—the very points on which he was so entirely astray. As to God, Elihu had declared Job's mistake in the following words: "Job hath spoken without knowledge, and his words were without wisdom. My desire is that Job may be tried unto the end, because of his answers for wicked men. For he addeth rebellion unto his sin; he clappeth his hands among us, and multiplieth his words against

God.... Thinkest thou this to be right, that thou saidst, 'My righteousness is more than God's'?" But mark the change. Hearken to the breathings of a truly repentant spirit; the brief yet comprehensive statement of a corrected judgment. "Then Job answered the Lord, and said, 'I know that Thou canst do every thing, and that no thought can be withholden from Thee. Who is he that hideth counsel without knowledge? therefore have I uttered that I understood not; things too wonderful for me, which I knew not. Hear, I beseech Thee, and I will speak. I will demand of thee, and declare thou unto Me. I have heard of Thee by the hearing of the ear, *but now mine eye seeth Thee.*'" (Chap. xlii. 1-9.)

Here, then, was the turning-point. All his previous statements as to God and His ways are now pronounced to be "words without knowledge." What a confession! What a moment in man's history when he discovers that he has been all wrong! What a thorough break-down! What profound humiliation! It reminds us of Jacob getting the hollow of his thigh touched, and thus learning his utter weakness and nothingness. These are weighty moments in the history of souls—great epochs, which leave an indelible impress on the whole moral being and character. To get right thoughts about God is to begin to get right about every thing. If I am wrong about God, I am wrong about myself, wrong about my fellows, wrong about all.

Thus it was with Job. His new thoughts as to God were immediately connected with new thoughts of himself; and hence we find that the elaborate self-vindication, the impassioned egotism, the vehement self-gratulation, the lengthened arguments in self-defense—all is laid aside; all is displaced by one short sentence of three words,—"*I am vile.*" And what is to be done with this vile self? Talk about it? Set it up? Be occupied with it? Take counsel for it? Make provision for it? Nay, "*I abhor it.*"

This is the true moral ground for every one of us. Job took a long time to reach it, and so do we. Many of us imagine that we have reached the end of self when we have given a nominal assent to the doctrine of human depravity, or judged some of those sprouts which have appeared above the surface of our practical life. But, alas! it is to be feared that very few of us indeed really know the full truth about ourselves. It is one thing to say, "*We* are all vile," and quite another to feel, deep down in the heart, that "*I* am vile." This latter can only be known and habitually realized in the immediate presence of God. The two things must ever go together, "Mine eye seeth *Thee,*" "Wherefore I abhor *myself.*" It is as the light of what God is shines in upon what I am that I abhor myself. And then my self-abhorrence is a real thing. It is not in word, neither in tongue, but in deed and in truth. It will be seen in a life of self-abnegation, a humble spirit, a lowly mind, a gracious carriage in the midst of the scenes through which I am called to pass. It is of little use to profess very low thoughts of self while, at the same time, we are quick to resent any injury done to us,—any fancied insult, slight, or disparagement. The true secret of a broken and contrite heart is, to abide ever in the divine presence, and then we are able to carry ourselves right toward those with whom we have to do.

Thus we find that when Job got right as to God and himself, he soon got right as to his friends, for he learned to pray for them. Yes, he could pray for the "miserable comforters," the "physicians of no value," the very men with whom he had so long, so stoutly, and so vehemently contended! "And the Lord turned the captivity of Job when he prayed for his friends."

This is morally beautiful. It is perfect. It is the rare and exquisite fruit of divine workmanship. Nothing can be more touching than to see Job's three friends exchanging their experience, their tradition, and their legality for the precious "burnt-offering;" and to see our dear patriarch exchanging his bitter invectives for the sweet prayer of charity. In short, it is a most soul-subduing scene altogether. The combatants are in the dust before God and in each other's arms. The strife is ended; the war of words is closed; and instead thereof, we have the tears of repentance, the sweet odor of the burnt-offering, the embrace of love.

Happy scene! Precious fruit of divine ministry! What remains? What more is needed? What but that the hand of God should lay the top-stone on the beauteous structure? Nor is this lacking, for we read, "The Lord gave Job twice as much as he had before." But how? By what agency? Was it by his own independent industry and clever management? No; all is changed. Job is on new moral ground. He has new thoughts of God, new thoughts of himself, new thoughts of his friends, new thoughts of his circumstances; all things are become new. "Then came there unto him all his brethren, and all his sisters, and all they that had been of his acquaintance before, and did eat bread with him in his house; and they bemoaned him, and comforted him over all the evil that the Lord had brought upon him; *every man also gave him a piece of money, and every one an earring of gold*. So the Lord blessed the latter end of Job more than his beginning.... After this lived Job a hundred and forty years, and saw his sons, and his sons' sons, even four generations. So Job died, being old and full of days."

WHAT RAISED THE WONDROUS THOUGHT?
(POEM)

What raised the wondrous thought?
Or who did it suggest?
"That we, the Church, to glory brought,
Should WITH the Son be blest."

O God, the thought was Thine!
(Thine only it could be,)
Fruit of the wisdom, love divine,
Peculiar unto Thee.

For, sure, no other mind,
For thoughts so bold, so free,
Greatness or strength, could ever find;
Thine only it could be.

The motives, too, Thine own,
The plan, the counsel, Thine! —
Made for Thy Son, bone of His bone
In glory bright to shine.

O God, with great delight
Thy wondrous thought we see,
Upon His throne, in glory bright,
The bride of Christ shall be.

Sealed with the Holy Ghost,
We triumph in that love,
Thy wondrous thought has made our boast,
"GloryWITH Christ above."

THE BIBLE: ITS SUFFICIENCY AND SUPREMACY

Some, we are aware, would fain persuade us that things are so totally changed since the Bible was penned, that we need other guidance than that which its precious pages supply. They tell us that Society is not what it was; that the human race has made progress; that there has been such a development of the powers of nature, the resources of science, and the appliances of philosophy, that to maintain the sufficiency and supremacy of the Bible, at such a point in the world's history as the nineteenth century of the Christian era, can only be regarded as childishness, ignorance, or imbecility.

Now, the men that tell us these things may be very clever and very learned; but we have no hesitation whatever in telling them that, in this matter, "they do greatly err, not knowing the Scriptures, nor the power of God." We certainly do desire to render all due respect to learning, genius, and talent, whenever we find them in their right place, and at their proper work; but when we find them lifting their proud heads above the word of God; when we find them sitting in judgment, and casting a slur upon that peerless revelation, we feel that we owe them no respect whatever; yea, we treat them as so many agents of the devil, in his efforts to shake those eternal pillars on which the faith of God's people has ever rested. We cannot listen for a moment to men, however profound in their reading and thinking, who dare to treat God's book as though it were man's book, and speak of those pages that were penned by the Allwise, Almighty, and Eternal God, as though they were the production of a shallow and short-sighted mortal.

It is important that the reader should see clearly that men must either deny that the Bible is the word of God, or admit its sufficiency and supremacy in all ages, and in all countries—in all stages and conditions of the human race. Grant us but this, that God has written a book for man's guidance, and we argue that that book *must* be amply sufficient for man, no matter when, where, or how we find him. "All scripture is given by inspiration of God ... that the man of God may be *perfect* (αρτιος), *thoroughly furnished* unto *all* good works." (2 Tim. iii. 16, 17.) This, surely, is enough. To be perfect and thoroughly furnished, must needs render a man independent of all the boasted powers of science and philosophy, falsely so called.

We are quite aware that, in writing thus, we expose ourselves to the sneer of the learned rationalist, and the polished and cultivated philosopher. But we are not very careful about this. We greatly admire the answer of a pious, but, no doubt, very ignorant woman to some very learned man who was endeavoring to show her that the inspired writer had made a mistake in asserting that Jonah was in the whale's belly. He assured her that such a thing could not possibly be, inasmuch that the natural history of the whale proved that it could not swallow anything so large. "Well," said the poor woman, "I do not know much about natural history; but this I know, that if the Bible were to tell me that Jonah swallowed the whale I would believe it." Now, it is quite possible many would pronounce this poor woman to have been under the influence of ignorance and blind credulity; but, for our part, we should rather be the ignorant woman, confiding in God's word, than the learned rationalist trying to pick holes in it. We have no doubt as to who was in the safer position.

But, let it not be supposed that we prefer ignorance to learning. Let none imagine that we despise the discoveries of science, or treat with contempt the achievements of sound philosophy. Far from it. We honor them highly in their proper sphere. We could not say how much we prize the labors of those learned men who have consecrated their energies to the work of clearing the sacred text of the various errors and corruptions which, from age to age, had crept into it, through the carelessness or infirmity of copyists, taken advantage of by a crafty and malignant foe. Every effort put forth to preserve, to unfold, to illustrate, and to enforce the precious truth of Scripture, we most highly esteem; but, on the other hand, when we find men making use of their learning, their science, and their philosophy, for the purpose of undermining the sacred edifice of divine revelation, we deem it our duty, to raise our voice, in the clearest and strongest way, against them, and to warn the reader, most solemnly, against their baneful influence.

We believe that the Bible, as written in the original Hebrew and Greek languages, is the very word of the only wise and the only true God, with whom one day is as a thousand years, and a thousand years as one day, who saw the end from the beginning, and not only the end, but every stage of the way. We therefore hold it to be nothing short of positive blasphemy to assert that we have arrived at a stage of our career in which the Bible is not sufficient, or that we are compelled to travel outside its covers to find ample guidance and instruction for the present moment, and for every moment of our earthly pilgrimage. The Bible is a perfect chart, in which every exigency of the Christian mariner has been anticipated. Every rock, every sand-bank, every shoal, every strand, every island, has been carefully noted down. All the need of the Church of God, its members, and its ministers, has been most fully provided for. How could it be otherwise, if we admit the Bible to be the word of God? Could the mind of God have devised, or His finger sketched an imperfect chart? Impossible. We must either deny the divinity or admit the sufficiency of THE BOOK. We are absolutely shut up to this alternative. There is not so much as a single point between these two positions. If the book is incomplete, it cannot be of God; if it be of God it must be perfect. But if we are compelled to betake ourselves to other sources for guidance and instruction, as to the path of the Church of God, its members or its ministers, then is the Bible incomplete, and being such, it cannot be of God at all.

What then, dear reader, are we to do? Whither can we betake ourselves? If the Bible be not a divine and therefore all-sufficient guide-book, what remains?

Some will tell us to have recourse to tradition. Alas! what a miserable guide. No sooner have we launched out into the wide field of tradition than our ears are assailed by ten thousand strange and conflicting sounds. We meet, it may be, with a tradition which seems very authentic, very venerable, well worthy of respect and confidence, and we commit ourselves to its guidance; but, directly we have done so, another tradition crosses our path, putting forth quite as strong claims on our confidence, and leading us in quite an opposite direction. Thus it is with tradition. The mind is bewildered, and one is reminded of the assembly at Ephesus, concerning which we read that, "Some cried one thing, and some another; for the assembly was confused." The fact is, we want a perfect standard, and this can only be found in a divine revelation, which, as we believe, is to be found within the covers of our most precious Bible. What a treasure! How we should bless God for it! How we should praise His name for His mercy in that He hath not left His Church dependent upon the *ignis fatuus* of human tradition, but upon the steady light of divine revelation! We do not want tradition to assist revelation, but we use revelation as the test of tradition. We should just as soon think of bringing out a rush-light to assist the sun's meridian beams, as of calling in human tradition to aid divine revelation.

But there is another very ensnaring and dangerous resource presented by the enemy of the Bible, and alas! accepted by too many of the people of God, and that is expediency, or the very attractive plea of doing all the good we can, without due attention to the way in which that good is done. The tree of expediency is a wide-spreading one, and yields most tempting clusters. But ah! beloved reader, remember its clusters will prove bitter as wormwood in the end. It is, no doubt, well to do all the good we can; but let us look well to the way in which we do it. Let us not deceive ourselves by the vain imagination that God will ever accept of services based upon positive disobedience to His word. "It is a gift," said the elders, as they boldly walked over the plain commandment of God, as if He would be pleased with a gift presented on such a principle. There is an intimate connection between the ancient "corban" and the modern "expediency," for, "there is nothing new under the sun." The solemn responsibility of obeying the word of God was got rid of under the plausible pretext of "corban," or "it is a gift" (Mark vii. 7-13).

Thus it was of old. The "corban" of the ancients justified, or sought to justify, many a bold transgression of the law of God; and the "expediency" of our times allures many to out-step the boundary line laid down by divine revelation.

Now, we quite admit that expediency holds out most attractive inducements. It does seem so very delightful to be doing a great deal of good, to be gaining the ends of a large-hearted benevolence, to be reaching tangible results. It would not be an easy matter duly to estimate the ensnaring influences of such objects, or the immense difficulty of throwing them overboard. Have we never been tempted as we stood upon the narrow path of obedience, and looked forth upon the golden fields of expediency lying on either side, to exclaim, "Alas! I am sacrificing my usefulness for an idea"? Doubtless; but then what if it should turn out that we have the very same foundation for that "idea" as for the fundamental doctrines of salvation? The question is, What is the idea? Is it founded upon "Thus saith the Lord"?

If so, let us tenaciously hold by it, though ten thousand advocates of expediency were hurling at us the grievous charge of narrow-mindedness.

There is immense power in Samuel's brief but pointed reply to Saul, "Hath the Lord as great delight in burnt offerings and sacrifices, as in obeying the voice of the Lord! Behold, to obey is better than sacrifice, and to hearken than the fat of rams." (1 Sam. xv. 22.) Saul's word was "*Sacrifice.*" Samuel's word was "*Obedience.*" No doubt the bleating of the sheep and the lowing of the oxen were most exciting. They would be looked upon as substantial proofs that something was being done; while on the other hand, the path of obedience seemed narrow, silent, lonely, and fruitless. But oh! those pungent words of Samuel! "*to obey is better than sacrifice.*" What a triumphant answer to the most eloquent advocates of expediency! They are most conclusive—most commanding words. They teach us that it is better, if it must be so, to stand, like a marble statue, on the pathway of obedience, than to reach the most desirable ends by transgressing a plain precept of the word of God.

But let none suppose that one must be like a statue on the path of obedience. Far from it. There are rare and precious services to be rendered by the obedient one—services which can only be rendered by such, and which owe all their preciousness to their being the fruit of simple obedience.[11] True, they may not find a place in the public record of man's bustling activity; but they are recorded on high, and they will be published at the right time. As a dear friend has often said to us, "Heaven will be the safest and happiest place to hear all about our work down here." May we remember this, and pursue our way, in all simplicity, looking to Christ for guidance, power, and blessing. May His smile be enough for us. May we not be found looking askance to catch the approving look of a poor mortal whose breath is in his nostrils, nor sigh to find our names amid the glittering record of the great men of the age. The servant of Christ should look far beyond all such things. The grand business of the servant is to obey. His object should not be to do a great deal, but simply to do what he is told. This makes all plain; and, moreover, it will make the Bible precious as the depository of the Master's will, to which he must continually betake himself to know what he is to do, and how he is to do it. Neither tradition nor expediency will do for the servant of Christ. The all-important enquiry is, "What saith the Scriptures."

This settles everything. From the decision of the word of God there must be no appeal. When God speaks man must bow. It is not by any means a question of obstinate adherence to a man's own notions. Quite the opposite. It is a reverent adherence to the word of God. Let the reader distinctly mark this. It often happens that, when one is determined, through grace, to abide by Scripture, he will be pronounced dogmatic, intolerant and imperious; and, no doubt, one has to watch over his temper, spirit, and style, even when seeking to abide by the word of God. But, be it well remembered, that obedience to Christ's commandments is the very opposite of imperiousness, dogmatism, and intolerance. It is not a little

---

[11] What a pattern of this we have in our blessed Lord! who for thirty years lived here in retirement, known by men only as "the carpenter" (Mark vi. 3), but known by, and the delight of, the Father, as the Holy One of God, the perfect meat-offering of Lev. vi. 19-33—wholly burnt upon the altar.—Ed.

strange that when a man tamely consents to place his conscience in the keeping of his fellow, and to bow down his understanding to the opinions of men, he is considered meek, modest, and liberal; but let him reverently bow to the authority of the holy Scripture, and he will be looked upon as self-confident, dogmatic, and narrow-minded. Be it so. The time is rapidly approaching when obedience shall be called by its right name, and meet its recognition and reward. For that moment the faithful must be content to wait, and while waiting for it, be satisfied to let men call them whatever they please. "The Lord knoweth the thoughts of man, that they are vanity."

But we must draw to a close, and would merely add, in conclusion, that there is a third hostile influence against which the lover of the Bible will have to watch, and that is *rationalism*—or the supremacy of man's reason. The faithful disciple of the word of God will have to withstand this audacious intruder, with the most unflinching decision. It presumes to sit in judgment upon the word of God—to decide upon what is and what is not worthy of God—to prescribe boundaries to inspiration. Instead of humbly bowing to the authority of Scripture, which continually soars into a region where poor blind reason can never follow, it proudly seeks to drag Scripture down to its own level. If the Bible puts forth aught which, in the smallest degree, clashes with the conclusions of rationalism, then there must be some flaw. God is shut out of His own book if He says anything which poor blind, perverted reason cannot reconcile with her own conclusions—which conclusions, be it observed, are not unfrequently the grossest absurdities.

Nor is this all. Rationalism deprives us of the only perfect standard of truth, and conducts us into a region of the most dreary uncertainty. It seeks to undermine the authority of a book in which we can believe everything, and carries us into a field of speculation in which we can be sure of nothing. Under the dominion of rationalism the soul is like a vessel broken from its safe moorings in the haven of divine revelation, to be tossed like a cork upon the wild watery waste of universal scepticism.

Now we do not expect to convince a thorough rationalist, even if such a one should condescend to scan our unpretending pages, which is most unlikely. Neither could we expect to gain over to our way of thinking the decided advocate of expediency, or the ardent admirer of tradition. We have neither the competency, the leisure, nor the space, to enter upon such a line of argument as would be required were we seeking to gain such ends as these. But we are most anxious that the Christian reader should rise up from the perusal of this little book with a deepened sense of the preciousness of his Bible. We earnestly desire that the words, *"The Bible: its sufficiency and supremacy,"* should be engraved, in deep and broad characters, upon the tablet of the reader's heart.

We feel that we have a solemn duty to perform, at a moment like the present, in the which Superstition, Expediency, and Rationalism are all at work, as so many agents of the devil, in his efforts to sap the foundations of our holy faith. We owe it to that blessed volume of inspiration, from which we have drunk the streams of life and peace, to bear our feeble testimony to the divinity of its every page—to give expression, in this permanent form, to our profound reverence for its authority, and our conviction of its divine sufficiency for every need, whether of the believer individually, or the church collectively.

We press upon our readers earnestly to set a higher value than ever upon the Holy Scriptures, and to warn them, in most urgent terms, against every influence, whether of tradition, expediency, or rationalism, which might tend to shake their confidence in those heavenly oracles. There is a spirit abroad, and there are principles at work, which make it imperative upon us to keep close to Scripture—to treasure it in our hearts—and to submit to its holy authority.

May God the Spirit, the Author of the Bible, produce, in the writer and reader of these lines, a more ardent love for that Bible! May He enlarge our experimental acquaintance with its contents, and lead us into more complete subjection to its teachings in all things, that God may be more glorified in us through Jesus Christ our Lord. Amen.

CHRISTIANITY: WHAT IS IT?

(Read Phil. iii.)

We have endeavored to hold up the Bible as the Church's supreme and all-sufficient guide, in all ages, in all climes, and under all circumstances. We now desire to hold up Christianity in its divine beauty and moral excellence, as illustrated in this well-known passage of Holy Scripture.

And be it observed that, as it was the Bible itself, and not any special system of theology deduced therefrom, that we sought to present to our readers; so now, it is Christianity, and not any peculiar form of human religiousness, that we desire to place before them. We are deeply thankful for this. We dare not enter upon the defence of men or their systems. Men err in their theology and fail in their ethics; but the Bible and Christianity remain unshaken and unshakeable. This is an unspeakable mercy. Who can duly estimate it? To be furnished with a perfect standard of divinity and morals is a privilege for which we can never be sufficiently thankful. Such a standard we possess, blessed be God! in the Bible and in the Christianity which the Bible unfolds to our view. Men may err in their creed and break down in their conduct, but the Bible is the Bible still, and Christianity is Christianity still.

Now, we believe that this third chapter of Philippians gives us the model of a true Christian—a model on which every Christian should be formed. The man who is here introduced to our notice could say, by the Holy Ghost, "Brethren, be ye followers together of me." Nor is it as an apostle that he here speaks to us— nor as one endowed with extraordinary gifts, and privileged to see unspeakable visions. It is not to Paul, the apostle, nor Paul, the gifted vessel, that we listen, in verse 17 of our chapter, but to Paul, the Christian. We could not follow him in his brilliant career, as an apostle. We could not follow him, in his rapture to Paradise; but we can follow him in his Christian course, in this world; and it seems to us that we have in our chapter a very full view of that course, and not only of the course itself, but also the starting-post and the goal. In other words, we have to consider, first, the Christian's *standing*; secondly, the Christian's *object*; and thirdly, the Christian's *hope*. May God the Holy Ghost be our teacher, while we dwell for a little on these most weighty and most interesting points! And first, as to

The Christian's Standing.

The point is unfolded, in a double way, in our chapter. We are not only told what the Christian's standing is, but also what it is not. If ever there was a man who could boast of having a righteousness of his own in which to stand before God, Paul was the man. "If," says he, "any other man thinketh that he hath whereof to trust in the flesh, I more: circumcised the eighth day, of the stock of Israel, of the tribe of Benjamin, an Hebrew of the Hebrews; as touching the law, a Pharisee; concerning zeal, persecuting the church; touching the righteousness which is in the law, blameless."

This is a most remarkable catalogue, presenting everything that one could possibly desire for the formation of a standing in the flesh. No one could excel Saul of Tarsus. He was a Jew, of pure pedigree, in orderly fellowship, of blameless walk, of fervid zeal and unflinching devotedness. He was, on principle, a persecutor of the Church. As a Jew, he could not but see that the very foundations of Judaism were assailed by the new economy of the Church of God. It was utterly impossible that Judaism and Christianity could subsist on the same platform, or hold sway over the same mind. One special feature of the former system was the strict separation of Jew and Gentile; a special feature of the latter was the intimate union of both in one body. Judaism erected and maintained the middle wall of partition; Christianity abolished that wall altogether.

Hence Saul, as an earnest Jew, could not but be a zealous persecutor of the Church of God. It was part of his religion—of that in which he "excelled many of his equals in his own nation"—of that in which he was "exceedingly zealous." Whatever was to be had, in the shape of religiousness, Saul would have it; whatever height was to be attained, he would attain. He would leave no stone unturned in order to build up the superstructure of his own righteousness—righteousness in the flesh—righteousness in the old creation. He was permitted to possess himself of all the attractions of legal righteousness in order that he might fling them from him amid the brighter glories of a righteousness divine. "But what things were gain to me, those I counted loss for Christ. Yea, doubtless, and I count all things but loss, for the excellency of the knowledge of Christ Jesus my Lord; for whom I have suffered the loss of all things, and do count them but dung, that I may win Christ, and be found in Him, not having mine own righteousness which is of the law, but that which is through the faith of Christ, the righteousness which is of God by faith."

And we should note here that the grand prominent thought, in the above passage, is not that of a guilty sinner betaking himself to the blood of Jesus for pardon, but rather of a legalist casting aside, as dross, his own righteousness, because of having found a better. We need hardly say that Paul was a sinner—"chief of sinners"—and that, as such, he betook himself to the precious blood of Christ, and there found pardon, peace, and acceptance with God. This is plainly taught us in many passages of the New Testament. But it is not the leading thought in the chapter now before us. Paul is not speaking of his *sins*, but of his *gains*. He is not occupied with his necessities, as a sinner, but with his advantages, as a man—a man in the flesh—a man in the old creation—a Jew—a legalist.

True it is, most blessedly true, that Paul brought all his sins to the cross, and had them washed away in the atoning blood of the divine Sin-offering. But, in this passage, we see another thing. We see a legalist flinging far away from him his own righteousness, and esteeming it as a worthless and unsightly thing in contrast with a risen and glorified Christ, who is the righteousness of the Christian—the righteousness which belongs to the new creation. Paul had sins to mourn over, and he had a righteousness to boast in. He had guilt on his conscience, and he had laurels on his brow. He had plenty to be ashamed of, and plenty to glory in. But the special point presented in Phil. iii. 4-8 is not a sinner getting his sins pardoned, his guilt cleared, his shame covered, but a legalist laying aside his righteousness, a scholar casting away his laurels, and a man abandoning his vain glory, simply because he had found true glory, unfading laurels, and an everlasting righteousness in the Person of a victorious and exalted Christ. It was not merely that Paul, the sinner, *needed* a righteousness because, in reality, he had none of his own; but that Paul, the Pharisee, *preferred* the righteousness which was revealed to him in Christ, because it was infinitely better and more glorious than any other.

No doubt Paul as a sinner needed, like every other sinner, a righteousness in which to stand before God; but that is not what he is bringing before us in our chapter. We are anxious that the reader should clearly apprehend this point. It is not merely that my sins *drive* me to Christ; but His excellences *draw* me to Him. True, I have sins and therefore I need Christ; but even if I had a righteousness, I should cast it from me, and gladly hide myself *"in Him."* It would be a positive "loss" to me to have any righteousness of my own, seeing that God has graciously provided such a glorious righteousness for me in Christ. Like Adam, in the garden of Eden, he was naked, and therefore he made himself an apron; but it would have been a "loss" to him to retain the apron after that the Lord God had made him a coat. It was surely far better to have a God-made coat than a man-made apron. So thought Adam, so thought Paul, and so thought all the saints of God whose names are recorded upon the sacred page. It is better to stand in the righteousness of God, which is by faith, than to stand in the righteousness of man, which is by works of law. It is not only mercy to get rid of our sins, through the remedy which God has provided, but to get rid of our righteousness, and accept, instead, the righteousness which God has revealed.

Thus, then, we see that the standing of a Christian is *in Christ*. "Found in Him." This is Christian standing. Nothing less, nothing lower, nothing different. It is not partly in Christ, and partly in law — partly in Christ and partly in ordinances. No; it is "Found in Him." This is the standing which Christianity furnishes. If this be touched, it is not Christianity at all. It may be some ancient *ism*, or some mediæval *ism*, or some modern *ism*; but most surely it is not the Christianity of the New Testament if it be aught else than this, "Found in Him."

We do therefore earnestly exhort the reader to look well to this our first point, "In Christ it is we stand." He is our righteousness. He Himself, the crucified, risen, exalted, glorified Christ. Yes; He is our righteousness. To be found in Him is proper Christian standing. It is not Judaism, Catholicism, nor any other *ism*. It is not the being a member of this church, that church, or the other church. It is to be in Christ. This is the great foundation of true practical Christianity. In a word this is the standing of the Christian.

Let us now in the second place, look at

THE CHRISTIAN'S OBJECT.

Here again, Christianity shuts us up to Christ: "That I may *know Him*," is the breathing of the true Christian. If to be "found in Him" constitutes the Christian's standing, then "to know Him" is the Christian's proper object. The ancient philosophy had a motto which it was constantly sounding in the ears of its votaries, and that motto was, "Know thyself." Christianity, on the contrary, has a loftier motto, pointing to a nobler object. It tells us to know Christ—to make Him our object—to fix our earnest gaze on Him.

This, and this alone, is the Christian's object. To have any other object is not Christianity at all. Alas! Christians have other objects. And that is precisely the reason why we said, at the opening of this paper, that it is Christianity, and not the ways of Christians, that we desire to hold up to the view of our readers. It matters not in the least what the object is; if it is not Christ, it is not Christianity. The true Christian's desire will ever be embodied in these words, "That I may know Him, and the power of His resurrection, and the fellowship of His sufferings, being made conformable unto His death." It is not that I may get on in the world—that I may make money—that I may attain a high position—that I may aggrandize my family—that I may make a name—that I may be regarded as a great man, a rich man, a popular man. No; not one of these is a Christian object. It may be all very well for a man, who has got nothing better, to make such things his object. But the Christian has got Christ. This makes all the difference. It may be all well enough for a man, who does not know Christ as his righteousness, to do the best he can in the way of working out a righteousness for himself; but to one whose standing is in a risen Christ, the very fairest righteousness that could be produced by human efforts would be an actual loss. So is it exactly in the matter of an object. The question is not, What harm is there in this or that? but, Is it a Christian object?

It is well to see this. We may depend upon it, beloved reader, that one great reason of the low tone which prevails amongst Christians will be found in the fact that the eye is taken off Christ and fixed upon some lower object. It may be a very laudable object for a mere man of the world—for one who merely sees his place in nature, or in the old creation. But the Christian is not this. He does not belong to this world at all. He is in it, but not of it. "They," says our blessed Lord, "are not of the world, even as I am not of the world." (John xvii.) "Our citizenship is in heaven;" and we should never be satisfied to propose to ourselves any lower object than Christ. It matters not in the least what a man's position may be. He may be only a scavenger, or he may be a prince, or he may stand at any one of the many gradations between these two extremes. It is all the same, provided Christ is his real, his only object. It is a man's object, not his position, that gives him his character.

Now Paul's one object was Christ. Whether he was stationary, or whether he travelled; whether he preached the gospel, or whether he gathered sticks; whether he planted churches, or made tents, Christ was his object. By night and by day, at home or abroad, by sea or by land, alone or in company, in public or private, he could say, "One thing I do." And this, be it remembered, was not merely Paul the laborious apostle, or Paul the raptured saint, but Paul the living, acting, walking Christian—the one who addresses us in these words, "Brethren, be ye followers together of me." Nor should we ever be satisfied with anything less than this. True, we fail sadly; but let us always keep the true object before us. Like the school-boy at his copy, he can only expect to succeed by keeping his eye fixed upon his head-line. His tendency is to look at his own last written line, and thus each succeeding line is worse than the preceding one. Thus it is in our own case. We take our eye off the blessed and perfect head-line, and begin to look at ourselves, our own productions, our own character, our interests, our reputation. We begin to think of what would be consistent with our own principles, our profession, or our standing, instead of fixing the eye steadily upon that one object which Christianity presents, even Christ Himself.

But some will say, "Where will you find this?" Well, if it be meant, where are we to find it amongst the ranks of Christians, now-a-days, it might be difficult indeed. But we have it in the third chapter of the epistle to the Philippians. This is enough for us. We have here a model of true Christianity, and let us ever and only aim thereat. If we find our hearts going after other things let us judge them. Let us compare our lines with the head-line, and earnestly seek to produce a faithful copy thereof. In this way, although we may have to weep over constant failure, we shall always be kept occupied with our proper object, and thus have our character formed; for, let it never be forgotten, it is the object which forms the character. If money be my object, my character is covetous; if power, I am ambitious; if books, I am literary; if Christ, I am a Christian. It is not here a question of life and salvation, but only of practical Christianity. If we were asked for a simple definition of a Christian, we should at once say: A Christian is a man who has Christ for his object. This is most simple. May we enter into its power, and thus exhibit a more healthy and vigorous discipleship in this day, when so many, alas! are minding earthly things.

We shall close this hasty and imperfect sketch of a wide and weighty subject, with a line or two on

THE CHRISTIAN'S HOPE.

This, our third and last point, is presented in our chapter in a manner quite as characteristic as the other two. The *standing* of the Christian is to be found in Christ; the *object* of the Christian is to know Christ; and the *hope* of the Christian is to be like Christ. How beautifully perfect is the connection between these three things. No sooner do I find myself in Christ as my righteousness, than I long to know Him as my object, and the more I know Him, the more ardently shall I long to be like Him, which hope can only be realized when I see Him as He is. Having a perfect righteousness, and a perfect object, I just want one thing more, and that is to be done with everything that hinders my enjoyment of that object. "For our conversation (or citizenship, πολιτυμα not αναστροφε, Phil. iii. 20), is in heaven; from whence also we look for the Saviour, the Lord Jesus Christ, who shall change our vile body, that it may be fashioned like unto His glorious body, according to the working whereby He is able even to subdue all things unto Himself."

Now putting all these things together, we get a very complete view of true Christianity. We cannot attempt to elaborate any one of the three points above referred to; for, it may be truly said, each point would demand a volume to treat it fully. But we would ask the reader to pursue the marvellous theme for himself. Let him rise above all the imperfections and inconsistencies of Christians, and gaze upon the moral grandeur of Christianity as exemplified in the life and character of the model man presented to our view in this chapter. And may the language of his heart be, "Let others do as they will, as for me, nothing short of this lovely model shall ever satisfy my heart. Let me turn away my eye from men altogether, and fix it intently upon Christ Himself, and find all my delight in Him as my righteousness, my object, my hope." Thus may it be with the writer and the reader, for Jesus' sake.

JEHOSHAPHAT

In tracing the inspired record of the houses of Israel and Judah, from the period of their separation, under Rehoboam, we can without difficulty recognize the marked distinction between them. The line of kings from Jeroboam to Hosea presents only a dark and sorrowful catalogue of evil-doers in the sight of the Lord: we look in vain for an exception. Even Jehu, who manifested so much zeal and energy in the abolition of idolatry, proved, in the sequel, that his heart was far from being right with God. In fact, a dark cloud of idolatry seems to have settled upon the whole house of Israel, until they were carried away beyond Babylon, and scattered amongst the Gentiles.

Not so, however, with Judah. Here we find some happy exceptions—some pleasant rays from that lamp which the Lord so graciously granted in Jerusalem for David His servant's sake. The soul is refreshed by the history of such men as Josiah, Asa, Joash, and Hezekiah,—men whose hearts were devoted to the service of the sanctuary, and who therefore exerted a holy influence on their times.

It is on the narrative of one of these blessed exceptions that I desire to dwell for a little, trusting the Lord to give instruction and profit in so doing.

Jehoshaphat, king of Judah, is introduced to our notice in 2 Chron. xvii. In this chapter, we find God, in His grace, establishing His servant in the kingdom, and the people of God acknowledging him therein. Jehoshaphat's first act was to "strengthen himself against Israel." This is worthy of notice. Israel and Israel's king were ever a snare to the heart of Jehoshaphat. But in the opening of his course, in the season of his early freshness, he was able to fortify his kingdom against the power of Israel. Now, one frequently observes this in the history of Christians; the evils which in after life prove their greatest snares are those against which there is the greatest watchfulness at first. Most happy is it when the spirit of watchfulness increases with our increasing knowledge of the tendencies and capabilities of our hearts. But this, alas! is not always the way: on the contrary, how frequently do we find Christians of some years' standing indulging in things which at first their consciences would have shrunk from. This may seem to be but a growing out of a legal spirit; but should it not rather be viewed as a growing out of a tender and sensitive conscience? It would be sad if the result of more enlarged views were to be a careless spirit or a seared conscience; or if high principles of truth did but tend to render those who were once self-denying and separated, self indulgent, careless, and worldly. But it is not so. To grow in the knowledge of truth is to grow in the knowledge of God, and to grow in the knowledge of God is to grow in practical holiness. The conscience that can let pass without reproof things from which it would formerly have shrunk is, it is much to be feared, instead of being under the action of the truth of God, under the hardening influence of the deceitfulness of sin.

The whole scene presented to us (chap. xvii.) is full of interest. Jehoshaphat not only retains the conquests of Asa, his father, but goes on to extend, by his personal exertions, the interests of his kingdom. All is well ordered. "The Lord was with Jehoshaphat, because he walked in *the first ways* of his father David, and sought not unto Baalim; but sought to the Lord God of his father, and walked in His commandments, and not after the doings of Israel. Therefore the Lord established the kingdom in his hand; and all Judah brought to Jehoshaphat presents; and he had riches and honor in abundance. And his heart was lifted up in the ways of the Lord: moreover, he took away the high places and groves out of Israel." Here was the true secret of his prosperity: "His heart was lifted up in the ways of the Lord." When the heart is *thus* lifted up, every thing goes well.

In chap. xviii., however, we have a very different state of things. Jehoshaphat's prosperity is used by the devil as a snare for him. "Jehoshaphat had riches and honors in abundance, and *joined affinity with Ahab.*" We have already observed Jehoshaphat fortifying his *kingdom*; but the enemy comes upon him in a way for which Jehoshaphat does not seem to have prepared himself; he does not attack his *kingdom*, he attacks his *heart*. He comes not as the lion, but as the serpent. Ahab's "sheep and oxen" are found more suitable and effectual than Ahab's men of war. Had Ahab declared war against Jehoshaphat, it would only have cast him upon the Lord; but he does not. Jehoshaphat's kingdom is fortified against Ahab's hostilities, but his heart lies open to Ahab's allurements. This is truly solemn! We often make a great effort against evil in one shape, while we are allowing it to get in upon us in another. Jehoshaphat had at first strengthened himself against Israel, but now he joins affinity with Israel's king. And why? Had any change for the better taken place? Had Ahab's heart become more tender toward the Lord? By no means. *He* was still the same, but Jehoshaphat's conscience had lost much of its early tenderness and sensitiveness: he had come near to the evil, and tampered with it; he had touched the pitch, and was defiled by it. "He joined affinity with Ahab." Here was the evil, — an evil which, however slow in its operation, would certainly produce its own fruit sooner or later. "He that soweth to his flesh shall of the flesh reap corruption." (Gal. vi. 8.) The truth of this must inevitably be realized. Grace may triumph in the forgiveness of sin, but the legitimate fruit will spring forth in due time. The Lord put away David's sin in the matter of Uriah, but the child died, and Absalom arose in rebellion. So it will ever be. If we sow to the flesh, we must reap corruption; the flesh can produce naught else.

In Jehoshaphat's case, it was not until *after years* that the results of his false steps began to show themselves: "And after certain years, he went down to Ahab to Samaria; and Ahab killed sheep and oxen for him in abundance, and for the people he had with him, and persuaded him to go up with him to Ramoth-gilead." Satan knows his ground; he knows where the seed of evil has taken root; he knows the heart that is prepared to respond to his temptation; he knew that the "affinity" into which the king of Judah had entered with the king of Israel had prepared him for further steps in a downward course. When a Christian enters into connection with the world, he lays himself open to be *"persuaded"* by the world, to enter upon an *un*christian course of action. David took Ziklag from Achish (1 Sam. xxvii. 6), and the next step was, to join Achish against Israel. (1 Sam. xxviii. 1.) The world will never give any thing to a child of God without making large demands in return. When the king of Judah had allowed Ahab to kill sheep and oxen for him, he would have found it difficult not to meet Ahab's desire in reference to Ramoth-gilead. The safest way therefore is, to be no debtor to the world. Jehoshaphat should have had nothing whatever to do with Ahab; he should have kept himself pure. The Lord was not with Ahab, and though it might seem a desirable thing to recover one of the cities of refuge out of the hand of the enemy, yet Jehoshaphat should have known that he was not to do evil that good might come. If we join with the world in its schemes, we must expect to be identified with it in its convulsions.

Ramoth-gilead had been of old assigned as a city of refuge for the slayer (Deut. iv. 43), and to recover this city from the king of Syria was the object of Ahab's expedition. But behind this we can detect the snare of the enemy, who cared little about the city, provided he could thereby betray a child of God from the path of purity and separation. The devil has always found religious and benevolent objects most effectual in their influence upon the people of God. He does not come at first with something openly ungodly; he does not tempt a believer to join the world for some wicked design, because he knows that the sensitive conscience would shrink from such a thing; his way is rather to present in the distance some desirable object—to cover his schemes with the cloak of religion or benevolence, and thus insnare. There is, however, one truth which would, if realized, effectually deliver the Christian from all connection with the men of this world. The apostle, by the Holy Ghost, teaches us that unbelievers are "unto *every* good work reprobate." (Tit. i. 16.) This is enough for an obedient soul. We must not join with those who are so represented. It matters not what they propose—be it a work of benevolence or a work of religion,—Scripture tells us they are reprobate, yes, "reprobate," though they profess that they know God. This should be sufficient. God cannot accept of or acknowledge the works or offerings of those whose hearts are far from Him; nor should the Church mingle with such, even though it be for the accomplishment of desirable ends. "Keep thyself pure" is a valuable admonition for us all. "To obey is better than sacrifice, and to hearken than the fat of rams." It would have been infinitely better and more acceptable for Jehoshaphat to have kept himself pure from all contact with Ahab's defilement than to have recovered Ramoth from the Syrians, even had he succeeded in doing so.

However, he had to learn this by painful experience. And thus it is that most of us learn our lessons. We may *speak* much of certain points of truth, while we know but little of having learnt them experimentally. When Jehoshaphat at the commencement of his career strengthened himself against Israel, he had little idea of the way in which he would afterward be insnared by the very worst of Israelites. The only effectual safeguard against evil is, to be in communion with God about it. When we look at evil in the light of the holiness of God, we not only look at the *act*, but at the *principle*; and if the principle be unsound, no matter what the result may be, we should have nothing to do with it. But to deal thus with evil requires much exercise of soul before God—much spirituality, much self-judgment, much prayer and watchfulness. The Lord grant us these, and also more tenderness and godly sensitiveness of conscience.

We have no idea of the sad consequences of a mistake on the part of a child of God. It is not always that the full results appear to us; but the enemy takes care to make his own use of the matter, not in injury done to the one who makes the mistake merely, but to others who witness and are influenced by it. Jehoshaphat did not only fall into the snare himself, but he led others in also. "I am as thou art," said he; and further, "My people as thy people." What miserably low ground for a man of God to take! and what a place to put the people of God into—"*I am as thou art*"! Thus spake Jehoshaphat, and well was it for him that his words were not verified throughout. God did not judge of *him* as He judged of *Ahab*; here was his real security, even in the midst of the terrible consequences of his unguarded conduct. He was not as Ahab in the close of his career, though he had joined affinity with him for the purpose of carrying out his plans; he was not as Ahab when Ahab was pierced by an arrow; he was not as Ahab when the dogs licked Ahab's blood. The Lord had made him to differ.

But we should remember that when the Christian joins with the world for any purpose whatsoever, whether of religion or of benevolence, he is just saying (as Jehoshaphat said to Ahab), "I am as thou art." Let the Christian reader ask his own heart, Is this right? Is he prepared to say this? It will not do to say, "We are not to judge others." Jehoshaphat ought to have judged, as is manifested from the language of Jehu the prophet, when he met him on his return from Ramoth, "Shouldst thou help the ungodly, and love them that hate the Lord?" How was he to know who was ungodly, or who hated the Lord, if he did not exercise judgment? We have certainly no right to judge those that are without, but we are bound to exercise judgment as to those with whom we enter into fellowship. Nor does this in the least involve of necessity the idea of one's own personal superiority in any one particular. No; it is not, "Stand by thyself: *I* am holier than *thou*;" but, "I must stand apart, because *God is holy*." This is the true principle. It is upon the ground of what God is (not of what we are) that we separate from known evil. "Be *ye* holy, for *I* am holy."

Jehoshaphat, however, failed to maintain this separation; and, as has been already remarked, in failing himself, led others into failure. In this we may learn a most solemn lesson. Jehoshaphat had, we may suppose, gained very considerable influence over the hearts of the people by his previous devotedness;—he had established himself in their confidence and affections; and, to a certain extent, rightly so. It is right that those who walk devotedly should be loved and confided in; but then we must watch most jealously against the dangerous tendency of mere personal influence. No one save a man of extensive influence could have said, "My people are as thy people." He might have said, "I am as thou art," but no more. His extensive influence, when used out of communion, only made him a more efficient instrument of evil. Satan knew this; he knew his mark; he did not fasten on an ordinary man of Judah, but on the most prominent and influential man he could find, well knowing that if he could only succeed in drawing him aside, others would follow in his train. Nor was he mistaken. Many would no doubt say, "What harm can there be in joining Ahab's expedition? Surely, if there were any thing wrong in it, such a good man as king Jehoshaphat would not engage in it. So long as we see *him* there, *we* may make our minds easy about the matter." But if this were not the language of some in Jehoshaphat's day, it certainly is of many in our own. How often do we hear Christians say, "How can such-and-such things be wrong, when we see such good men in connection with them, or engaging in them?" Now all that can be said of such reasoning is that it is utterly false; it is beginning quite at the wrong end. We are responsible to God to act upon principle, let others do as they may. We should be able, through grace, humbly, yet decidedly, to render a sound and intelligent reason for whatever course of action we may adopt, without any reference to the conduct of others. Moreover, we know full well that good men go astray, and do wrong things. They are not, therefore, nor can they be, our guides. "To his own master he standeth or falleth." A spiritual mind, a conscience enlightened by the Word of God, a real sense of personal responsibility, together with honesty of purpose, are what we specially need. If we lack these, our path will be defective.

But it may be said, there are few, if any, who occupy a position in which their conduct could exert such an extensive influence as that of king Jehoshaphat. To meet this, it may be needful to dwell a little upon a truth sadly neglected in the present day, namely, that of *the unity of the body of Christ, and the consequent effect which the conduct of each member, however obscure, must produce upon the whole body.*

The great doctrine of the unity of the Church upon earth is, it is to be feared, feebly apprehended and feebly carried out, even by the most spiritually minded and intelligent of the Lord's people. The reason of this is very apparent. The doctrine is viewed rather in the light of the Church's present condition, than of her condition as presented in the New Testament; and this being so, the unity never can be understood. If we simply take Scripture for our guide, we shall have no difficulty about it. There we read, "If *one* member suffer, *all* the members suffer with it." This principle did not hold good in the days of king Jehoshaphat, because the body of Christ, properly so called, had no actual existence. All the members of it were written in God's book; but "as yet there was none of them"—they existed in the purpose of God, but that purpose had not been actualized. Hence, though so many were led astray by the influence of Jehoshaphat, it was not by any means on the principle stated in the above passage; it was not all suffering from the act of one because they were one body, but many being led astray by one because they followed his example. The distinction is very important. There is no member of the Church, how obscure soever, whose path and conduct do not affect, in some measure, all the members. "By one Spirit are we all baptized into one body, whether we be Jews or Gentiles, whether we be bond or free; and have been all made to drink into one Spirit." Hence, if a Christian be walking loosely or carelessly,—if he be out of communion,—if he fail in prayer, in watchfulness, or in self-judgment, he is really injuring the whole body; and, on the contrary, when he is walking in spiritual health and vigor, he is promoting the blessing and interest of all.

It was not without a struggle that Jehoshaphat yielded to the solicitations of Ahab. The working of conscience is observable in the words, "Inquire, I pray thee, at the word of the Lord to-day." But ah! how futile was prayer for guidance, when he had already said, "I am as thou art, and my people as thy people; and we will be with thee in the war"! It is but solemn mockery to ask for guidance when we have made up our minds; and yet how frequently we do so! How frequently do we decide on a course of action, and then go and ask the Lord about it! All this is wretched; it is only honoring God with the lips, while the heart is in positive rebellion against Him. Instead of getting that guidance for which we profess to ask, may we not rather expect a lying spirit to be sent forth to us? (*v.* 21.) Ahab was at no loss for counselors. He speedily "gathered together four hundred prophets," who were ready to counsel him according to his heart's desire: "Go up, for God will deliver it into the king's hand." This was what he wanted. Nor need we marvel at Ahab's being quite satisfied with prophets like these. They suited him well.

But surely Jehoshaphat should not have even appeared to acknowledge them to be prophets of the Lord, as he evidently did, by saying, "Is there not here a prophet of the Lord *besides*?" (or, as the margin reads, "yet one more?") Had he been faithful to the Lord, he would at once have denied the right of these false prophets to give counsel. But, alas! he was giving full countenance to the religion of the world, and to these its ministers. He could not bring himself to hurt Ahab's feelings by dealing faithfully with his prophets. They were all, it would seem, proper men. How dreadful a thing it is to allow ourselves to get into a condition of soul in which we are unable to bear distinct and faithful testimony against the ministers of Satan! "We must," it is said, "be liberal;" "we must not hurt people's feelings;" "there are good men every where." But truth is truth, and we are not to put error for truth, nor truth for error. Nothing but a secret desire to stand well with the world will ever lead to this careless method of dealing with evil. Now, if we want to stand well with the world, let us do it at our own charges, and not at the expense of God's truth. It is often urged, "We must present truth in such an aspect as will attract," when what is really meant is this, that truth is to be made a kind of variable, elastic thing, which can be turned into any shape, or stretched to any length, to suit the taste and habits of those who would fain put it out of the world altogether. Truth, however, cannot be thus treated; it can never be made to reduce itself to the level of this world. Those who profess to hold it may seek to use it thus, but it will ever be found the same pure, holy, faithful witness against the world and all its ways. It will speak distinctly, if its voice be not stifled by connection with the practice of its faithless professors. When Jehoshaphat had stooped so low as to acknowledge the false prophets for the purpose of gratifying Ahab, who could observe any distinct testimony for God? All seemed to sink down to the one common level, and the enemy to have it all his own way. The voice of truth was hushed: the prophets prophesied falsely: God was forgotten. Thus must it ever be. The attempt to accommodate truth to those who are of the world can only end in complete failure. There can be no accommodation. Let it stand upon its own heavenly height; let saints stand fully and firmly with it; let them invite sinners up to them; but let them not descend to the low and groveling pursuits and habits of the world, and thus rob truth, so far as in them lies, of all its edge and power. It is far better to allow the contrast between God's truth and our ways to be fully seen, than to attempt to identify them in appearance, when they really do not agree. We may think to commend truth to the minds of worldly people by an effort to conform to their ways; but, so far from commending it, we in reality expose it to secret contempt and scorn. Jehoshaphat certainly did not further the cause of truth by conforming to Ahab's ways, or by acknowledging the claims of his false prophets. The man who conforms to the world will be the enemy of Christ, and the enemy of Christ's people. It cannot be otherwise. "The friendship of the world is enmity with God; whosoever, therefore, will be a friend of the world is the enemy of God."

How fully was this proved in the case of king Jehoshaphat! He became the friend and companion of Ahab, who hated Micaiah, the servant of God; and as a consequence, although he did not himself positively persecute the righteous witness, yet he did what was as bad; for he sat beside Ahab, and beheld the Lord's prophet first struck, and then committed to prison, simply because he would not tell a lie to please a wicked king, and harmonize with four hundred wicked prophets. What must have been the feelings of Jehoshaphat when he beheld his brother smitten and imprisoned for his faithfulness in testifying against an expedition in which he himself was engaged! Yet such was the position into which his connection with Ahab had forced him that he could not avoid being a witness of these wicked proceedings; yea, and moreover, a partaker of them also. When a man associates himself with the world, he must do so thoroughly. The enemy will not be satisfied with half measures; on the contrary, he will use every effort to force a saint out of communion into the most terrible extremes of evil.

The beginning of evil is like the letting out of water. Small beginnings lead to fearful results. There is first a slight tampering with evil at a distance; then, by degrees, a nearer approach to it; after this, a taking hold of it more firmly; and finally, a deliberate plunge into it, whence nothing but the most marked interposition of God can rescue. Jehoshaphat "joined affinity with Ahab;" then accepted of his hospitality; after that, was "persuaded" into open association with him; and finally, took *his* place at the battle of Ramoth-gilead. He had said to Ahab, "I am as thou art," and Ahab takes him at his word; for he says to him, "I will disguise myself, and will go to the battle; but put thou on thy robes." Thus, so completely did Jehoshaphat surrender his personal identity, in the view of the men of the world, that "it came to pass, when the captains of the chariots saw Jehoshaphat, that they said, *'It is the king of Israel.'*" Terrible position for Jehoshaphat! To find him personating, and thus mistaken for, the worst of Israel's kings is a sad proof of the danger of associating with the men of the world. Happy was it for Jehoshaphat that the Lord did not take him at his word when he said to Ahab, "I am as thou art." The Lord knew that Jehoshaphat was not Ahab, though he might personate and be mistaken for him. Grace had made him to differ, and conduct should have *proved* him to be what grace had made him. But, blessed be God, "He knows how to deliver the godly out of temptation," and He graciously delivered His poor servant out of the evil into which he had plunged himself, and in which he would have perished, had not the hand of God been stretched out to rescue him. "Jehoshaphat cried out, and the Lord helped him; and God moved them to depart from him."[12]

Here we have the turning-point in this stage of Jehoshaphat's life. His eyes were opened to see the position into which he had brought himself; at least, he saw his danger, if he did not apprehend the moral evil of his course. Encompassed by the captains of Syria, he could feel something of what it was to have taken Ahab's place. Happily for him, however, he could look up to the Lord from the depth of his distress,—he could cry out to Him in the time of his extremity; had it not been thus, the enemy's arrow, lodged deep in his heart, might have told out the sorrowful result of his ungodly association. "Jehoshaphat cried out," and his cry came up before the Lord, whose ear is ever open to hear the cry of such as feel their need. "Peter went out and wept bitterly." The prodigal said, "I will arise, and go to my father;" and the father ran to meet him, and fell on his neck, and kissed him. Thus is it that the blessed God ever meets those who, feeling that they have hewn out for themselves broken cisterns, which can hold no water, return to Him, the fountain of living waters. Would that all who feel that they have in any measure departed from Christ and slipped into the current of this present world might find their way back, in true humility and contrition of spirit, to Him who says, "Behold, I stand at the door, and knock; if any man hear My voice, and open the door, I will come in to him, and will sup with him, and he with Me."

How different Ahab's case! He, though carrying in his bosom a mortal wound, propped himself up in his chariot until the evening, fondly desiring to hide his weakness, and accomplish the object of his heart. We find no cry of humility, no tear of penitence, no looking upward. Ah, no; we find not any thing but what is in full keeping with his entire course. He died as he had lived—doing evil in the sight of the Lord. How fruitless were his efforts to prop himself up! Death had seized upon him; and though he struggled for a time to keep up an appearance, yet "about the time of the sun going down he died." Terrible end!—the end of one who had "sold himself to work wickedness." Who would be the votary of the world? Who that valued a life of simplicity and purity would mix himself up with its pursuits and habits? Who that valued a peaceful and happy termination of his career would link himself with its destinies?

Dear Christian reader, let us, with the Lord's help, endeavor to shake off the world's influence, and purge ourselves from its ways. We have no idea how insidiously it creeps in upon us. The enemy at first weans from really simple and Christian habits, and by degrees we drop into the current of the world's thoughts.

---

[12] The reader will doubtless observe how the inspired writer presents God under two different titles in the above verse. *"The Lord"* brings out His connection with His distressed servant—His connection in grace; while the expression *"God"* shows out the powerful control which He exercised over the Syrian captains. It is needless to say that this distinction is divinely perfect. As Lord, He deals with His own redeemed people,—meeting all their weakness, and supplying all their need; but as God, He holds in His omnipotent hand the hearts of all men, to turn them whithersoever He will. Now we generally find unconverted persons using the expression "God," and not "Lord." They think of Him as One exercising an influence from a distance, rather than as One standing in near relationship. Jehoshaphat knew who it was that *"helped him,"* but the Syrian captains did not know who it was that *"moved them."*

Oh that we may, with more holy jealousy and tenderness of conscience, watch against the approach of evil, lest the solemn statement of the prophet should apply to us, "Her Nazarites *were* purer than snow, they *were* whiter than milk, they *were* more ruddy in body than rubies, their polishing *was* of sapphire: (but such is the sorrowful change, that) their visage *is* blacker than a coal, *they are not known in the streets*, their skin cleaveth to their bones; it is withered, it is become like a stick"!

We shall now look a little at chap. xix. Here we see some blessed results from all that Jehoshaphat had passed through. "He returned to his house in peace to Jerusalem." Happy escape! The Lord's hand had interposed for him, and delivered him from the snare of the fowler, and, we may say, he would no doubt have his heart full of gratitude to Him who had so made him to differ from Ahab, though he had said, "I am as thou art." Ahab had gone down to his grave in shame and degradation, while Jehoshaphat returned to his house in peace. But what a lesson he had learned! How solemn to think of his having been so near the brink of the precipice! Yet the Lord had a controversy with him about what he had done. Though He allowed him to return in peace to Jerusalem, and did not suffer the enemy to hurt him, He would speak to his conscience about his sin; He would bring him aside from the field of battle, to deal with him in private. "And Jehu, the son of Hanani the seer, went out to meet him, and said to king Jehoshaphat, 'Shouldst thou help the ungodly, and love them that hate the Lord? therefore is wrath upon thee from before the Lord." This was a solemn appeal, and it produced its own effect. Jehoshaphat "went out again through the people, from Beersheba to mount Ephraim, and brought them back unto the Lord God of their fathers." "When thou art converted, strengthen thy brethren." Thus did Peter; thus too did king Jehoshaphat; and blessed is it when lapses and failings lead, through the Lord's tender mercy, to such a result. Nothing but divine grace can ever produce this. When, after beholding Jehoshaphat surrounded by the Syrian captains (chap. xviii.), we find him here going out through the length and breadth of the land to instruct his brethren in the fear of the Lord, we can only exclaim, "What hath God wrought!" But he was just the man for such a work. It is one who has felt in his own person the terrible fruits of a careless spirit that can most effectually say, *"Take heed what ye do."* A restored Peter, who had himself denied the Holy One, was the chosen vessel to go and charge others with having done the same, and to offer them that precious blood which had cleansed his conscience from the guilt of it. So likewise the restored Jehoshaphat came from the battle of Ramoth-gilead to sound in the ears of his brethren with solemn emphasis, "Take heed what ye do." He that had just escaped from the snare could best tell what it was, and tell how to avoid it.

And mark the special feature in the Lord's character which engaged Jehoshaphat's attention: "There is no iniquity with the Lord our God, *nor respect of persons, nor taking of gifts*." Now his snare seems to have been the gift of Ahab: "Ahab slew sheep and oxen for him in abundance, and for the people he had with him, and persuaded him to go up with him to Ramoth-gilead." He allowed his heart to be warmed by Ahab's gift, and was thereby the more easily swayed by Ahab's arguments. Just as Peter accepted the compliment of being let into the high-priest's fire, and, being warmed thereby, denied his Lord. We can never canvass, with spiritual coolness, the world's arguments and suggestions, while we are breathing its atmosphere, or accepting its compliments. We must keep outside and independent of it, and thus we shall find ourselves in a better position to reject its proposals, and triumph over its allurements.

But it is instructive to mark how Jehoshaphat, after his restoration, dwells upon that feature in the divine character from the lack of which he had so grievously failed. Communion with God is the great safeguard against all temptation; for there is no sin to which we are tempted, of which we cannot find the opposite in God; and we can only avoid evil by communion with good. This is a very simple but deeply practical truth. Had Jehoshaphat been in fellowship with God, he could not have sought fellowship with Ahab. And may we not say this is the only divine way in which to look at the question of worldly association. Let us ask ourselves, Can our association with the world go hand in hand with our fellowship with God? This is really the question. It is a miserable thing to ask, May I not partake of all the benefits of the name of Christ, and yet dishonor that name by mixing myself up with the people of the world, and taking common ground with them? How easily the matter is settled when we bring it into the divine presence, and under the searching power of the truth of God: "Shouldst thou help the ungodly, and love them that hate the Lord?" Truth strips off all the false covering which a heart out of communion is wont to throw around things. It is only when *it* casts its unerring beams on our path that we see things in their true character. Mark the way in which divine truth exposed the actings of Ahab and Jezebel. Jezebel would fain put a fair cloak on her shocking wickedness: "Arise," said she, "and take possession of the vineyard of Naboth the Jezreelite, which he refused to give thee for money; for Naboth is not alive but dead." Such was her way of putting the matter. But how did the Lord view it? "Thus saith the Lord, 'Hast thou killed, and also taken possession'" (in other words, Hast thou committed murder and robbery?) God deals with realities. In His estimation, men and things get their proper place and value; there is no gilding, no affectation, no assumption—all is real. Just so was it with Jehoshaphat; his scheme which might in human estimation be regarded as a religious one, was in the divine judgment pronounced to be simply a helping of the ungodly, and loving them that hated the Lord. While men might applaud him, "there was wrath upon him from before the Lord."

However, Jehoshaphat had to be thankful for the salutary lesson which his fall had taught him; it had taught him to walk more in the fear of the Lord, and caused him to impress that more upon others also. This was doing not a little. True, it was a sad and painful way to learn; but it is well when we learn even by our falls,—it is well when we can tell even by painful experience the terrible evil of being mixed up with the world. Would to God we all felt it more! Would that we more walked in the solemn apprehension of the defiling nature of all worldly association, and of our own tendency to be defiled thereby! we should then be more efficient teachers of others! we should be able to say, with somewhat more weight, "Take heed what ye do;" and again, "Deal courageously, and the Lord shall be with the good."

In chap. xx. we find Jehoshaphat in far more healthful circumstances than in chap. xviii. He is here seen under trial from the hand of the enemy: "It came to pass after this also, that the children of Moab, and the children of Ammon, and with them others beside the Ammonites, came against Jehoshaphat to battle." We are in far less apprehension for Jehoshaphat when we behold him the object of the enemy's hostilities than when we beheld him the subject of Ahab's kindness and hospitality. And very justly so; for in the one case he is about to be cast simply on the God of Israel, whereas in the other he was about to fall into the snare of Satan. The proper place for the man of God is to be in positive opposition to the enemies of the Lord, and not in conjunction with them. We never can count upon divine sympathy or guidance when we join with the enemies of the Lord. Hence we observe what an empty thing it was of Jehoshaphat to ask counsel of the Lord in a matter which he knew to be wrong. Not so, however, in the scene before us. He is really in earnest when "he sets himself to seek the Lord, and proclaims a fast throughout all Judah." This is real work. There is nothing like trial from the hand of the world for driving the saint into a place of separation from it. When the world smiles, we are in danger of being attracted; but when it frowns, we are driven away from it into our stronghold; and this is both happy and healthful. Jehoshaphat did not say to a Moabite or an Ammonite, "I am as thou art." No; he knew well this was not so, for they would not let him think so. And how much better it is to know our true position in reference to the world!

There are three special points in Jehoshaphat's address to the Lord (*vv.* 6-12).

1. The greatness of God.

2. The oath to Abraham about the land.

3. The attempt of the enemy to drive the seed of Abraham out of that land.

The prayer is most precious and instructive—full of divine intelligence. He makes it altogether a question between the God of Abraham and the children of Ammon, Moab, and Mount Seir. This is what faith ever does, and the issue will ever be the same. "They come," says he, "to cast us out of *Thy possession, which Thou hast given us to inherit.*" How simple! *They* would take what *Thou* hast given! This was putting it, as it were, upon God to maintain His own covenant. "O our God, *wilt Thou not judge them? for we have no might* against this great company that cometh against us; neither know we what to do; but our eyes are upon Thee." Surely, we may say, victory was already secured to one who could thus deal with God. And so Jehoshaphat felt. For "when he had consulted with the people, *he appointed singers unto the Lord,* and that should praise the beauty of holiness, as they went out before the army, and to say, Praise the Lord; for His mercy endureth forever." Nothing but faith could raise a song of praise before even the battle had begun

"Faith counts the promise sure."

And as it had enabled Abraham to believe that God would put his seed into the possession of Canaan, so it enabled Jehoshaphat to believe that He would keep them therein, and he therefore did not need to wait for victory in order to praise; he already stood in the full results of victory. Faith could say, "Thou *hast guided* them in Thy strength unto Thy holy habitation," though they had but just entered upon the wilderness.

But what a strange sight it must have been for the enemies of Jehoshaphat, to see a band of men with musical instruments instead of weapons in their hands. It was something of the same principle of warfare as that adopted by Hezekiah afterward, when he clothed himself in sackcloth instead of armor. (Isa. xxxvii. 1.)[13]

[13] "The proud king of Assyria was at the gates of Jerusalem with a mighty conquering host, and one would naturally expect to find Hezekiah in the midst of his men of war, buckling on his armor, girding on his sword, mounting his chariot; but no; Hezekiah was different from most kings and captains,—he had found out a place of strength which was quite unknown to Sennacherib—he had discovered a field of battle in which he could conquer without striking a blow. And mark the armor with which he girds himself: 'And it came to pass, when Hezekiah heard it, that he rent his clothes, and *covered himself with sackcloth*, and went into the house of the Lord.' Here was the armor in which the king of Judah was about to cope with the king of Assyria. Strange armor!—the armor of the sanctuary. What would Sennacherib have said had he seen this? He had never met such an antagonist before—he had never come in contact with a man who, instead of covering himself with a coat of mail, would *cover himself* with sackcloth; and instead of rushing forth into the field of battle in his chariot, would fall upon his knees in the temple. This would have appeared a novel mode of warfare in the eyes of the king of Assyria. He had met the kings of Hamath and Arphad, etc.; but if he had, it was upon his own principle, and in his own way; but he had never encountered such an antagonist as Hezekiah. In fact, what gave the latter such uncommon power in this contest was the feeling that *he* was nothing—that an 'arm of flesh' was of no avail;—in a word, that it was just Jehovah or nothing. This is specially seen in the act of spreading the letter before the Lord. Hezekiah was enabled by faith to retire out of the scene, and make it altogether a question between Jehovah and the king of Assyria. It was not Sennacherib and Hezekiah, but Sennacherib and Jehovah. This tells us the meaning of the sackcloth. Hezekiah felt himself to be utterly helpless, and he took the place of helplessness. He tells the Lord that the king of Assyria had reproached *Him*; he calls upon Him to vindicate His own glorious name, feeling assured that in so doing He would deliver His people. Mark, then, this wondrous scene. Repair to the sanctuary, and there behold one poor, weak, solitary man on his knees, pouring out his soul to Him who dwelt between the cherubim. No military preparations,—no reviewing of troops: the elders of the priests, covered with sackcloth, pass to and fro from Hezekiah to the prophet Isaiah: all is apparent weakness. On the other hand, see a mighty conqueror leading on a numerous army flushed with victory, eager for spoil. Surely, one might say, speaking after the manner of men, all is over with Hezekiah and Jerusalem!—surely Sennacherib and his proud host will swallow up in a moment such a feeble band! And observe, further, the ground which Sennacherib takes in all this. (Isa. xxxvi. 4-7.) Here we observe that Sennacherib makes the very reformation which Hezekiah had effected a ground of reproach; thus leaving him, as he vainly thought, no resting-place or foundation for his confidence. Again, he says, 'Am I come up without the Lord against this land to destroy it? *The Lord said unto me, Go up against this land, and destroy it.*' (*v. 10*) This was indeed putting Hezekiah's faith to the test: faith must pass through the furnace. It will not do to say that we trust in the Lord; we must *prove* that we do, and that too when every thing apparently is against us. How, then, does Hezekiah meet all these lofty words? In the silent dignity of faith. 'The king's commandment was, saying, Answer him not.' (v. 21.) Such was the king's bearing in the eyes of the people; yea, rather, such is ever the bearing of faith: calm, self-possessed, dignified, in the presence of man; while, at the same time, ready to sink into the very dust in self-abasement in the presence of God. The man of faith can say to his fellow, 'Stand still, and see the salvation of God!' and, at the same moment, send up to God the cry of conscious weakness. (See Ex. xiv. 13-15.) So it was with the king of Judah at this solemn and trying crisis. Hearken to him while, in the retirement of the sanctuary, shut in with God, he pours out the anxieties of his soul in the

Yes, it was the same, for both had been trained in the same school, and both fought under the same banner. Would that our warfare with the present age—with its habits, manners, and maxims—were more conducted on the same principle. "Above all, taking the shield of faith, wherewith ye shall be able to quench all the fiery darts of the wicked one."

What a contrast between Jehoshaphat personating Ahab at Ramoth-gilead, and standing with the Lord against his enemies the Moabites! Yes, what a contrast, in every particular! His mode of seeking help and guidance of the Lord was different, his mode of proceeding to battle was different; and oh, how different too the end! Instead of being well-nigh overwhelmed by the enemy, and crying out in the depth of his distress and danger, we find him joining in a loud chorus of praise to the God of his fathers, who had given him a victory without his striking a blow,—who had made his enemies destroy one another, and who had graciously conducted him from the dark valley of Achor into the valley of Berachah. Blessed contrast! May it lead us to seek a more decided path of separation, and of abiding dependence on the Lord's grace and faithfulness. The valley of Berachah, or praise, is ever the place into which the Spirit of God would conduct; but He cannot lead us thither when we join ourselves with the "Ahabs" of this world, for the purpose of carrying out their schemes. The word is, "Come out from among them, and be ye separate, saith the Lord, and touch not the unclean thing; and I will receive you, and will be a Father unto you, and ye shall be My sons and daughters, saith the Lord Almighty." (2 Cor. vi. 17, 18.)

It is wonderful how worldliness hinders, yea, rather destroys, a spirit of praise; it is positively hostile to such a spirit, and, if indulged in, it will either lead to deep anguish of soul, or to the most thorough and open abandonment of all semblance of godliness. In Jehoshaphat's case, it was happily the former. He was humbled, restored, and led into larger blessedness.

But it would be sad indeed were any one to plunge into worldliness with the hope that it might lead to an issue similar to that of Jehoshaphat. Vain, presumptuous hope! Sinful expectation! Who that valued a pure, calm, and peaceful walk could for a moment entertain it? "The Lord knoweth how to deliver the godly out of temptation," but shall we, on that account, go and deliberately plunge ourselves into it? God forbid!

Yet, ah! who can sound the depths of the human heart—its profound, malignant depths? Who can disentangle its complicated mazes? Could any one imagine that Jehoshaphat would again, after such solemn lessons, join himself with the ungodly, to further their ambitious, or rather their avaricious, schemes? No one could imagine it, save one who had learned something of his own heart. Yet so he did. "He joined himself with Ahaziah, king of Israel, who did very wickedly. And he joined himself with him, to make ships to go to Tarshish; and they made the ships in Ezion-gaber. Then Eliezer, the son of Dodavah of Mareshah, prophesied against Jehoshaphat, saying, 'Because thou hast joined thyself with Ahaziah, the Lord hath broken thy works.' And the ships were broken, and they were not able

ear of One who was willing to hear and ready to help. (Chap. xxxvii. 15-20.)" —(*Practical Reflections on the Life and Times of Hezekiah.*)

to go to Tarshish." (*vv.* 35-37.) What is man! A poor, stumbling, failing, halting creature; ever rushing into some new folly or evil. Jehoshaphat had, as it were, but just recovered from the effects of his association with Ahab, and he forthwith joins himself with Ahaziah. He had with difficulty, or rather through the special and most gracious interference of the Lord, escaped from the arrows of the Syrians, and again we find him in league with the kings of Israel and Edom, to fight against the Moabites.

Such was Jehoshaphat—such his extraordinary course. There were some "good things found in him;" but his snare was, worldly association; and the lesson which we learn from the consideration of his history is, to beware of that evil. Yes; we would need to have sounded in our ears, with ceaseless solemnity, the words, "COME OUT, AND BE SEPARATE." We cannot, by any possibility, mix ourselves up with the world, and allow ourselves to be governed and led by its maxims and principles, without suffering in our own souls, and marring our testimony.

I would only remark, in conclusion, that it seems like a relief to the spirit to read the words, "Jehoshaphat slept with his fathers" (chap. xxi. 1), as we feel assured, that he has at last got beyond the reach of the enemy's snares and devices; and further, that he comes under the Spirit's benediction, "Blessed are the dead which die in the Lord; for they rest from their labors,"—yes, a rest from their conflicts, snares, and temptations also.

LIFE AND TIMES OF JOSIAH

(2 Chron. xxxiv., xxxv.)

PART I

Two thousand four hundred years have rolled away since king Josiah lived and reigned; but his history is pregnant with instruction, which can never lose its freshness or its power. The moment at which he ascended the throne of his fathers was one of peculiar gloom and heaviness. The tide of corruption, swollen by many a tributary stream, had risen to the highest point; and the sword of judgment, long held back in divine patience and long-suffering, was about to fall in terrible severity upon the city of David. The brilliant reign of Hezekiah had been followed by a long and dreary period of fifty-five years under the sway of his son Manasseh; and albeit the rod of correction had proved effectual in leading this great sinner to repentance and amendment, yet no sooner had the sceptre fallen from his hand than it was seized by his godless and impenitent son Amon, who "did that which was evil in the sight of the Lord, as did Manasseh his father: for Amon sacrificed unto all the carved images which Manasseh his father had made, and served them; and humbled not himself before the Lord, as Manasseh his father had humbled himself: but Amon trespassed more and more. And his servants conspired against him, and slew him in his own house.... And the people of the land made Josiah his son king in his stead" (2 Chron. xxxiii. 22-25).

Thus, then, Josiah, a child of eight years, found himself on the throne of David, surrounded by the accumulated evils and errors of his father and his grandfather—yea, by forms of corruption which had been introduced by no less a personage than Solomon himself. If the reader will just turn for a moment to 2 Kings xxiii., he will find a marvelous picture of the condition of things at the opening of Josiah's history. There were "idolatrous priests, whom the kings of Judah had ordained to burn incense in the high places, in the cities of Judah, and in the places round about Jerusalem; those also that burned incense unto Baal, to the sun, and to the moon, and to the planets, and to all the host of heaven."

Reader, ponder this! Only think of kings of Judah, successors of David, ordaining priests to burn incense to Baal! Bear in mind too that each of these kings of Judah was responsible to "write him a copy of the book of the law," which he was to keep by him, and in which he was to "read *all the days of his life*, that he may learn to fear the Lord his God, to keep *all the words of this law*, and those statutes to do them." (See Deut. xvii. 18, 19.) Alas! alas! how sadly had they departed from "all the words of the law," when they could actually set about ordaining priests to burn incense to false gods!

But further, there were "horses that the kings of Judah had given *to the sun*," and that, moreover, "at the entering in of the house of the Lord," and "chariots of the sun," and "high places which *Solomon* the king of Israel had builded for Ashtoreth the abomination of the Zidonians, and for Chemosh the abomination of the Moabites, and for Milcom the abomination of the children of Ammon."

All this is most solemn, and worthy of the serious consideration of the Christian reader. We certainly ought not to pass it over as a mere fragment of ancient history. It is not as though we were reading the historic records of Babylon, of Persia, of Greece, or of Rome. We should not marvel at the kings of those nations burning incense to Baal, ordaining idolatrous priests, and worshiping the host of heaven; but when we see kings of Judah, the sons and successors of David, children of Abraham, men who had access to the book of the law of God, and who were responsible to make that book the subject of their profound and constant study,—when we see such men falling under the power of dark and debasing superstition, it sounds in our ears a warning voice, to which we cannot with impunity refuse to give heed. We should bear in mind that all these things have been written for our learning; and although it may be said that we are not in danger of being led to burn incense to Baal, or to worship the host of heaven, yet we may be assured we have need to attend to the admonitions and warnings with which the Holy Ghost has furnished us in the history of God's ancient people. "Now all these things happened unto them for ensamples; and they are written for our admonition, on whom the ends of the ages have come" (1 Cor. x. 11). These words of the inspired apostle, though directly referring to the actings of Israel in the wilderness, may nevertheless apply to the entire history of that people—a history fraught with the deepest instruction from first to last.

But how are we to account for all those gross and terrible evils into which Solomon and his successors were drawn? What was their origin? NEGLECT OF THE WORD OF GOD. This was the source of all the mischief and all the sorrow. Let professing Christians remember this; let the whole Church of God remember it. The neglect of the Holy Scriptures was the fruitful source of all those errors and corruptions which blot the page of Israel's history, and which brought down upon them many heavy strokes of Jehovah's governmental rod. "Concerning the works of men, by the word of Thy lips, I have kept me from the paths of the destroyer" (Psa. xvii. 4). "*From a child* thou hast known the Holy Scriptures, which are able to make thee wise unto salvation through faith which is in Christ Jesus. All Scripture is given by inspiration of God, and is profitable for doctrine, for reproof, for correction, for instruction in righteousness, that the man of God may be perfect [ἄρτιος], throughly furnished unto all good works» (2 Tim. iii. 15-17).

In these two precious quotations we have the word of God presented in its twofold virtue; it not only perfectly preserves us from evil, but perfectly furnishes us unto all good,—it keeps us from the paths of the destroyer, and guides us in the ways of God.

How important, then, is the study—the diligent, earnest, prayerful study of

Holy Scripture! How needful to cultivate a spirit of reverential submission, in all things, to the authority of the word of God! Mark how continually and how earnestly this was impressed upon the ancient people of God. How often were such accents as the following sounded in their ears!—"Now therefore harken, O Israel, unto the statutes and unto the judgments which I teach you, for to do them, that ye may live, and go in and possess the land which the Lord God of your fathers giveth you. Ye shall not add unto the word which I command you, neither shall ye diminish aught from it, that ye may keep the commandments of the Lord your God which I command you.... Behold, I have taught you statutes and judgments, even as the Lord my God commanded me, that ye should do so in the land whither ye go to possess it. Keep, therefore, and do them; *for this is your wisdom and your understanding in the sight of the nations*, which shall hear all the statutes, and say, Surely, this great nation is a wise and understanding people. For what nation is there so great, who hath God so nigh unto them, as the Lord our God is in all things that we call upon Him for? And what nation is there so great, that hath statutes and judgments so righteous as all this law, which I set before you this day? *Only take heed to thyself, and keep thy soul diligently*, lest thou forget the things which thine eyes have seen, and lest they depart from thy heart all the days of thy life; but teach them thy sons, and thy sons' sons" (Deut. iv. 1-9).

Let it be carefully noticed here, that "wisdom and understanding" consist simply in having the commandments of God treasured in the heart. This, moreover, was to be the basis of Israel's moral greatness, in view of the nations around them. It was not the learning of the schools of Egypt, or of the Chaldeans. No; it was the knowledge of the word of God, and attention thereto—the spirit of implicit obedience in all things to the holy statutes and judgments of the Lord their God. This was Israel's wisdom; this their true and real greatness; this their impregnable bulwark against every foe—their moral safeguard against every evil.

And does not the self-same thing hold good with respect to God's people at the present moment? Is not obedience to the word of God our wisdom, our safeguard, and the foundation of all true moral greatness? Assuredly. Our wisdom is to obey. The obedient soul is wise, safe, happy, and fruitful. As it was, so it is. If we study the history of David and his successors, we shall find (without so much as a single exception) that those who yielded obedience to the commandments of God were safe, happy, prosperous, and influential. And so it will ever be. Obedience will always yield its own precious and fragrant fruits,—not that its fruits should be our *motive* for rendering obedience; we are called to be obedient, irrespective of everything.

Now it is obvious that in order to be obedient to the word of God, we must be acquainted with it, and in order to be acquainted with it, we must carefully study it. And how should we study it? With an earnest desire to understand its contents, with profound reverence for its authority, and with an honest purpose to obey its dictates, cost what it may. If we have grace to study Scripture in some small degree after this fashion, we may expect to grow in knowledge and wisdom.

But alas! there is a fearful amount of ignorance of Scripture in the professing Church. We are deeply impressed with a sense of this; and we may as well, at this point, just tell the reader that our main object in calling his attention to the subject of "Josiah and his times" is to wake up in his soul an intense desire after a closer acquaintance with God's holy Word, and a more entire bowing down of his whole moral being—heart, conscience, and understanding—to that perfect standard.

We feel the commanding importance of this subject, and we must discharge what we believe to be a sacred duty to the souls of our readers and to the truth of God. The powers of darkness are abroad. The enemy is succeeding to an appalling extent in drawing hearts after various forms of error and evil, in casting dust in the eyes of God's people, and in blinding the minds of men. True we have not got Ashtoreth, Chemosh, and Milcom; but we have ritualism, infidelity, spiritualism, etc. We have not to cry against burning incense to Baal, and worshiping the host of heaven, but we have something far more ensnaring and dangerous. We have the ritualist, with his sensuous and attractive rites and ceremonies; we have the rationalist, with his learned and plausible reasonings; we have the spiritualist, with his boasted converse with the spirits of the departed,—and what multitude of other delusions and insidious attacks upon the truth!

We doubt if the minds of Christians generally are alive to the real character and extent of these formidable influences. There are at this moment millions of souls throughout the length and breadth of the professing Church who are building their hopes for eternity upon the sandy foundation of ordinances, rites, and ceremonies. There is a very marked return to the traditions of the fathers, as they are called; an intense longing after those things which gratify the senses—music, painting, architecture, vestments, lights, incense,—all the appliances, in short, of a gorgeous and sensuous religion. The theology, the worship, and the discipline of the various churches of the Reformation are found insufficient to meet the religious cravings of the people. They are too severely simple to satisfy hearts that long for something tangible on which to lean for support and comfort—something to feed the senses, and fan the flame of devotion.

Hence the strong tendency of the religious mind in the direction of what is called ritualism. If the soul has not got hold of *the truth*, if there is not the living link with Christ, if the supreme authority of Holy Scripture be not set up in the heart, there is no safeguard against the powerful and fascinating influences of ceremonial religiousness. The most potent efforts of mere intellectualism, eloquence, logic, all the varied charms of literature, are found to be utterly insufficient to hold that class of minds to which we are now referring. They *must* have the forms and offices of religion; to these they will flock; around these they will gather; on these they will build.

It is painfully interesting to mark the efforts put forth in various quarters to act upon the masses and keep the people together. It is very evident to the thoughtful Christian that those who put forth such efforts must be sadly deficient in that profound faith in the power of the Word of God and of the cross of Christ which swayed the heart of the apostle Paul. They cannot be fully aware of the solemn fact that Satan's grand object is to keep souls in ignorance of divine revelation, to hide from them the glory of the cross and of the person of Christ. For this end he is using ritualism, rationalism, and spiritualism now, just as he used Ashtoreth,

Chemosh, and Milcom in the days of Josiah. "There is nothing new under the sun." The devil has ever hated the truth of God, and he will leave no stone unturned to keep it from acting on the heart of man. Hence it is that he has rites and ceremonies for one man, the powers of reason for another; and when men tire of both, and begin to sigh for something satisfying, he leads them into converse and communion with the spirits of the departed. By all alike are souls led away from the Holy Scriptures, and from the blessed Saviour which those Scriptures reveal.

It is solemn and affecting beyond expression to think of all this, and not less so to contemplate the lethargy and indifference of those who profess to have the truth. We do not stop to inquire what it is that ministers to this lethargic state of many professors. That is not our object. We desire, by the grace of God, to see them thoroughly roused out of it, and to this end it is that we call their attention to the influences that are abroad, and to the only divine safeguard against them. We cannot but feel deeply for our children, growing up in such an atmosphere as that which at present surrounds us, and which will become yet darker and darker. We long to see more earnestness on the part of Christians in seeking to store the minds of the young with the precious and soul-saving knowledge of the word of God. The child Josiah, and the child Timothy, should incite us to greater diligence in the instruction of the young, whether in the bosom of the family, in the Sunday-school, or in any way we can reach them. It will not do for us to fold our arms, and say, "When God's time comes, our children will be converted; and till then, our efforts are useless." This is a fatal mistake. "God is a rewarder of them that diligently seek Him." (Heb. xi.) He blesses our prayerful efforts in the instruction of our children. And further, who can estimate the blessing of being early led in the right way—of having the character formed amid holy influences, and the mind stored with what is true and pure and lovely? On the other hand, who will undertake to set forth the evil consequences of allowing our children to grow up in ignorance of divine things? Who can portray the evils of a polluted imagination—of a mind stored with vanity, folly, and falsehood—of a heart familiarized from infancy with scenes of moral degradation? We do not hesitate to say that Christians incur very heavy and awful responsibility in allowing the enemy to preoccupy the minds of their children at the very period when they are most plastic and susceptible.

True, there must be the quickening power of the Holy Ghost. It is as true of the children of Christians as of any other that they "must be born again." We all understand this. But does this fact touch the question of our responsibility in reference to our children? Is it to cripple our energies or hinder our earnest efforts? Assuredly not. We are called upon by every argument, divine and human, to shield our precious little ones from every evil influence, and to train them in that which is holy and good. And not only should we so act in respect to our own children, but also in respect to the thousands around us, who are like sheep having no shepherd, and who may each say, alas, with too much truth, "No man careth for my soul."

May the foregoing pages be used by God's Spirit to act powerfully on the hearts of all who may read them, that so there may be a real awakening to a sense of our high and holy responsibilities to the souls around, and a shaking off of that terrible deadness and coldness over which we all have to mourn.

PART II

In studying the history of Josiah and his times, we learn one special and price-less lesson, namely, *the value and authority of the word of God*. It would be utterly im-possible for human language to set forth the vast importance of such a lesson—a lesson for every age, for every clime, for every condition—for the individual be-liever and for the whole Church of God. The supreme authority of Holy Scripture should be deeply impressed on every heart. It is the only safeguard against the many forms of error and evil which abound on every hand. Human writings, no doubt, have their value; they may interest the mind as a reference, but they are perfectly worthless as authority.

We need to remember this. There is a strong tendency in the human mind to lean upon human authority. Hence it has come to pass that millions throughout the professing Church have virtually been deprived altogether of the word of God, from the fact that they have lived and died under the delusion that they could not know it to be the word of God apart from human authority. Now this is, in reality, throwing the word of God overboard. If that Word is of no avail without man's authority, then, we maintain, it is not God's Word at all. It does not matter, in the smallest degree, what the authority is, the effect is the same. God's Word is declared to be insufficient without something of man to give the certainty that it is God that is speaking.

This is a most dangerous error, and its root lies far deeper in the heart than many of us are aware. It has often been said to us, when quoting passages of Scrip ture, "How do you know that that is the word of God?" What is the point of such a question? Plainly to overthrow the authority of the Word. The heart that could suggest such an inquiry does not want to be governed by Holy Scripture at all. The *will* is concerned. Here lies the deep secret. There is the consciousness that the Word condemns something that the heart wants to hold and cherish, and hence the effort to set the Word aside altogether.

But how are we to know that the book which we call the Bible is the word of God? We reply, It carries its own credentials with it. It bears its own evidence upon every page, in every paragraph, in every line. True, it is only by the teaching of the Holy Spirit, the divine Author of the book, that the evidence can be weighed and the credentials appreciated. But we do not want man's voice to accredit God's book; or, if we do, we are most assuredly on infidel ground as regards divine rev-elation. If God cannot speak directly to the heart—if He cannot give the assurance that it is He Himself who speaks, then where are we? whither shall we turn? If God cannot make Himself heard and understood, can man do it better?—can he improve upon God? Can man's voice give us more certainty? Can the authority of the Church, the decrees of general councils, the judgment of the fathers, the opin-ion of the doctors, give us more certainty than God Himself? If so, we are just as completely at sea—just as thoroughly in the dark as though God had not spoken at all. Of course, if God has not spoken, we are completely in the dark; but if He has spoken, and yet we cannot know His voice without man's authority to accredit it, where lies the difference? Is it not plain to the reader of these lines that if God in His great mercy has given us a revelation, it must be sufficient of itself; and on the other hand, that any revelation which is not sufficient of itself cannot possibly be divine? And further, is it not equally plain that if we cannot believe what God says because He says it, we have no safer ground to go upon when man presumes to affix his accrediting seal?

Let us not be misunderstood. What we insist upon is this: the all-sufficiency of a divine revelation apart from and above all human writings—ancient, mediæval, or modern. We value human writings; we value sound criticism; we value profound and accurate scholarship; we value the light of *true* science and philosophy; we value the testimony of pious travelers who have sought to throw light upon the sacred text; we value all those books that open up to us the intensely interesting subject of biblical antiquities; in short, we value everything that tends to aid us in the study of the Holy Scriptures: but after all, we return with deeper emphasis to our assertion as to the all-sufficiency and supremacy of the word of God. That Word must be received on its own divine authority, without any human recommendation, or else it is not the word of God to us. We believe that God can give us the certainty in our own souls that the Holy Scriptures are, in very deed, His own word. If He does not give it, no man can; and if He does, no man need. Thus the inspired apostle says to his son Timothy, "Continue thou in the things which thou hast learned, and *hast been assured of* knowing *of whom* thou hast learned; and that from a child thou hast known the Holy Scriptures, which are able to make thee wise unto salvation through faith which is in Christ Jesus" (2 Tim. iii. 14, 15).

How did Timothy know that the Holy Scriptures were the word of God? He knew it by divine teaching. He knew of *whom* he had learned. Here lay the secret. There was a living link between his soul and God, and he recognized in Scripture the very voice of God. Thus it must ever be. It will not do merely to be convinced in the intellect, by human arguments, human evidences, and human apologies, that the Bible is the word of God; we must know its power in the heart and on the conscience by divine teaching; and when this is the case, we shall no more need human proofs of the divinity of the book than we need a rushlight at noonday to prove that the sun is shining. We shall then believe what God says because He says it, and not because man accredits it, nor because we feel it. "Abraham *believed God,* and it was counted unto him for righteousness." He did not want to go to the Chaldeans, or to the Egyptians, in order to find out from them if what he had heard was in reality the word of God. No, no; he knew *whom* he had believed, and this gave him holy stability. He could say, beyond all question, "God has established a link between my soul and Himself, by means of His Word, which no power of earth or hell can ever snap." This is the true ground for every believer—man, woman, or child, in all ages and under all circumstances. This was the ground for Abraham and Josiah, for Luke and Theophilus, for Paul and Timothy; and it must be the ground for the writer and the reader of these words, else we shall never be able to stand against the rising tide of infidelity, which is sweeping away the very foundations on which thousands of professors are reposing.

However, we may well inquire, can a merely national profession, a hereditary faith, an educational creed, sustain the soul in the presence of an audacious skepticism that reasons about everything and believes nothing? Impossible! We must be able to stand before the skeptic, the rationalist, and the infidel, and say, in all the calmness and dignity of a divinely wrought faith, *"I know whom I have believed."* Then we shall be little moved by such books as, "The Phases of Faith," "Essays and Reviews," "Broken Lights," "Ecce Homo," or "Colenso." They will be no more to us than gnats in the sunshine. They cannot hide from our souls the heavenly beams of our Father's revelation. God has spoken, and His voice reaches the heart. It makes itself heard above the din and confusion of this world, and all the strife and controversy of professing Christians. It gives rest and peace, strength and fixedness, to the believing heart and mind. The opinions of men may perplex and confound. We may not be able to thread our way through the labyrinths of human systems of theology; but God's voice speaks in Holy Scripture—speaks to the heart—speaks to *me*. This is life and peace. It is all I want. Human writings may now go for what they are worth, seeing I have all I want in the ever-flowing fountain of inspiration—the peerless, precious volume of my God.

But let us now turn to Josiah, and see how all that we have been dwelling upon finds its illustration in his life and times.

"Josiah was eight years old when he began to reign" (2 Chron. xxxiv. 1). This tells a tale as to the condition and ways of God's people. Josiah's father had been murdered by his own servants, after a brief and evil reign of two years, in the twenty-fourth year of his age. Such things ought not to have been. They were the sad fruit of sin and folly—the humiliating proofs of Judah's departure from Jehovah. But God was above all; and although we should not have expected ever to find a child of eight years of age on the throne of David, yet that child could find his sure resource in the God of his fathers: so that in this case, as in all others, "where sin abounded, grace did much more abound." The very fact of Josiah's youth and inexperience only afforded an occasion for the display of divine grace, and the setting forth of the value and the power of the word of God.

This pious child was placed in a position of peculiar difficulty and temptation. He was surrounded by errors in various forms and of long standing; but "he did that which was right in the sight of the Lord, and walked in the ways of David his father, and declined neither to the right hand nor to the left. For in the eighth year of his reign, while he was yet young, he began to seek after the God of David his father: and in the twelfth year began to purge Judah and Jerusalem from the high places, and the groves, and the carved images, and the molten images."

This was a good beginning. It is a great matter, while the heart is yet tender, to have it impressed with the fear of the Lord. It preserves it from a host of evils and errors. "The fear of the Lord is the beginning of wisdom," and it taught this pious youth to know what was "right," and to adhere to it with unswerving fixedness of purpose. There is great force and value in the expression, "He did that which was right *in the sight of the Lord.*" It was not that which was right in his own eyes, nor yet in the eyes of the people, nor in the eyes of those that had gone before him; but simply what was right in the sight of the Lord. This is the solid foundation of all right action. Until the fear of the Lord gets its true place in the heart, there can be nothing right, nothing wise, nothing holy. How can there be, if indeed that fear is the *beginning* of wisdom? We may do many things through the fear of man, many things through force of habit, through surrounding influences; but never can we do what is really right in the sight of the Lord until our hearts are brought to understand the fear of His holy name. This is the grand regulating principle. It imparts seriousness, earnestness, and reality—rare and admirable qualities! It is an effectual safeguard against levity and vanity. A man, or a child, who habitually walks in the fear of God is always earnest and sincere, always free from trifling and affectation, from assumption and bombast, life has a purpose, the heart has an object, and this gives intensity to the whole course and character.

But further, we read of Josiah that "he walked in the ways of David his father, and *declined neither to the right hand nor to the left.*" What a testimony for the Holy Ghost to bear concerning a young man! How we do long for this plain decision! It is invaluable at all times, but especially in a day of laxity and latitudinarianism—of false liberality and spurious charity like the present. It imparts great peace of mind. A vacillating man is never peaceful; he is always tossed to and fro. "A double-minded man is unstable in all his ways." He tries to please everybody, and in the end pleases nobody. The decided man, on the contrary, is he who feels he has "to please but *One.*" This gives unity and fixedness to the life and character. It is an immense relief to be thoroughly done with men-pleasing and eye-service—to be able to fix the eye upon the Master alone, and go on with Him through evil report and through good report. True, we may be misunderstood and misrepresented; but that is a very small matter indeed; our great business is to walk in the divinely appointed path, "declining neither to the right hand nor to the left." We are convinced that plain decision is the only thing for the servant of Christ at the present moment; for so surely as the devil finds us wavering, he will bring every engine into play in order to drive us completely off the plain and narrow path. May God's Spirit work more mightily in our souls, and give us increased ability to say, "My heart is fixed, O God; my heart is fixed: I will sing and give praise."

We shall now proceed to consider the great work which Josiah was raised up to accomplish; but ere doing so, we must ask the reader to notice particularly the words already referred to, namely, "In the eighth year of his reign, while he was yet young, *he began to seek after the God of David his father.*" Here, we may rest assured, lay the true basis of all Josiah's valuable service. He began by seeking after God. Let young Christians ponder this deeply. Hundreds, we fear, have made shipwreck by rushing prematurely into work. They have become occupied and engrossed with their service before the heart was rightly established in the fear and love of God. This is a very serious error indeed, and we have met numbers, within the last few years, who have fallen into it. We should ever remember that those whom God uses much in public He trains in secret; and further, that all His most honored servants have been more occupied with their Master than with their work. It is not that we undervalue work; by no means; but we do find that all those who have been signally owned of God, and who have pursued a long and steady course of service and Christian testimony, have begun with much deep and earnest heart-work, in the secret of the divine presence. And on the other hand, we have noticed that when men have rushed prematurely into public work—when they began to teach before they had begun to learn, they have speedily broken down and gone back.

It is well to remember this. God's plants are deeply rooted, and often slow of growth. Josiah "began to seek God" four years before he began his public work. There was in his case a firm ground-work of genuine personal piety, on which to erect the superstructure of active service. This was most needful. He had a great work to do. "High places and groves, carved images and molten images," abounded on all hands, and called for no ordinary faithfulness and decision. Where were these to be had? In the divine treasury, and there alone. Josiah was but a child, and many of those who had introduced the false worship were men of years and experience. But he set himself to seek the Lord. He found his resource in the God of his father David. He betook himself to the fountain-head of all wisdom and power, and there gathered up strength wherewith to gird himself for what lay before him.

This, we repeat, was most needful; it was absolutely indispensable. The accumulated rubbish of ages and generations lay before him. One after another of his predecessors had added to the pile; and notwithstanding the reformation effected in the days of Hezekiah, it would seem as though all had to be done over again. Harken to the following appalling catalogue of evils and errors: "In the twelfth year, Josiah began to purge Judah and Jerusalem from the high places, and the groves, and the carved images, and the molten images. And they break down the altars of Baalim in his presence; and the images that were on high above them he cut down; and the groves, and the carved images, and the molten images, he brake in pieces, and *made dust* of them, and strewed it upon the graves of them that had sacrificed unto them. And he burnt the bones of the priests upon their altars, and cleansed Judah and Jerusalem. And so did he in the cities of Manasseh and Ephraim and Simeon, even unto Naphtali, with their mattocks round about. And when he had broken down the altars and the groves, and had beaten the graven images into *powder*, and cut down all the idols throughout *all the land of Israel*, he returned to Jerusalem."

See also the narrative given in 2 Kings xxiii, where we have a much more detailed list of the abominations with which this devoted servant of God had to grapple. We do not quote any further. Enough has been given to show the fearful lengths to which even the people of God may go when once they turn aside, in the smallest measure, from the authority of Holy Scripture. We feel that this is one special lesson to be learned from the deeply interesting history of this best of Judah's kings, and we fondly trust it may be learned effectually. It is indeed a grand and all-important lesson. The moment a man departs, the breadth of a hair, from Scripture, there is no accounting for the monstrous extravagance into which he may rush. We may feel disposed to marvel how such a man as Solomon could ever be led to "build high places for Ashtoreth the abomination of the Zidonians, and for Chemosh the abomination of the Moabites, and for Milcom the abomination of the children of Ammon." But then we can easily see how that having in the first place disobeyed the word of his Lord in going to those nations for wives, he easily enough fell into the deeper error of adopting their worship.

But, Christian reader, let us remember that all the mischief, all the corruption and confusion, all the shame and dishonor, all the reproach and blasphemy, had its origin in the neglect of the word of God. We cannot possibly ponder this fact too deeply. It is solemn, impressive, and admonitory beyond expression. It has ever been a special design of Satan to lead God's people away from Scripture. He will use anything and everything for this end—tradition, the Church so-called, expediency, human reason, popular opinion, reputation and influence, character, position, and usefulness—all those he will use in order to get the heart and conscience away from that one golden sentence—that divine, eternal motto, "It is written." All that enormous pile of error which our devoted young monarch was enabled to "grind into *dust*, and beat into *powder*"—all, all had its origin in the gross neglect of this most precious sentence. It mattered little to Josiah that all these things could boast of antiquity, and the authority of the fathers of the Jewish nation. Neither was he moved by the thought that these altars and high places, these groves and images, might be regarded as proofs of largeness of heart, breadth of mind, and a liberality of spirit that spurned all narrowness, bigotry, and intolerance—that *would* not be confined within the narrow bounds of Jewish prejudice, but could travel forth through the wide, wide world, and embrace all in a circle of charity and brotherhood. None of these things, we are persuaded, moved him. If they were not based upon "Thus saith the Lord," he had but one thing to do with them, and that was to *"beat them into powder."*

PART III

The various periods in the life of Josiah are very strongly marked. "In the *eighth* year of his reign, he began to seek after the God of David his father;" "in the *twelfth* year he began to purge Judah and Jerusalem;" and "in the *eighteenth* year of his reign, when he had purged the land and the house, he sent Shaphan the son of Azaliah, and Maaseiah the governor of the city, and Joah the son of Joahaz the recorder, to repair the house of the Lord his God."

Now in all this we can mark that progress which ever results from a real purpose of heart to serve the Lord. "The path of the just is as a shining light, which shineth more and more unto the perfect day." Such was the path of Josiah; and such, too, may be the path of the reader, if only he is influenced by the same earnest purpose. It does not matter what the circumstances may be. We may be surrounded by the most hostile influences, as Josiah was in his day; but a devoted heart, an earnest spirit, a fixed purpose, will, through grace, lift us above all, and enable us to press forward from stage to stage of the path of true discipleship.

If we study the first twelve chapters of the book of Jeremiah, we shall be able to form some idea of the condition of things in the days of Josiah. There we meet with such passages as the following: "I will utter My judgments against them touching *all their wickedness*, who have forsaken Me, and have *burned incense unto other gods*, and *worshiped the works of their own hands*. Thou therefore gird up thy loins, and arise, and speak unto them all that I command thee: *be not dismayed at their faces*, lest I confound thee before them." "Wherefore I will yet plead with you, saith the Lord, and with your children's children will I plead. For pass over the isles of Chittim, and see; and send unto Kedar, and consider diligently, and see if there be such a thing. Hath a nation changed their gods, which are yet no gods? but My people have changed their glory for that which doth not profit." So also in the opening of chap. iii., we find the most terrible imagery used to set forth the base conduct of "backsliding Israel and treacherous Judah." Harken to the following glowing language in chap. iv.: "Thy way and thy doings have procured these things unto thee; this is thy wickedness, because it is bitter, because it reacheth unto thy heart. My bowels! my bowels! I am pained at my very heart; my heart maketh a noise in me; I cannot hold my peace, because thou hast heard, O my soul, the sound of the trumpet, the alarm of war. Destruction upon destruction is cried; for the whole land is spoiled: suddenly are my tents spoiled, and my curtains in a moment. How long shall I see the standard, and hear the sound of the trumpet? For My people are foolish, they have not known Me; they are sottish children, and they have none understanding: they are wise to do evil, but to do good they have no knowledge. I beheld the earth, and, lo it was without form and void; and the heavens, and they had no light. I beheld the mountains, and, lo, they trembled, and all the hills moved lightly. I beheld, and, lo, there was no man, and all the birds of the heavens were fled. I beheld, and, lo, the fruitful place was a wilderness, and all the cities thereof were broken down at the presence of the Lord, and by His fierce anger."

What vivid language! The whole scene seems, in the vision of the prophet, reduced to primæval chaos and darkness. In short, nothing could be more gloomy than the aspect here presented. The whole of these opening chapters should be carefully studied, if we would form a correct judgment of the times in which Josiah's lot was cast. They were evidently times characterized by deep-seated and wide-spread corruptions, in every shape and form. High and low, rich and poor, learned and ignorant, prophets, priests, and people—all presented an appalling picture of hollowness, deceit, and heartless wickedness, which could only be faithfully portrayed by an inspired pen.

But why dwell upon this? Why multiply quotations in proof of the low moral condition of Israel and Judah in the days of king Josiah? Mainly to show that, no matter what may be our surroundings, we can individually serve the Lord, if only there be the purpose of heart to do so. Indeed, it is in the very darkest times that the light of true devotedness shines forth most brightly. It is thrown into relief by the surrounding gloom. The very circumstances which indolence and unfaithfulness would use as a plea for yielding to the current will only furnish a devoted spirit with a plea for making head against it. If Josiah had looked around him, what would he have seen? Treachery, deceit, corruption, and violence. Such was the state of public morals. And what of religion? Errors and evils in every imaginable shape. Some of these were hoary with age. They had been instituted by *Solomon* and left standing by *Hezekiah*. Their foundations had been laid amid the splendors of the reign of Israel's wisest and wealthiest monarch, and the most pious and devoted of Josiah's predecessors had left them as they found them.

Who, then, was Josiah, that he should presume to overturn such venerable institutions? What right had he, a mere youth, raw and inexperienced, to set himself in opposition to men so far beyond him in wisdom, intelligence, and mature judgment? Why not leave things as he found them? Why not allow the current to flow peacefully on through those channels which had conducted it for ages and generations? Disruptions are hazardous. There is always great risk in disturbing old prejudices.

These and a thousand kindred questions might doubtless have exercised the heart of Josiah; but the answer was simple, direct, clear and conclusive. It was not the judgment of Josiah against the judgment of his predecessors, but it was the judgment of God against all. This is a most weighty principle for every child of God and every servant of Christ. Without it, we can never make head against the tide of evil which is flowing around us. It was this principle which sustained Luther in the terrible conflict which he had to wage with the whole of Christendom. He too, like Josiah, had to lay the axe to the root of old prejudices, and shake the very foundation of opinions and doctrines which had held almost universal sway in the Church for over a thousand years. How was this to be done? Was it by setting up the judgment of Martin Luther against the judgment of popes and cardinals, councils and colleges, bishops and doctors? Assuredly not. This would never have brought about the Reformation. It was not Luther *versus* Christendom, but Holy Scripture *versus* Error.

Reader, ponder this! Yes, ponder it deeply. We feel it is a grand and all-important lesson for this moment, as it surely was for the days of Luther and for the days of Josiah. We long to see the supremacy of Holy Scripture—the paramount authority of the word of God—the absolute sovereignty of divine revelation reverently owned throughout the length and breadth of the Church of God. We are convinced that the enemy is diligently seeking, in all quarters and by all means, to undermine the authority of the Word, and to weaken its hold upon the human conscience. And it is because we feel this that we seek to raise, again and again, a note of solemn warning, as also to set forth, according to our ability, the vital importance of submitting, in all things, to the inspired testimony—the voice of God in Scripture. It is not sufficient to render a merely formal assent to that popular statement, "The Bible, and the Bible alone, is the religion of Protestants." We want more than this. We want to be, in all things, absolutely governed by the authority of Scripture—not by our fellow-mortal's interpretation of Scripture, but by Scripture itself. We want to have the conscience in a condition to yield, at all times, a true response to the teachings of the divine Word.

This is what we have so vividly illustrated in the life and times of Josiah, and particularly in the transactions of the eighteenth year of his reign, to which we shall now call the reader's attention. This year was one of the most memorable, not only in the history of Josiah, but in the annals of Israel. It was signalized by two great facts, namely, *the discovery of the book of the law* and *the celebration of the feast of the Passover*. Stupendous facts!—facts which have left their impress upon this most interesting period, and rendered it pre-eminently fruitful in instruction to the people of God in all ages.

It is worthy of note that the discovery of the book of the law was made during the progress of Josiah's reformatory measures. It affords one of the ten thousand proofs of that great practical principle that "to him that hath shall more be given;" and again, "If any man *will do* His will, he *shall know* of the doctrine."

"Now in the eighteenth year of his reign, when he had purged the land and the house, he sent Shaphan the son of Azaliah, and Maaseiah the governor of the city, and Joah the son of Joahaz the recorder, to repair the house of the Lord his God. And when they came to Hilkiah the priest, they delivered the money that was brought into the house of God.... And when they brought out the money that was brought into the house of the Lord, Hilkiah the priest found a book of the law of the Lord given by Moses. And Hilkiah the priest answered and said to Shaphan the scribe, I have found the book of the law in the house of the Lord. And Hilkiah delivered the book to Shaphan. And Shaphan carried the book to the king.... And Shaphan read it before the king. And it came to pass, when the king had heard the words of the law, that he rent his clothes" (2 Chron. xxxiv. 8-19).

Here we have a tender conscience bowing under the action of the word of God. This was one special charm in the character of Josiah. He was, in truth, a man of a humble and contrite spirit, who trembled at the word of God. Would that we all knew more of this! It is a most valuable feature of the Christian character. We certainly do need to feel much more deeply the weight, authority, and seriousness of Scripture. Josiah had no question whatever in his mind as to the genuineness and authenticity of the words which Shaphan had read in his hearing. We do not read of his asking, "How am I to know that this is the word of God?" No; he trembled at it; he bowed before it; he was smitten down under it; he rent his garments. He did not presume to sit in judgment upon the word of God, but, as was meet and right, he allowed the Word to judge him.

Thus it should ever be. If man is to judge Scripture, then Scripture is not the word of God at all; but if Scripture is in very truth the word of God, then it must judge man. And so it is and so it does. Scripture *is* the word of God, and it judges man thoroughly. It lays bare the very roots of his nature—it opens up the foundations of his moral being. It holds up before him the only faithful mirror in which he can see himself perfectly reflected. This is the reason why man does not like Scripture—cannot bear it—seeks to set it aside—delights to pick holes in it—dares to sit in judgment upon it. It is not so in reference to other books. Men do not trouble themselves so much to discover and point out flaws and discrepancies in Homer or Herodotus, Aristotle or Shakespeare. No; but Scripture judges them—judges their ways, their lusts. Hence the enmity of the natural mind to that most precious and marvelous Book, which, as we have already remarked, carries its own credentials with it to every divinely prepared heart. There is a power in Scripture which must bear down all before it. All must bow down under it, sooner or later. "The word of God is quick and powerful, and sharper than any two-edged sword, piercing even to the dividing asunder of soul and spirit, and of the joints and marrow, and is a discerner of the thoughts and intents of the heart. Neither is there any creature that is not manifest in His sight; but all things are naked and opened unto the eyes of Him with whom we have to do" (Heb. iv. 12, 13).

Josiah found it to be even so. The word of God pierced him through and through. "And it came to pass, when the king had heard the words of the law, that he rent his clothes. And the king commanded Hilkiah, and Ahikam the son of Shaphan, and Abdon the son of Micah, and Shaphan the scribe, and Asaiah a servant of the king's, saying, Go inquire of the Lord for me, and for them that are left in Israel and in Judah, concerning the words of the book that is found; for great is the wrath of the Lord that is poured out upon us, because our fathers have not kept the word of the Lord, to do after all that is written in this book." What a striking contrast between Josiah, with contrite heart, exercised conscience, and rent garments, bowing down under the mighty action of the word of God, and our modern skeptics and infidels, who, with appalling audacity, dare to sit in judgment upon that very same Word! Oh that men would be wise in time, and bow their hearts and consciences in reverent submission to the word of the living God before that great and terrible day of the Lord in the which they shall be compelled to bow, amid "weeping and wailing and gnashing of teeth."

God's word shall stand forever, and it is utterly vain for man to set himself up in opposition to it, or seek by his reasonings and skeptical speculations to find out errors and contradictions in it. "Forever, O Lord, Thy word is settled in heaven." "Heaven and earth shall pass away, but My words shall not pass away." "The word of the Lord endureth forever." Of what possible use is it, therefore, for man to resist the word of God? He can gain nothing; but oh! what may he lose? If man could prove the Bible false, what should he gain? but if it be true after all, what does he lose? A serious inquiry! May it have its weight with any reader whose mind is at all under the influence of rationalistic or infidel notions.

We shall now proceed with our history.

"And Hilkiah and they that the king had appointed went to Huldah the prophetess, the wife of Shallum the son of Tikvath, the son of Hasrah, keeper of the wardrobe; (now she dwelt in Jerusalem, in the college;) and they spake to her to that effect." At the opening of this paper we referred to the fact of a child of eight years old being on the throne of David as indicative of the condition of things amongst the people of God. Here, too, we are arrested by the fact that the prophetic office was filled by a woman. It surely tells a tale. Things were low; but the grace of God was unfailing and abundant, and Josiah was so thoroughly broken down that he was prepared to receive the communication of the mind of God through whatever channel it might reach him. This was morally lovely. It might, to nature's view, seem very humiliating for a king of Judah to have recourse to a woman for counsel; but then that woman was the depositary of the mind of God, and this was quite enough for a humble and a contrite spirit like Josiah's. He had thus far proved that his one grand desire was to know and do the will of God, and hence it mattered not by what vehicle the voice of God was conveyed to his ear, he was prepared to hear and obey.

Christian reader, let us consider this. We may rest assured that herein lies the true secret of divine guidance. "The meek will He guide in judgment, and the meek will He teach His way" (Ps. xxv. 9). Were there more of this blessed spirit of meekness among us, there would be less confusion, less controversy, less striving about words to no profit. If we were all meek, we should all be divinely guided and divinely taught, and thus we should see eye to eye; we should be of one mind, and speak the same thing, and avoid much sad and humbling division and heart-burning.

See what a full answer the meek and contrite Josiah received from Huldah the prophetess—an answer both as to his people and as to himself. "And she answered them, Thus saith the Lord God of Israel, Tell ye the man that sent you to me, Thus saith the Lord, Behold, I will bring evil upon this place, and upon the inhabitants thereof, even all the curses that are written in the book which they have read before the king of Judah. Because *they have forsaken Me*, and have burned incense unto other gods, that they might provoke Me to anger with all the works of their hands; therefore My wrath shall be poured out upon this place, and shall not be quenched."

All this was but the solemn reiteration and establishment of what had already fallen upon the open and attentive ear of the king of Judah; but then it came with fresh force, emphasis, and interest, as a direct personal communication to himself. It came enforced and enhanced by that earnest sentence, "Tell ye *the man* that sent you to me."

But there was more than this. There was a gracious message directly concerning Josiah himself. "And as for the king of Judah, who sent you to inquire of the Lord, so shall ye say unto him, Thus saith the Lord God of Israel concerning the words which thou hast heard: BECAUSE THY HEART WAS TENDER, and thou didst *humble thyself before God* when thou heardest His words against this place, and against the inhabitants thereof, and *humbledst thyself before Me*, and didst rend thy clothes and *weep before Me*; I have even heard thee also, saith the Lord. Behold, I will gather thee to thy fathers, and thou shalt be gathered to thy grave in peace, neither shall thine eyes see all the evil that I will bring upon this place and upon the inhabitants of the same. So they brought the king word again" (2 Chron. xxxiv. 23-28).

All this is full of instruction and encouragement for us in this dark and evil day. It teaches us the immense value, in the divine estimation, of deep personal exercise of soul and contrition of heart. Josiah might have deemed the case hopeless—that nothing could avert the mighty tide of wrath and judgment which was about to roll over the city of Jerusalem and the land of Israel—that any movement of his must prove utterly unavailing—that the divine purpose was settled—the decree gone forth, and that, in short, he had only to stand by and let things take their course. But Josiah did not reason thus. No; he bowed before the divine testimony. He humbled himself, rent his clothes, and wept. God took knowledge of this. Josiah's penitential tears were precious to Jehovah, and though the appalling judgment had to take its course, yet the penitent escaped. And not only did he himself escape, but he became the honored instrument in the Lord's hand of delivering others also. He did not abandon himself to the influence of a pernicious fatalism, but in brokenness of spirit and earnestness of heart he cast himself upon God, confessing his own sins and the sins of his people. And then, when assured of his own personal deliverance, he set himself to seek the deliverance of his brethren also. This is a fine moral lesson for the heart. May we learn it thoroughly.

PART IV

It is deeply interesting and instructive to mark the actings of Josiah when his heart and conscience had been brought under the powerful influence of the word of God. He not only bowed down under that Word himself, but he sought to lead others to bow likewise. This must ever be the case where the work is real. It is impossible for a man to feel the weight and solemnity of truth and not seek to bring others under its action. No doubt a quantity of truth may be held in the intellect—held superficially—held in a merely speculative, notional way; but this will have no practical effect; it does not tell upon the heart and conscience after a divine, living fashion; it does not affect the life and character. And inasmuch as it does not affect our own souls, neither will our mode of presenting it be very likely to act with much power upon others. True, God is sovereign, and He may use His own Word even when spoken by one who has never really felt its influence; but we are speaking now of what may properly and naturally be looked for; and we may rest assured that the best way in which to make others feel deeply is to feel deeply ourselves.

Take any truth you please. Take, for example, the glorious truth of the Lord's coming. How is a man most likely to affect his hearers by the presentation of this truth? Unquestionably by being deeply affected himself. If the heart be under the power of that solemn word, "the Lord is at hand,"—if this fact be realized in all its solemnity as to the world, and in its sweet attractiveness as to the believer individually and the Church collectively, then it will assuredly be presented in a way calculated to move the hearts of the hearers. It is easy to see when a man *feels* what he is saying. There may be a very clear and clever exposition of the doctrine of the second advent, and of all the collateral truths; but if it be cold and heartless, it will fall powerless on the ears of the audience. In order to speak to *hearts*, on any subject, the heart of the speaker must feel it. What was it that gave such power to Whitefield's discourses? It was not the depth or the range of truth contained in them, as is manifest to any intelligent reader. No. The secret of their mighty efficacy lay in the fact that the speaker *felt* what he was saying. Whitefield wept over the people, and no marvel if the people wept under Whitefield. He must be a hardened wretch indeed who can sit unmoved under a preacher who is shedding tears for his soul's salvation.

Let us not be misunderstood. We do not mean to say that anything in a preacher's manner can of itself convert a soul. Tears cannot quicken: earnestness cannot regenerate. It is "not by might, nor by power, but by My Spirit, saith the Lord." It is only by the powerful action of the Word and Spirit of God that any soul can be born again. All this we fully believe, and would ever bear in mind; but at the same time, we as fully believe and would also bear in mind that God blesses earnest preaching, and souls are moved by it. We have far too much mechanical preaching—too much routine work—too much of what may justly be called *going through* a service. We want more earnestness, more depth of feeling, more intensity, more power to weep over the souls of men, a more influential and abiding sense of the awful doom of impenitent sinners, the value of an immortal soul, and the solemn realities of the eternal world. We are told that the famous Garrick was once asked by a bishop how it was that he produced far more powerful results by his fiction than the bishop could by preaching truth. The reply of the actor is full of force. "My lord," said he, "the reason is obvious: I speak fiction as though it were truth, whereas you speak truth as though it were fiction."

Alas! it is much to be feared that too many of us speak truth in the same way, and hence the little result. We are persuaded that earnest, faithful preaching is one of the special wants of this our day. There are a few here and there, thank God, who seem to *feel* what they are at—who stand before their audience as those who consider themselves as channels of communication between God and their fellows—men who are really bent on their work—bent, not merely on preaching and teaching, but on saving and blessing souls. The grand business of the evangelist is to *bring* the soul and Christ together; the business of the teacher and pastor is to *keep* them together. True it is, most blessedly true, that God is glorified and Jesus Christ magnified by the unfolding of truth, whether men will hear or whether they will forbear; but is this fact to be allowed to interfere, in the smallest degree, with the ardent desire for *results* in reference to souls? We do not for a moment believe it. The preacher should look for results, and should not be satisfied without them. He should no more think of being satisfied to go on without results than the husbandman thinks of going on from year to year without a crop. Some preachers there are who only succeed in preaching their hearers away, and then they content themselves by saying, "We are a sweet savor to God." Now, we believe this is a great mistake, and a fatal delusion. What we want is to live before God for the results of our work—to wait upon Him—to agonize in prayer for souls—to throw all our energies into the work—to preach as though the whole thing depended upon us, although knowing full well that we can do just nothing, and that our words must prove as the morning cloud if not fastened as a nail in a sure place by the Master of assemblies. We are convinced that, in the divine order of things, the earnest workman must have the fruit of his labor; and that according to his faith, so shall it be. There may be exceptions, but as a general rule, we may rest assured that a faithful preacher, will, sooner or later, reap fruit.

We have been drawn into the foregoing line of thought while contemplating the interesting scene in the life of Josiah presented to us at the close of 2 Chronicles xxxiv. It will be profitable for us to dwell upon it. Josiah was a man thoroughly in earnest. He felt the power of truth in his own soul, and he could not rest satisfied until he gathered the people around him, in order that the light which had shone upon him might shine upon them likewise. He did not, he could not, rest in the fact that he was to be gathered to his grave in peace—that his eyes were not to see the evil that was coming upon Jerusalem—that he was to escape the appalling tide of judgment which was about to roll over the land. No; he thought of others, he felt for the people around him; and inasmuch as his own personal escape stood connected with and based upon his true penitence and humiliation under the mighty hand of God, so he would seek, by the action of that Word which had wrought so powerfully in his own heart, to lead others to like penitence and humiliation.

"Then the king sent and gathered together all the elders of Judah and Jerusalem. And the king went up into the house of the Lord, and all the men of Judah, and the inhabitants of Jerusalem, and the priests, and the Levites, and all the people, great and small; and he read in their ears all the words of the book of the covenant that was found in the house of the Lord. And the king stood in his place, and made a covenant before the Lord, to walk after the Lord, and to keep His commandments and His testimonies and his statutes *with all his heart* and *with all his soul,* to perform the words of the covenant which are written in this book. And he caused all that were present in Jerusalem and Benjamin to stand to it. And the inhabitants of Jerusalem did according to the covenant of God, the God of their fathers. And Josiah took away all the abominations out of all the countries that pertained to the children of Israel, and made all that were present in Israel to serve, even to serve the Lord their God. And all his days they departed not from following the Lord, the God of their fathers."

There is a fine moral lesson in all this for us—yea, many lessons to which we, with all our light, knowledge, and privilege, may well sit down. What first of all strikes us at this moment is the fact that Josiah felt his responsibility to those around him. He did not put his light under a bushel, but rather allowed it to shine for the full benefit and blessing of others. This is all the more striking, inasmuch as that great practical truth of the unity of all believers in one body was not known to Josiah, because not revealed by God. The doctrine contained in that one brief sentence, "There is one body and one Spirit," was not made known until long after the times of Josiah, even when Christ the risen Head had taken His seat at the right hand of the Majesty in the heavens.

But although this truth was "hid in God," nevertheless there was the unity of the nation of Israel. There was a national unity, though there was not the unity of a body; and this unity was always recognized by the faithful, whatever might be the outward condition of the people. The twelve loaves on the table of show-bread in the sanctuary were the divine type of the perfect unity and yet the perfect distinctness of the twelve tribes. The reader can see this in Leviticus xxiv. It is full of interest, and should be deeply pondered by every student of Scripture and every earnest lover of the ways of God. During the dark and silent watches of the night, the seven lamps of the golden candlestick threw their light upon the twelve loaves ranged by the hand of the high-priest according to the commandment of God upon the pure table. Significant figure!

It was on this grand truth that Elijah the Tishbite took his stand, when on Mount Carmel he built an altar "with twelve stones, according to the number of the tribes of the sons of Jacob, unto whom the word of the Lord came, saying, 'Israel shall be thy name'" (1 Kings xviii). To this same truth Hezekiah had regard when he commanded "that the burnt-offering and the sin-offering should be made for *all Israel*" (2 Chron. xxix. 24). Paul, in his day referred to this precious truth, when in the presence of king Agrippa he spoke of "our twelve tribes, instantly serving God day and night" (Acts xxvi. 7).

Now, if any one of those men of faith had been asked, "Where are the twelve tribes?" could he have given an answer? could he have pointed them out? Assuredly he could; but not to sight—not to man's view, for the nation was divided—its unity was broken. In the days of Elijah and Hezekiah there were the ten tribes and the two; and in the days of Paul, the ten tribes were scattered abroad, and only a remnant of the two in the land of Palestine, under the dominion of Daniel's fourth beast. What then? Was the truth of God made of none effect by Israel's outward condition? Far be the thought! "Our twelve tribes" must never be given up. The unity of the nation is a grand reality to faith. It is as true at this moment as when Joshua pitched the twelve stones at Gilgal. The word of our God shall stand forever. Not one jot or tittle of aught that He has spoken shall ever pass away. Change and decay may mark the history of human affairs,—death and desolation may sweep like a withering blast over earth's fairest scenes, but Jehovah will make good His every word, and Israel's twelve tribes shall yet enjoy the promised land, in all its length, breadth, and fulness. No power of earth or hell shall be able to hinder this blessed consummation. And why? What makes us so sure? How can we speak with such absolute certainty? Simply because the mouth of the Lord hath spoken it. We may be more sure that Israel's tribes shall yet enjoy their fair inheritance in Palestine than that the house of Tudor once held sway in England. The former we believe on the testimony of God, who cannot lie; the latter on the testimony of man only.

It is of the utmost importance that the reader should be clear as to this, not only because of its special bearing upon Israel and the land of Canaan, but also because it affects the integrity of Scripture as a whole. There is a loose mode of handling the word of God, which is at once dishonoring to Him and injurious to us. Passages which apply distinctly and exclusively to Jerusalem and to Israel are made to apply to the spread of the gospel and the extension of the Christian Church. This, to say the least of it, is taking a very unwarrantable liberty with divine revelation. Our God can surely say what He means, and as surely He means what He says; hence, when He speaks of Israel and Jerusalem, He does not mean the Church; and when He speaks of the Church, He does not mean Israel or Jerusalem.

Expositors the students of Scripture should ponder this. Let no one suppose that it is merely a question of prophetic interpretation. It is far more than this. It is a question of the integrity, value, and power of the word of God. If we allow ourselves to be loose and careless in reference to one class of scriptures, we are likely to be loose and careless as to another, and then our sense of the weight and authority of all Scripture will be sadly enfeebled.

But we must return to Josiah, and see how he recognized, according to his measure, the great principle on which we have been dwelling. He certainly proved no exception to the general rule, namely, that all the pious kings of Judah had regard to the unity of the nation of Israel, and never suffered their thoughts, their sympathies, or their operations to be confined within any narrower range than "our twelve tribes." The twelve loaves on the pure table were ever before the eye of God and ever before the eye of faith. Nor was this a mere speculation—a none-practical dogma—a dead letter. No; it was in every case a great practical, influential truth. "Josiah took away *all* the abominations out of *all the countries that pertained to the children of Israel.*" This was acting in the fullest harmony with his pious predecessor, Hezekiah, who "commanded that the burnt-offering and the sin-offering should be made for *all Israel*".

And now, Christian reader, mark the application of all this to our own souls at this present moment. Do you heartily believe, upon divine authority, in the doctrine of the unity of the body of Christ? Do you believe that there is such a body on this earth now, united to its divine and living Head in heaven by the Holy Ghost? Do you hold this great truth from God Himself, upon the authority of Holy Scripture? Do you, in one word, hold as a cardinal and fundamental truth of the New Testament the indissoluble unity of the Church of God? Do not turn round and ask, "Where is this to be *seen*?" This is the question which unbelief must ever put, as the eye rests upon Christendom's numberless sects and parties, and to which faith replies, as the eye rests upon that imperishable sentence, "There is one body and one Spirit." Mark the words!—"There *is*." It does not say there *was* at one time and there shall be again "one body." Neither does it say that such a thing exists in heaven. No; but it says, "There *is* one body and one Spirit" now on this earth. Can this truth be touched by the condition of things in the professing Church? Has God's Word ceased to be true because man has ceased to be faithful? Will any one undertake to say that the unity of the body was only a truth for apostolic times, and that it has no application now, seeing that there is no exhibition of it?

Reader, we solemnly warn you to beware how you admit into your heart a sentiment so entirely infidel as this. Rest assured it is the fruit of positive unbelief in God's Word. No doubt, appearances argue against this truth; but what truth is it against which appearances do not argue? And say, is it on appearances that faith ever builds? Did Elijah build on appearances when he erected his altar of twelve stones, according to the number of the tribes of the sons of Jacob? Did king Hezekiah build on appearances when he issued that fine commandment that the burnt-offering and the sin-offering should be made for *all Israel*? Did Josiah build on appearances when he carried his reformatory operations into all the countries that pertained to the children of Israel? Surely not. They built upon the faithful word of the God of Israel. That Word was true whether Israel's tribes were scattered or united. If God's truth is to be affected by outward appearances, or by the actings of men, then where are we? or what are we to believe? The fact is, there is hardly a truth in the entire compass of divine revelation to which we could with calm confidence commit our souls if we suffer ourselves to be affected by outward appearances.

No, reader; the only ground on which we can believe anything is this one eternal clause, "*It is written*"! Do you not admit this? Does not your whole soul bow down to it? Do you not hold it to be a principle entirely vital? We believe you do, as a Christian, hold, admit, and reverently believe this. Well, then, *it is written*, "There is one body and one Spirit" (Eph. iv.). This is as clearly revealed in Scripture as that "we are justified by faith," or any other truth. Do outward appearances affect the saving, fundamental doctrine of justification by faith? Are we to call in question this precious truth because there is so little exhibition of its purifying power in the lives of believers? Who could admit such a fatal principle as this? What a complete upturning of all the foundations of our faith is necessarily involved in the admission of this most mischievous line of reasoning! We believe because it is written in the Word, not because it is exhibited in the world. Doubtless it ought to be exhibited, and it is our sin and shame that it is not. To this we shall afterward refer more fully; but we must insist upon the proper ground of belief, namely, divine revelation; and when this is clearly seen and fully admitted, it applies as distinctly to the doctrine of the unity of the body as it does to the doctrine of justification by faith.

PART V

We feel it to be of real moment to insist upon this principle, namely, that the *only* ground on which we can believe any doctrine is its being revealed in the divine Word. It is thus we believe all the great truths of Christianity. We know nothing and can believe nothing of what is spiritual, heavenly, or divine, save as we find it revealed in the word of God. How do I know I am a sinner? Because Scripture hath declared that "all have sinned." No doubt I feel that I am a sinner; but I do not believe because I feel, but I feel because I believe, and I believe because God has spoken. Faith rests upon divine revelation, not on human feelings or human reasonings. "It is written" is quite sufficient for faith. It can do with nothing less, but it asks nothing more. God speaks: faith believes. Yes, it believes simply because God speaks. It does not judge God's Word by outward appearances, but it judges outward appearances by the word of God.

Thus it is in reference to all the cardinal truths of the Christian religion, such as the Trinity, the deity of our Lord Jesus Christ, His atonement, His priesthood, His advent, the doctrine of original sin, of justification, judgment to come, eternal punishment. We believe these grand and solemn truths, not on the ground of feeling, of reason, or of outward appearances, but simply on the ground of divine revelation.

Hence, then, if it be asked, On what ground do we believe in the doctrine of the unity of the body? we reply, Upon the self-same ground that we believe the doctrine of the Trinity, the deity of Christ, and the atonement. We believe it because it is revealed in sundry places in the New Testament. Thus, for example, in 1 Cor. xii. we read, "For as *the body is one*, and hath many members, and all the members of that *one body*, being many, are *one body*; so also *is Christ*. For by one Spirit are we all baptized into *one body*, whether we be Jews or Gentiles, whether we be bond or free; and have been all made to drink into one Spirit." Again, "God hath tempered the body together, having given more abundant honor to that part which lacked, that there should be no schism in the body.... Now, *ye are the body of Christ*, and members in particular."

Here we have distinctly laid down the perfect and indissoluble unity of the Church of God, the body of Christ, on precisely the same authority as any other truth commonly received amongst us; so that there is just as much ground for calling in question the deity of Christ as there is for calling in question the unity of the body. The one is as true as the other; and both are divinely true, because divinely revealed. We believe that Jesus Christ is God over all, blessed forever, because Scripture tells us so; we believe that there is one body because Scripture tells us so. We do not reason in the one case, but believe and bow; nor should we reason in the other case, but believe and bow. "There is one body and one Spirit."

Now, we must bear in mind that this truth of the unity of the body is not a mere abstraction—a barren speculation—a powerless dogma. It is a practical, formative, influential truth, in the light of which we are called to walk, to judge ourselves and all around us. It was so with the faithful in Israel of old. The unity of the nation was a real thing to them, and not a mere theory to be taken up or laid down at pleasure. It was a great formative, powerful truth. The nation was one in God's thoughts; and if it was not manifestly so, the faithful had only to take the place of self-judgment, brokenness of spirit, and contrition of heart. Witness the case of Hezekiah, Josiah, Daniel, Nehemiah, and Ezra. It never once occurred to these faithful men that they were to give up the truth of Israel's unity because Israel had failed to maintain it. They did not measure the truth of God by the actings of men; but they judged the actings of men, and themselves likewise, by the truth of God. This was the only true way to act. If the manifested unity of Israel was marred through man's sin and folly, the true-hearted members of the congregation owned and mourned over the sin, confessed it as their own, and looked to God. Nor was this all. They felt their responsibility to act on the truth of God whatever might be the outward condition of things.

This, we repeat, was the meaning of Elijah's altar of twelve stones, erected in the face of Jezebel's eight hundred false prophets, and despite the division of the nation in man's view. (1 Kings xviii.) This, too, was the meaning of Hezekiah's letters sent to "*all Israel*" to invite them to "come to the house of the Lord at Jerusalem, to keep the passover unto the Lord God of Israel." Nothing can be more touching than the spirit and style of these letters. "*Ye children of Israel*, turn again unto the Lord God of Abraham, Isaac, and Israel, and He will return to the remnant of you that are escaped out of the hand of the kings of Assyria. And be not ye like your fathers and like your brethren, which trespassed against the Lord God of their fathers, who therefore gave them up to desolation, as ye see. Now, *be ye not stiff-necked*, as your fathers were, but *yield yourselves unto the Lord*, and enter into His sanctuary, which He *hath sanctified forever*; and serve the Lord your God, that the fierceness of His wrath may turn away from you. *For if ye turn again unto the Lord, your brethren and your children shall find compassion* before them that lead them captive, so that they shall come again into this land; for the Lord your God is gracious and merciful, and will not turn away His face from you" (2 Chron. xxx. 6-9).

What was all this but simple faith acting on the grand, eternal, immutable truth of the unity of the nation of Israel? The nation was *one* in the purpose of God, and Hezekiah looked at it from the divine standpoint, as faith ever does, and he acted accordingly. "So the posts passed from city to city, through *the country of Ephraim and Manasseh*, even unto Zebulun; but *they laughed them to scorn, and mocked them*." This was very sad, but it is only what we must expect. The actings of faith are sure to call forth the scorn and contempt of those who are not up to the standard of God's thoughts. Doubtless these men of Ephraim and Manasseh regarded Hezekiah's message as a piece of presumption or wild extravagance. Perhaps the great truth that was acting with such power on his soul, forming his character and ruling his conduct, was in their judgment a myth, or at best a valueless theory—a thing of the past—an institution of bygone ages, having no present application. But faith is never moved by the thoughts of men, and therefore Hezekiah went on with his work, and God owned and blessed him. He could afford to be laughed at and turned into ridicule, while he beheld divers of Asher and

Manasseh and Zebulun humbling themselves and coming to Jerusalem. Hezekiah and all who thus humbled themselves under the mighty hand of God reaped a rich harvest of blessing, while the mockers and scorners were left in the barrenness and deadness with which their own unbelief had surrounded them.

And let the reader mark the force of those words of Hezekiah, "If *ye* turn again unto the Lord, *your brethren and your children shall find compassion* before them that lead them captive." Does not this approach very near to that precious truth of the New Testament times, that we are members one of another, and that the conduct of one member affects all the rest? Unbelief might raise the question as to how this could possibly be—as to how the actings of one could possibly affect others far away; yet so it was in Israel, and so it is now in the Church of God. Witness the case of Achan, in Joshua vii. There, one man sinned; and, so far as the narrative informs us, the whole congregation was ignorant of the fact; and yet we read that "*the children of Israel* committed a trespass in the accursed thing." And again, "*Israel* hath sinned." How could this be? Simply because the nation was one, and God dwelt among them. This, plainly, was the ground of a double responsibility, namely, a responsibility to God, and a responsibility to the whole assembly and to each member in particular. It was utterly impossible for any one member of the congregation to shake off this high and holy responsibility. A person living at Dan might feel disposed to question how his conduct could affect a man living at Beersheba; yet such was the fact, and the ground of this fact lay in the eternal truth of Israel's indissoluble unity and Jehovah's dwelling in the midst of His redeemed assembly. (See Exodus xv. 2, and the many passages which speak of God's dwelling in the midst of Israel.)

We do not attempt even to quote the numerous scriptures which speak of God's presence in the congregation of Israel—His dwelling in their midst. But we would call the attention of the reader to the all-important fact that those scriptures *begin* with Exodus xv. It was when Israel stood, as a fully redeemed people, on Canaan's side of the Red Sea that they were able to say, "The Lord is my strength and my song, and He is become my salvation: He is *my God*, and I will prepare Him a *habitation*." Redemption formed the ground of God's dwelling among His people, and His presence in their midst secured their perfect unity. Hence no one member of the congregation could view himself as an isolated independent atom. Each one was called to view himself as part of a whole, and to view his conduct in reference to all those who, like himself, formed part of that whole.

Now, reason could never grasp a truth like this. It lay entirely beyond the ken of the most powerful human intellect. Faith alone could receive it and act upon it, and it is of the deepest interest to see that the faithful in Israel ever recognized it and acted upon it. Why did Hezekiah send letters to "all Israel"? Why did he expose himself to scorn and ridicule in so doing? Why did he command that "the burnt-offering and the sin-offering should be made for all Israel"? Why did Josiah carry his reformatory operations into all "the countries that pertained to the children of Israel"? Because those men of God recognized the divine truth of Israel's unity, and they did not think of throwing this grand reality overboard because so few saw it or sought to carry it out. "The people shall dwell alone;" and "I, the

Lord, will dwell among the children of Israel." These imperishable truths shine, like most precious gems of heavenly lustre, all along the page of Old Testament Scripture; and we invariably find that, just in proportion as any one was living near to God—near to the living and ever-gushing fountain of life and light and love—just in proportion as he entered into the thoughts, purposes, sympathies, and counsels of the God of Israel, did he apprehend and seek to carry out that which God had declared to be true of His people, though His people had proved so untrue to Him.

And now, Christian reader, we would ask you a very plain and pointed question, which is this: Do you not recognize in the unity of the Jewish nation the foreshadowing of a higher unity now existing in that one body of which Christ is the Head? We trust you do. We fondly hope that your whole moral being bows down, with reverent submission, to the mighty truth, "There *is* one body." But then we can well imagine that you feel yourself not a little perplexed and confounded when you cast your eye around you through the length and breadth of the professing Church, in search of any positive expression of this unity. You see Christians scattered and divided—you see innumerable sects and parties; and what perhaps puzzles you most of all, you see those who profess to believe and act upon the truth of the unity of the body divided amongst themselves, and presenting anything but a spectacle of unity and harmony. All this, we confess, is very perplexing to one who looks at it from a merely human standpoint. We are not the least surprised at people being stumbled and hindered by these things. Still the foundation of God standeth sure. His truth is perfectly indestructible; and if we gaze with admiration upon the faithful worthies of a bygone age who believed and confessed the unity of Israel when there was not a trace of that unity visible to mortal eyes, why should we not heartily believe and diligently carry out the higher unity of the one body? "There is one body and one Spirit," and herein lies the basis of our responsibility to one another and to God. Are we to surrender this all-important truth because Christians are scattered and divided? God forbid. It is as real and as precious as ever, and it ought to be as formative and as influential. We are bound to act upon the truth of God, irrespective of consequences, and utterly regardless of outward appearances. It is not for us to say, as so many do, "The case is hopeless: everything has gone to pieces. It is impossible to carry out the truth of God amid the heaps of rubbish which lie around us. The unity of the body was a thing of the *past*; it may be a thing of the *future*, but it cannot be a thing of the *present*. The idea of unity must be abandoned as thoroughly Utopian, it cannot be maintained in the face of Christendom's numberless sects and parties. Nothing remains now but for each one to look to the Lord for himself, and to do the best he can, in his own *individual* sphere, and according to the dictates of his own conscience and judgment."

Such is, in substance, the language of hundreds of the true people of God; and as is their language, so is their practical career. But we must speak plainly, and we have no hesitation in saying that this language savors of sheer unbelief in that great cardinal verity of the unity of the body; and, moreover, that we have just as much warrant for rejecting the precious doctrine of Christ's deity, of His perfect humanity, or of His vicarious sacrifice, as we have for rejecting the truth of the perfect unity of His body, inasmuch as this latter rests upon precisely the same foundation as the former, namely, the eternal truth of God—the absolute statement of Holy Scripture. What right have we to set aside any one truth of divine revelation? What authority have we to single out any special truth from the word of God and say that it no longer applies? We are bound to receive *all truth*, and to submit our souls to its authority. It is a dangerous thing to admit for a moment the idea that any one truth of God is to be set aside, on the plea that it cannot be carried out. It is sufficient for us that it is revealed in the Holy Scriptures: we have only to *believe* and to *obey*. Does Scripture declare that there is "one body"? Assuredly it does. This is enough. We are responsible to maintain this truth, cost what it may; we can accept nothing else—nothing less—nothing different. We are bound, by the allegiance which we owe to Christ the Head, to testify, practically, against everything that militates against the truth of the indissoluble unity of the Church of God, and to seek earnestly and constantly a faithful expression of that unity.

True, we shall have to contend with false unity on the one hand and false individuality on the other; but we have only to hold fast and confess the truth of God, looking to Him, in humility of mind and earnest purpose of heart, and He will sustain us in the path, let the difficulties be what they may. No doubt there are difficulties in the way—grave difficulties, such as we in our own strength cannot cope with. The very fact that we are told to "*endeavor* to keep the unity of the Spirit in the bond of peace" is sufficient to prove that there are difficulties in the way; but the grace of our Lord Jesus Christ is amply sufficient for all the demands that may be made upon us in seeking to act upon this most precious truth.

In contemplating the present condition of the professing Church we may discern two very distinct classes. In the first place, there are those who are seeking unity on false grounds; and secondly, those who are seeking it on the ground laid down in the New Testament. This latter is distinctly a spiritual, living, divine unity, and stands out in vivid contrast with all the forms of unity which man has attempted, whether it be national, ecclesiastical, ceremonial, or doctrinal. The Church of God is not a nation, not an ecclesiastical or political system. It is a body united to its divine Head in heaven, by the presence of the Holy Ghost. This is what it was, and this is what it is. "There is one body and one Spirit." This remains unalterably true. It holds good now just as much as when the inspired apostle penned Ephesians iv. Hence anything that tends to interfere with or mar this truth must be wrong, and we are bound to stand apart from it and testify against it. To seek to unite Christians on any other ground than the unity of the body is manifestly opposed to the revealed mind of God. It may seem very attractive, very desirable, very reasonable, right, and expedient; but it is contrary to God, and this should be enough for us. God's Word speaks *only* of the unity of the body and the unity of the Spirit. It recognizes no other unity: neither should we.

The Church of God is one, though consisting of many members. It is not local, or geographical; it is corporate. All the members have a double responsibility; they are responsible to the Head, and they are responsible to one another. It is utterly impossible to ignore this responsibility. Men may seek to shirk it; they may deny it; they may assert their individual rights, and act according to their own reason, judgment, or will; but they cannot get rid of the responsibility founded upon the fact of the one compact body. They have to do with the Head in heaven and with the members on earth. They stand in this double relationship—they were incorporated thereinto by the Holy Ghost, and to deny it is to deny their very spiritual existence. It is founded in life, formed by the Spirit, and taught and maintained in the Holy Scriptures. There is no such thing as independency. Christians cannot view themselves as mere individuals—as isolated atoms. "We are members one of another." This is as true as that we are "justified by faith." No doubt there is a sense in which we are individual: we are individual in our repentance; individual in our faith; individual in our justification; individual in our walk with God and in our service to Christ; individual in our rewards for service, for each one shall get a white stone and a new name engraved thereon known only to himself. All this is quite true, but it in no wise touches the other grand practical truth of our union with the Head above and with each and all of the members below.

And we would here call the reader's attention to two very distinct lines of truth flowing out of two distinct titles of our blessed Lord, namely, Headship and Lordship. He is Head of His body the Church, and He is Lord of all, Lord of each. Now, when we think of Christ as Lord, we are reminded of our individual responsibility to Him, in the wide range of service to which He, in His sovereignty, has graciously called us. Our reference must be to Him in all things. All our actings, all our movements, all our arrangements, must be placed under the commanding influence of that weighty sentence (often, alas! lightly spoken and penned), "If *the Lord* will." And, moreover, no one has any right to thrust himself between the conscience of a servant and the commandment of his Lord. All this is divinely true, and of the very highest importance. The Lordship of Christ is a truth the value of which cannot possibly be overestimated.

But we must bear in mind that Christ is *Head* as well as *Lord*;—He is Head of a body, as well as Lord of individuals. These things must not be confounded. We are not to hold the truth of Christ's Lordship in such a way as to interfere with the truth of His Headship. If we merely think of Christ as Lord, and ourselves as individuals responsible to Him, then we shall ignore His Headship, and lose sight of our responsibility to every member of that body of which He is Head. We must jealously watch against this. We cannot look at ourselves as isolated, independent atoms; if we think of Christ as Head, then we must think of all His members, and this opens up a wide range of practical truth. We have holy duties to discharge to our fellow-members, as well as to our Lord and Master; and we may rest assured that no one walking in communion with Christ can ever lose sight of the grand fact of his relationship to every member of His body. Such an one will ever remember that his walk and ways exert an influence upon Christians living at the other side of the globe. This is a wondrous mystery, but it is divinely true. "If one member suffer, *all* the members suffer with it" (1 Cor. xii. 26). You cannot reduce the body of Christ to a matter of locality: the body is one, and we are called to maintain this practically in every possible way, and to bear a decided testimony against everything which tends to hinder the expression of the perfect unity of the body, whether it be false unity or false individuality. The enemy is seeking to associate Christians on a false ground, and gather them around a false centre; or, if he cannot do this, he will send them adrift upon the wide and tumultuous ocean of a desultory individualism. *We are throughly persuaded, before God, that the only safeguard against both these false and dangerous extremes is divinely wrought faith in the grand foundation-truth of the unity of the body of Christ.*

PART VI

It may here be proper to inquire what is the suited attitude of the Christian in view of the grand foundation-truth of the unity of the body. That it is a truth distinctly laid down in the New Testament cannot possibly be questioned. If any reader of these pages be not fully established in the knowledge and hearty belief of this truth, let him prayerfully study 1 Corinthians xii. and xiv., Ephesians ii. and iv., Colossians ii. and iii. He will find the doctrine referred to in a practical way in the opening of Romans xii; though it is not the design of the Holy Ghost, in that magnificent epistle, to give us a full unfolding of the truth respecting the Church. What we have to look for there is rather the soul's relationship with God through the death and resurrection of Christ. We might pass through the first eleven chapters of Romans and not know that there is such a thing as the Church of God, the body of Christ; and when we reach chap. xii., the doctrine of the one body is assumed, but not dwelt upon.

There is, then, "one body" actually existing on this earth, formed by the "one Spirit," and united to the living Head in heaven. This truth cannot be gainsaid. Some may not see it; some may find it very hard to receive it, in view of the present condition of things; but nevertheless it remains a divinely established truth that "there is one body," and the question is, how are we individually affected by this truth? It is as impossible to shake off the responsibility involved therein as it is to set aside the truth itself. If there is a body of which we are members, then do we, in every truth, stand in a holy relationship to every member of that body on earth, as well as to the Head in heaven; and this relationship, like every other, has its characteristic affections, privileges, and responsibilities.

And be it remembered, we are not speaking now of the question of association with any special company of Christians, but of the whole body of Christ upon earth. No doubt each company of Christians, wherever assembled, should be but the local expression of the whole body. It should be so gathered and so ordered, on the authority of the Word, and by the power of the Holy Ghost, as that all Christ's members who are walking in truth and holiness might happily find their place there. If an assembly be not thus gathered and thus ordered, it is not on the ground of the unity of the body at all. If there be anything, no matter what, in order, discipline, doctrine, or practice, which would prove a barrier to the presence of any of Christ's members whose faith and practice are according to the word of God, then is the unity of the body practically denied. We are solemnly responsible to own the truth of the unity of the body. We should so meet that all the members of Christ's body might, simply as such, sit down with us and exercise whatever gift the Head of the Church has bestowed upon them. The body is one. Its members are scattered over the whole earth. Distance is nothing: locality nothing. It may be New

Zealand, London, Paris, or Edinburgh; it matters not. A member of the body in one place is a member of the body everywhere, for there is but "one body and one Spirit." It is the Spirit who forms the body, and links the members with the Head and with one another. Hence, a Christian coming from New Zealand to London ought to expect to find an assembly so gathered as to be a faithful expression of the unity of the body, to which he might attach himself; and furthermore, any such Christian ought to find his place in the bosom of that assembly, provided always there be nothing in doctrine or walk to forbid his hearty reception.

Such is the divine order, as laid down in 1 Cor. xii. and xiv.; Eph. ii. and iv. and assumed in Rom. xii. Indeed, we cannot study the New Testament and not see this blessed truth. We find in various cities and towns saints gathered by the Holy Ghost in the name of our Lord Jesus Christ; as, for example, at Rome, Corinth, Ephesus, Philippi, Colosse, and Thessalonica. These were not independent, isolated, fragmentary assemblies, but parts of the one body, so that a member of the Church in one place was a member of the Church everywhere. Doubtless, each assembly, as guided by the one Spirit, and under the one Lord, acted in all local matters, such as receiving to communion, or putting away any wicked person from their midst; meeting the wants of their poor, and such like; but we may be quite assured that the act of the assembly at Corinth would be recognized by all other assemblies, so that if any one was separated from communion there, he would, if known, be refused in all other places; otherwise it would be a plain denial of the unity of the body. We have no reason to suppose that the assembly at Corinth communicated or conferred with any other assembly previous to the putting away of "the wicked person" in chap. v., but we are bound to believe that that act would be duly recognized and sanctioned by every assembly upon the earth, and that any assembly knowingly receiving the excommunicated man would have cast a slur upon the assembly at Corinth, and practically denied the unity of the body.

This we believe to be the plain teaching of the New Testament Scriptures—this, the doctrine which any simple, true-hearted student of these scriptures would gather up. That the Church has failed to carry out this precious truth is, alas! alas! painfully true; and that we are all participators in this failure is equally true. The thought of this should humble us deeply before God. Not one can throw a stone at another, for we are all verily guilty in this matter. Let not the reader suppose for a single moment that our object in these pages is to set up anything like high ecclesiastical pretensions, or to afford countenance to hollow assumption, in the face of manifest sin and failure. God forbid! we say with our very heart of hearts. We believe that there is a most urgent call upon all God's people to humble themselves in the dust on account of our sad departure from the truth so plainly laid down in the word of God.

Thus it was with the pious and devoted king Josiah, whose life and times have suggested this entire line of thought. He found the book of the law, and discovered in its sacred pages an order of things wholly different from what he saw around him. How did he act? Did he content himself by saying, "The case is hopeless: the nation is too far gone: ruin has set in, and it is utterly vain to think of aiming at the divine standard; we must only let things stand, and do the best we can"? Nay, reader, such was not Josiah's language or mode of action; but he humbled himself before God, and called upon others to do the same. And not only so, but he sought to carry out the truth of God. He aimed at the very loftiest standard, and the consequence was, that "from the days of Samuel the prophet, there was no passover like to Josiah's kept in Israel; neither did all the kings of Israel keep such a passover."

Such was the result of faithful reference and adherence to the word of God, and thus it will ever be, for "God is a rewarder of them that diligently seek Him." Look at the actings of the remnant that returned from Babylon in the days of Ezra and Nehemiah. What did they do? They set up the altar of God; they built the temple, and repaired the walls of Jerusalem. In other words, they occupied themselves with the true worship of the God of Israel, and with the grand centre or gathering-point of His people. This was right. It is what faith always does, regardless of circumstances. If the remnant had looked at circumstances, they could not have acted. They were a poor contemptible handful of people, under the dominion of the uncircumcised Gentiles. They were surrounded by active enemies on all sides, who, instigated by the enemy of God, of His city, of His people, left nothing undone to hinder them in their blessed work. These enemies ridiculed them, and said, "What do these feeble Jews? Will they fortify themselves? will they sacrifice? will they make an end in a day? will they revive the stones out of the heaps of the rubbish which are burned?" Nor was this all; not only had they to contend with powerful foes without, there was also internal weakness, for "Judah said, The strength of the bearers of burdens is decayed, and there is much rubbish, so that we are not able to build the wall." (Neh. iv.) All this was very depressing. It was very different from the brilliant and palmy days of Solomon. His burden-bearers were many and strong, and there was no rubbish covering the great stones and costly with which he built the house of God, nor any contemptuous foe to sneer at his work. And yet, for all that, there were features attaching to the work of Ezra and Nehemiah which are not to be found in the days of Solomon. Their very feebleness, the piles of rubbish which lay before them, the proud and insulting enemies who surrounded them — all these things conspired to add a peculiar halo of glory to their work. They built and prospered, and God was glorified, and He declared in their ears these cheering words: "The glory of this latter house shall be greater than of the former, saith the Lord of Hosts: and in this place will I give peace, saith the Lord of Hosts." (Hag. ii. 9.)

It is of importance, in connection with the subject that has been engaging our attention, that the reader should carefully study the books of Ezra and Nehemiah, Haggai and Zechariah. They are full of most blessed instruction, comfort, and encouragement in a day like the present. Many, nowadays, it may be, are disposed to smile at the bare mention of such a subject as the unity of the body; but let them ask themselves, Is it the smile of calm confidence, or the sneer of unbelief? One thing is certain, the devil as cordially hates the doctrine of the unity of the body as he hates any other doctrine of divine revelation, and he will as assuredly seek to hinder any attempt to carry it out as he sought to hinder the rebuilding of Jerusalem in the days of Nehemiah. But let us not be discouraged. It is enough for us that we find in God's Word the precious truth of the one body. Let us bring the light of this to bear upon the present condition of the professing Church, and see what it will reveal to our eyes. It will most assuredly put us on our faces in the dust before our God because of our ways; but at the same time, it will lift our hearts up to the contemplation of the divine standard. It will so enlighten and elevate our souls as to render us thoroughly dissatisfied with everything that does not present some expression, however feeble, of the unity of the body of Christ. It is wholly impossible that any one can drink into his soul the truth of the one body and rest satisfied with any thing short of the practical recognition thereof. True, he must make up his mind to bear the brunt of the enemy's opposition. He will meet a Sanballat here, and a Rehum there, but faith can say,—

> "Is God for me? I fear not, though all against me rise;
> When I call on Christ my Saviour, the host of evil flies."

There is ample encouragement for our souls in the word of God. If we look at Josiah, just *before the captivity*, what do we see? A man simply taking the Word as his guide—judging himself and all around by its light—rejecting all that was contrary to it, and seeking, with earnest purpose of heart, to carry out what he found written there. And what was the result? The most blessed passover that had been celebrated since the days of Samuel.

Again, if we look at Daniel, *during the captivity*, what do we see? A man acting simply on the truth of God and praying toward Jerusalem, though death stared him in the face as the consequence of his act. What was the result? A glorious testimony to the God of Israel, and the destruction of Daniel's enemies.

Finally, if we look at the remnant, *after the captivity*, what do we see? Men, in the face of appalling difficulties, rebuilding that city which was, and shall be, God's earthly centre. And what was the result? The joyous celebration of the feast of tabernacles, which had not been known since the days of Joshua the son of Nun.

Now, if we take any of the above interesting cases, and inquire as to the effect of their looking at surrounding circumstances, what answer shall we get? Take Daniel, for instance. Why did he open his window toward Jerusalem? Why look toward a city of ruins? Why call attention to a spot which only bore testimony to Israel's sin and shame? Would it not be better to let the name of Jerusalem sink into oblivion? Ah? we can guess at Daniel's reply to all such inquiries. Men might smile at him too, and deem him a visionary enthusiast; but he knew what he was doing. His heart was occupied with God's centre, the city of David, the grand gathering-point for Israel's twelve tribes. Was he to give up God's truth because of outward circumstances? Surely not. He could not consent to lower the standard even the breadth of a hair. He would weep, and pray, and fast, and chasten his soul before God, but never lower the standard. Was he going to give up God's thoughts about Zion because Israel had proved unfaithful? Not he. Daniel knew better than this. His eye was fixed on God's eternal truth, and hence, though he was in the dust because of his own sins and his people's, yet the divine banner floated above his head, in its unfading glory.

Just so now, dear Christian reader, we are called to fix the gaze of faith upon the imperishable truth of the one body; and not only to gaze upon it, but seek to carry it out in our feeble measure. This should be our one definite and constant aim. We should ever and only seek the expression of the unity of the body. We are not to ask, "How can this be?" Faith never says, "How?" in the presence of divine revelation; it believes and acts. We are not to surrender the truth of God on the plea that we cannot carry it out. The truth is revealed, and we are called to bow to it. We are not called to form the unity of the body. Very many seem to think that this unity is a something which they themselves are to set up or form in some way or another. This is a mistake. The unity exists. It is the result of the presence of the Holy Ghost in the body, and we have to recognize it, and walk in the light of it. This will give great definiteness to our course. It is always immensely important to have a distinct object before the heart, and to work with direct reference thereto. Look at Paul, that most devoted of workmen. What was his aim?—for what did he work? Hear the answer in his own words: "I now rejoice in my sufferings for you, and fill up that which is behind of the afflictions of Christ in my flesh for *His body's sake, which is the Church*: whereof I am made a minister, according to the dispensation of God which is given to me for you, to fulfil the word of God; even the mystery which hath been hid from ages and from generations, but now is made manifest to His saints: to whom God would make known what is the riches of the glory of this mystery among the Gentiles; which is Christ in you, the hope of glory: whom we preach, warning every man, and teaching every man in all wisdom; that we may present every man perfect in Christ Jesus; whereunto I also labor, striving according to His working, which worketh in me mightily" (Col. i. 24-29).

Now, this was a great deal more than the mere conversion of souls, precious as that is, most surely. Paul preached the gospel with a direct view to the body of Christ; and this is the pattern for all evangelists. We should not rest in the mere fact that souls are quickened; we should keep before our minds their incorporation, by the one Spirit, into the one body. This would effectually preserve us from sect-making—from preaching to swell the ranks of a party—from seeking to get persons to *join* this, that, or the other denomination. We should know nothing whatever but the one body, because we find nothing else in the New Testament. If this be lost sight of, the evangelist will not know what to do with souls when they are converted. A man may be used in the conversion of hundreds—a most precious work indeed—precious beyond all expression,—and if he does not see the unity of the body, he must be at sea as to their further course. This is very serious, both as to himself and them, and also as to the testimony for Christ.

May God's Spirit lead all Christians to see this great truth in all its bearings. We have but glanced at it, in connection with our theme; but it demands much serious attention at the present moment. It may be that some of our readers are disposed to find fault with what they may deem a long digression from the subject of "Life and Times of Josiah;" but in truth it should not be looked on as a digression, but as a line of truth flowing naturally out of that subject—a line, too, which cannot possibly be over-estimated.

PART VII

In closing our remarks on "the life and times of Josiah," we shall in few words advert, first, to the fact of his celebration of the passover; and secondly, to the solemn close of his history. Our sketch of this truly interesting period would unquestionably be incomplete were these things omitted.

And first, then, as to the fact—so full of interest and encouragement—that at the very close of Israel's history there should be one of the brightest moments that Israel had ever known. What does this teach us? It very manifestly teaches us that in darkest times it is the privilege of the faithful soul to act on divine principles and to enjoy divine privileges. We look upon this as a most weighty fact for all ages, but specially weighty at the present moment. If we did nothing more by writing our papers on Josiah than to impress this great fact on the mind of the Christian reader, we should consider that we had not written in vain. If Josiah had been influenced by the spirit and principle which, alas! seem to actuate so many in this our day, he never could have attempted to celebrate the passover at all. He would have folded his arms and said, "It is useless to think of maintaining any longer our great national institutions. It can only be regarded as a piece of presumption to attempt the celebration of that ordinance which was designed to set forth Israel's deliverance from judgment by the blood of the lamb, when Israel's unity is broken, and its national glory faded and gone."

But Josiah did not reason like this; he simply acted upon the truth of God. He studied the Scriptures, and rejected what was wrong and did what was right. "Moreover, Josiah kept a passover unto the Lord in Jerusalem; and they killed the passover on the fourteenth day of *the first month*." (2 Chron. xxxv. 1). This was taking higher ground than Hezekiah had taken, inasmuch as he kept his passover "on the fourteenth day of *the second month*." (Chap. xxx. 15). In so doing, Hezekiah was, as we know, availing himself of the provision which grace had made for cases of defilement. (See Num. ix. 9-11). The divine order, however, had fixed "the first month" as the proper period, and to this order Josiah was enabled to conform. In short, he took the very highest ground, according to the truth of God, while lying low under the deep sense of personal and national failure. This is ever the way of faith.

"And he set the priests in their charges, and encouraged them to the service of the house of the Lord, and said unto the Levites that taught *all Israel*, which were holy unto the Lord, Put the holy ark in the house which *Solomon*, the *son of David, king of Israel*, did build: it shall not be a burden on your shoulders; serve now the Lord your God, and *His people Israel*. And prepare yourselves by the houses of your fathers, after your courses, *according to the writing of David king of Israel*, and according to the writing of Solomon his son, and stand in the holy place, according to the divisions of the families of the fathers of your brethren the people, and after the division of the families of the Levites. So kill the passover, and sanctify yourselves, and prepare your brethren, *that they may do according to the word of the Lord by the hand of Moses*."

Here we have Josiah taking the loftiest ground and acting on the highest authority. The most cursory reader cannot fail to be arrested, as he scans the lines just quoted from the inspired record, by the names of "Solomon," "David," "Moses," "all Israel," and above all, by the expression—so full of dignity, weight, and power, —"That they may do according to the word of the Lord." Most memorable words! May they sink down into our ears and into our hearts. Josiah felt it to be his high and holy privilege to conform to the divine standard, notwithstanding all the errors and evils which had crept in from age to age. God's truth must stand forever. Faith owns and acts on this precious fact, and reaps accordingly. Nothing can be more lovely than the scene enacted on the occasion to which we are now referring. Josiah's strict adherence to the word of the Lord is not more to be admired than his large-hearted devotedness and liberality. "He gave to the people of the flock, lambs and kids, all for the passover-offerings, for all that were present, to the number of thirty thousand, and three thousand bullocks: these were of the king's substance. And his princes gave willingly unto the people, to the priests, and to the Levites.... So the service was prepared, and the priests stood in their place, and the Levites in their courses, according to the king's commandment.... And the singers, the sons of Asaph, were in their place, according to the commandment of David, and Asaph, and Heman, and Jeduthun the king's seer; and the porters waited at every gate; they might not depart from their service; for their brethren the Levites prepared for them. So all the service of the Lord was prepared the same day, to keep the passover, and to offer burnt-offerings upon the altar of the Lord, according to the commandment of king Josiah. And *the children of Israel* that were present kept the passover at that time, and the feast of unleavened bread seven days. And there was no passover like to that kept in Israel from the days of Samuel the prophet; neither did all the kings of Israel keep such a passover as Josiah kept, and the priests, and the Levites, and all Judah and Israel that were present, and the inhabitants of Jerusalem. In the eighteenth year of the reign of Josiah was this passover kept."

What a picture! King, princes, priests, Levites, singers, porters, all Israel, Judah, and the inhabitants of Jerusalem—all gathered together—all in their true place and at their appointed work, "according to the word of the Lord,"—and all this "in the eighteenth year of the reign of Josiah," when the entire Jewish polity was on the very eve of dissolution. Surely this must speak to the heart of the thoughtful reader. It tells its own impressive tale, and teaches its own peculiar lesson. It tells us that no age, no circumstances, no influence, can ever change the truth of God or dim the vision of faith. "The word of the Lord endureth forever," and faith grasps that word and holds it fast in the face of everything. It is the privilege of the believing soul to have to do with God and His eternal truth; and, moreover, it is the duty of such an one to aim at the very loftiest standard of action, and to be satisfied with nothing lower. Unbelief will draw a plea from the condition of things around to lower the standard, to relax the grasp, to slacken the pace, to lower the tone. Faith says, "No!"—emphatically and decidedly, "No!" Let us bow our heads in shame and sorrow on account of our sin and failure, but keep the standard up. The failure is ours: the standard is God's. Josiah wept and rent his clothes, but he did not surrender the truth of God. He felt and owned that he and his brethren and his fathers had sinned, but that was no reason why he should not celebrate the passover according to the divine order. It was as imperative upon him to do right as it was upon Solomon, David, or Moses. It is our business to obey the word of the Lord, and we shall assuredly be blessed in our deed. This is one grand lesson to be drawn from the life and times of Josiah, and it is undoubtedly a seasonable lesson for our own times. May we learn it thoroughly. May we learn to adhere with holy decision to the ground on which the truth of God has set us, and to occupy that ground with a larger measure of true devotedness to Christ and His cause.

Most gladly would we linger over the brilliant and soul-stirring scene presented in the opening verses of 2 Chronicles xxxv, but we must bring this paper to an end, and we shall merely glance very rapidly at the solemn and admonitory close of Josiah's history. It stands in sad and painful contrast with all the rest of his most interesting career, and sounds in our ears a note of warning to which we are bound to give our most serious attention. We shall do little more than quote the passage, and then leave the reader to reflect upon it, prayerfully and humbly, in the presence of God.

"After all this, when Josiah had prepared the temple, Necho king of Egypt came up to fight against Charchemish by Euphrates; and Josiah went out against him. But he sent ambassadors to him, saying, What have I to do with thee, thou king of Judah? I come not against thee this day, but against the house wherewith I have war; for God commanded me to make haste: forbear thee from meddling with God, who is with me, that He destroy thee not. Nevertheless, Josiah would not turn his face from him, but *disguised himself*, that he might fight with him, and harkened not to the words of Necho *from the mouth of God*, and came to fight in the valley of Megiddo. And the archers shot at king Josiah; and the king said to his servants, Have me away, for I am sore wounded. His servants therefore took him out of that chariot and put him in the second chariot that he had; and they brought him to Jerusalem, and he died, and was buried in one of the sepulchres of his fathers. And all Judah and Jerusalem mourned for Josiah" (2 Chron. xxxv. 20-24).

All this is very sad and humbling. We do not wish to dwell upon it further than is absolutely needful for the purpose of instruction and admonition. The Holy Spirit does not expatiate, but He has recorded it for our learning. It is ever His way to give us men as they were,—to write the history of their "deeds, *first and last*"— good and bad—one as well as another. He tells us of Josiah's piety at the "first," and of his wilfulness at the "last." He shows us that so long as Josiah walked in the light of divine revelation, his path was illuminated by the bright beams of the divine countenance; but the moment he attempted to act for himself—to walk by the light of his own eyes—to travel off the straight and narrow way of simple obedience, that moment dark and heavy clouds gathered around him, and the course that had opened in sunshine ended in gloom. Josiah went against Necho without any command from God—yea, he went in direct opposition to words spoken "from the mouth of God." He meddled with strife that belonged not to him, and he reaped the consequences.

"He disguised himself." Why do this, if he was conscious of acting for God? Why wear a mask, if treading the divinely appointed pathway? Alas! alas! Josiah failed in this, and in his failure he teaches us a salutary lesson. May we profit by it. May we learn more than ever to seek a divine warrant for all we do, and to do nothing without it. We can count on God to the fullest extent if we are walking in His way, but we have no security whatever if we attempt to travel off the divinely appointed line. Josiah had no command to fight at Megiddo, and hence he could not count on divine protection. "He disguised himself," but that did not shield him from the enemy's arrow. "The archers shot him"—they gave him his death wound, and he fell, amid the tears and lamentations of a people to whom he had endeared himself by a life of genuine piety and earnest devotedness.

May we have grace to imitate him in his piety and devotedness, and to guard against his wilfulness. It is a serious thing for a child of God to persist in doing his own will. Josiah went to Megiddo when he ought to have tarried at Jerusalem, and the archers shot him, and he died: Jonah went to Tarshish when he ought to have gone to Nineveh, and he was flung into the deep: Paul persisted in going to Jerusalem though the Spirit told him not, and he fell into the hands of the Romans. Now, all these were true, earnest, devoted servants of God; but they failed in these things; and though God overruled their failure for blessing, yet they had to reap the fruit of their failure, for *our* God is a consuming fire" (Heb. xii. 29).

Lector House believes that a society develops through a two-fold approach of continuous learning and adaptation, which is derived from the study of classic literary works spread across the historic timeline of literature records. Therefore, we aim at reviving, repairing and redeveloping all those inaccessible or damaged but historically as well as culturally important literature across subjects so that the future generations may have an opportunity to study and learn from past works to embark upon a journey of creating a better future.

This book is a result of an effort made by Lector House towards making a contribution to the preservation and repair of original ancient works which might hold historical significance to the approach of continuous learning across subjects.

HAPPY READING & LEARNING!

LECTOR HOUSE LLP
E-MAIL: lectorpublishing@gmail.com

* 9 789389 582864 *